THREE EARLY WORKS

THE BARNES & NOBLE LIBRARY OF ESSENTIAL READING

THREE EARLY WORKS

A Book of Prefaces
Damn! A Book of Calumny
The American Credo

H. L. MENCKEN

INTRODUCTION BY RICHARD J. SCHRADER

BARNES & NOBLE
NEW YORK

THE BARNES & NOBLE
LIBRARY OF ESSENTIAL READING

Originally published in 1917 *(A Book of Prefaces)*, 1918 *(Damn!)*,
and 1920 *(The American Credo)*

This edition published by Barnes & Noble Publishing, Inc.

2006 Barnes & Noble Publishing

ISBN-13: 978-0-7607-8057-2
ISBN-10: 0-7607-8057-9

Printed and bound in the United States of America

1 3 5 7 9 10 8 6 4 2

Contents

THE AMERICAN CREDO

INTRODUCTION

HENRY LOUIS MENCKEN WAS POSSIBLY AMERICA'S GREATEST AND most wide-ranging man of letters, in that he excelled as a journalist, essayist, philologist, satirist, political commentator, magazine editor, and literary critic. The various skills he demonstrated throughout his careers are amply displayed in the three works collected here: *A Book of Prefaces* (1917), *Damn! A Book of Calumny* (1918), and *The American Credo: A Contribution Toward the Interpretation of the National Mind* (1920). They were written at the end of his critical and journalistic apprenticeship, during World War I and its aftermath. By this time, he had perfected his inimitable satiric style and had found among the disillusioned an audience for his literary and political theories. Mencken hurled his invective against the complacencies of the Jazz Age, and in the 1920s, as in the previous two decades, he had the most authoritative voice of any American writer. Novelist Richard Wright claimed in his memoir *Black Boy* that he discovered from *A Book of Prefaces* how words could be used as weapons. Edmund Wilson, a leading man of letters in the next generation, made the broader claim that Mencken's public role was "the civilized consciousness of modern America."

H. L. Mencken (1880–1956) lived his whole life in Baltimore. He graduated valedictorian (1896) from the Baltimore Polytechnic Institute, a high school, and was self-taught thereafter. As a newspaperman he was primarily associated with the Baltimore *Sun*, from 1906 until 1948 when a debilitating stroke prevented further writing. His columns reached a national audience through syndication, making him a well-known critic of war fever, every president from "Roosevelt I" to "Roosevelt II," censorship, the Ku Klux Klan and rampant lynching in the South, Prohibition, and the residual Puritanism which, in his definition, underlay most of America's problems. He directed his writing to what he called the "civilized minority." He had another significant platform in the pages of two influential magazines. Mencken joined *The Smart Set* as book reviewer in 1908 and, with drama critic George Jean Nathan (1882–1958), edited it from 1914 to 1923. They resigned to become founding editors of *The American Mercury* the next year; Mencken stayed until 1933. Both journals featured his reviews and essays, as well as writing by others that bore his editorial stamp and usually reflected his point of view. His critical task, which is manifest in *A Book of Prefaces*, was to bring to the foreground the kind of realistic and naturalistic writing that had been developing since the end of the previous century. He advanced authors like Theodore Dreiser and Sinclair Lewis (and published James Joyce for the first time in America). He recruited women writers and gave more space to minority authors than any other white editor of his time. Mencken's most famous work is his monumental *The American Language*, whose first edition (1919) appeared in the same fruitful period as the three books presented here. It was thoroughly revised for three later editions, the last in 1936. The latest version has been reprinted many times, along with two supplements (1945, 1948). It remains an enjoyable and respected survey of the subject. For all that, Mencken may be remembered just as long for the humorous *New Yorker* reminiscences that were collected into *Happy Days* (1940), *Newspaper Days* (1941), and *Heathen Days* (1943).

Mencken had to suspend many of his journalistic activities because of increasing restrictions on free speech during the lead-up to America's entry into World War I. His loyalty was suspected because he supported Germany and opposed the calls for the United States to side with Britain and France. When he could no longer print such opinions, he began putting together the four essays that would comprise *A Book of Prefaces*: "Joseph Conrad," "Theodore Dreiser," "James Huneker," and "Puritanism as a Literary Force." He did so, as he said in the preface to the first printing, in hopes that "they may at least blow a wind through the prevailing fogs, and reveal what is sound and important in some first-rate books." He later wrote that they set forth "my objections to the whole Puritan *Kultur* in a large and positive way." The challenge was heard around the country, and the ensuing intellectual battle energized a generation. Because of the effect it had on his professional career, Mencken considered *Prefaces* to be his most important book.

Only marginally connected to the New England culture of colonial times, "Puritanism" was Mencken's comprehensive term for what ailed the America he knew. It embraced such things as religious fundamentalism, Prohibition, the world-saving idealism of Woodrow Wilson, book-banning on the one hand, and literary timidity on the other. His chapter on the subject, the longest and most important in the book, assails classic American writers, including William Dean Howells (his immediate predecessor as chief man of letters), for their excessive restraint. Too often, he claims, moralism weakened their writing, and moralists set up hedges against those who would rebel. Puritanism was kept alive by such defenders of the "genteel tradition" as Paul Elmer More, Irving Babbitt, and Mencken's arch-enemy among the critics, Stuart P. Sherman.

One aim of the chapter on Joseph Conrad (1857–1924) was to bring further recognition to this great novelist, whom Mencken had been one of the earliest American critics to promote. The effort was part of his campaign to arouse interest in the new literature and new ideas being produced in Europe. To that end he had written the first book on Irish playwright George Bernard

Shaw (1905) and the first in English on German philosopher Friedrich Nietzsche (1908). He had even co-translated two plays by the Norwegian Henrik Ibsen (1909), at a time when the American stage was badly in need of models for the new trends in realism.

Like Conrad, Theodore Dreiser (1871–1945) is praised for not being a moralist. The chapter on him demonstrates why Mencken is still considered one of the best champions and most incisive critics of the novelist. *Sister Carrie* (1900), the manuscript of which Dreiser presented to Mencken in gratitude for his support, has been thought of as the literary fanfare for the twentieth century. Dreiser's subsequent fiction realized Mencken's ideas on what a novelist ought to be saying about the true (meaningless) nature of life, no matter the graceless style. In the fascinating correspondence between the two, published in 1986, one can see them working out their common agenda, despite misgivings on both sides and the occasional need to defend Dreiser against prudish censors. It was an agenda that benefited all subsequent authors who strove to write realistically about the American scene.

James Gibbons Huneker (1857–1921), whom Mencken had known since 1905, fascinated him primarily as a raconteur. Their friendship gave Mencken access to the larger esthetic world, both European and American. Huneker's lush style, moreover, was a major influence on that of Mencken, who soaked it in over beer at Lüchow's restaurant in New York City and from reading the extensive criticism of art, music, literature, and culture that flowed from Huneker's pen. He was a fellow anti-philistine and, for Mencken, that rarest of Americans, "a civilized man." In fact, like Conrad and Dreiser, he is praised for his decidedly non-American qualities.

As a defender of Germany, Mencken was limited by the censorship of the times in what he could criticize about America. His choice of essays for the book continued his assault by indirection, generally avoiding the political commentary that might have gotten him into trouble. (The United States declared war on

April 6, 1917, and *Prefaces* appeared on October 8.) It was the first of his books to be published by his friend Alfred A. Knopf, who had gone into business just two years before. Their stars would rise together, and Knopf's famous Borzoi device appeared on posthumously published Mencken works as late as 1995.

Much of the material for the four essays in *Prefaces* was revised from work that Mencken had done for the Baltimore *Sun* and *The Smart Set.* He had been writing about Conrad, Dreiser, and Huneker for years, and his task now was mostly to make judicious selections. The freshest revision stemmed from his recent canvass of American public libraries to find the distribution of Dreiser's books. (Only the "intellectual slums" of New Orleans and Providence had no Dreiser books at all.) "Puritanism as a Literary Force" drew upon a *Smart Set* series called "The American" and other articles, but it also contained a great deal that was original. While it was, by his standards, somewhat tempered, Mencken wanted it to be the most "headlong and uncompromising" attack on American culture ever made, leaving no doubt where he stood on the war and the Wilsonian ideals behind it.

Some tinkering was done at Knopf's behest to avoid trouble with the censors, but even so a number of reviewers denounced the book for its defense of Dreiser and its assault on the "Comstocks," who were anti-vice crusaders in the mold of the leading figure of that endeavor, Anthony Comstock. The most notorious attack was by Stuart P. Sherman, who is discussed in the Dreiser chapter as "the moralist turned critic." He had criticized Mencken and Dreiser before, and now, in the *Nation* of November 29, 1917, he took advantage of the wartime hysteria to assail Mencken's fondness for European culture and his pro-German stance. Mencken never forgave him—in spite of Sherman's later change of heart—not because of the critical sparring, which Mencken enjoyed, but because of the ethnic slurs against himself and Dreiser as German-Americans that Sherman employed in this and other pieces.

Such attacks confirmed Mencken in his belief that a strain of Puritanism still infected the national letters. However, not all the reviews were negative, and *Prefaces* sold well for a book of literary criticism: some 6,300 copies of six Knopf printings, the last in 1928. The second of them was revised, and Mencken wrote new prefaces for the second through fifth printings. Doubleday sold 10,000 more as one-dollar reprints in the late 1920s. The fourth printing, which is reproduced here, was also used for the London issue by Jonathan Cape (1922). Mencken recognized that, for all the hurtful personal attacks, he had gained the kind of authority that his newspaper and magazine reviews alone could not provide. Here and abroad his audience widened, and the discussion he initiated would carry on for years.

Damn! A Book of Calumny was another project in which Mencken assembled and revised material that he had published before. Some of it had appeared in *The Smart Set*; even more came from pieces he had done for the New York *Evening Mail*, which had also printed two of his most famous essays: "The Sahara of the Bozart" (an attack on Southern culture with far-reaching effects) and "A Neglected Anniversary" (wherein he created the Bathtub Hoax, a fictional history of the bathtub that his later disclaimers have not kept out of standard reference works). His usual practice was to work up an idea as a newspaper article, develop it later for a magazine audience, then rewrite it for a book. After the monograph on Nietzsche in 1908, he did not create a book out of entirely new matter until *Treatise on the Gods* (1930).

Apart from containing some of Mencken's wittier turns in its forty-nine short essays, *Damn!* was an interesting experiment in literary marketing. It was one of two Mencken books published in 1918 by his friend Philip Goodman—the other is the often-reprinted *In Defense of Women*. Though a newly fledged Knopf author, Mencken kept a promise to Goodman by allowing him to put out these two works.

Goodman's novel idea was to avoid relying solely on bookstores, for both he and Mencken thought that they were "run by idiots." Instead, he would look to places like pharmacies, which were beginning to handle merchandise other than drugs. Mencken observed that he was ahead of his time in this attempt; twenty years later the idea would be a commonplace. But for various reasons, including inadequate advertising, Goodman could not make it work in 1918.

Damn! was published on April 1, 1918, five months before *In Defense of Women*. One of three titles in the same small format, it was offered to druggists and other retailers at a fifty-percent discount. Goodman promoted it with circulars and a dust jacket that exaggerated its naughtiness. In fact, the front of the jacket contained denunciations of Mencken, not the usual praise-filled blurbs. The ploy did not do much for sales, though it probably increased the hostility of the reviews, which in turn brought further publicity. In the long run, these notices were helpful in calling attention to Mencken's writing, but *Damn!* was a financial failure.

Goodman initially blamed the small format, so after the first edition of 1,000 copies ("divided bogusly into Second Printing and Third Printing" by claims on the title page, according to Mencken) he had the book reset for a second edition in July. There were some revisions, a preface was inserted, and larger type was used, adding about forty pages. The price went up from 90¢ to $1.25. Mencken used the preface to lament the title, which was Goodman's idea. It "has libelled the book, which is moral and reassuring in character, and not only libelled it, but also brought down upon it the indignation of the right-thinking." He noted that, because of the title, the New York *Times* refused to print more than one ad for it so as not to outrage its subscribers. Mencken continued the joke by claiming that many critics had misrepresented the book, which "is obviously not cynical or immoral or pessimistic, but full of high hope and rectitude, and not strutting and squalling, but extremely polite and *pianissimo*."

Sales remained sluggish, and Knopf took over the remaining sheets later in the year; he would do the same for *In Defense of Women* in 1919. (Unlike Knopf, Goodman failed as a publisher, but he later enjoyed success as a theatrical producer.) Knopf reissued the book without "Damn!" in the title and without the preface, adding a dime to the price. Despite everything, the book sold only about 1,800 copies altogether. While it has been mined for anthologies, it has never before been reprinted as a whole.

When the war ended, so did most of the constraints on Mencken's method of attack. He no longer had to demonstrate the gullibility of the American "booboisie" by such indirect means as the Bathtub Hoax. One of the fruits of the postwar environment was "Répétition Générale," a department in *The Smart Set* that he created with co-editor Nathan. It ran from April 1919 until they left the magazine. With an early installment, Mencken and Nathan began the practice of including what they imagined were items of American popular belief, and from these they constructed *The American Credo: A Contribution Toward the Interpretation of the National Mind.* Knopf published the book on February 6, 1920.

Of the 488 articles, Mencken contributed about half, and though the long preface (more than half the book) is jointly signed, he wrote all of it. The preface gave Mencken a chance to revenge himself on those who had attacked him for his stance during the war and to elaborate on such perennial Menckenian themes as intolerance and conformity. Here is the satiric voice that would be heard in his writing throughout the rest of the 1920s, including the *Prejudices* series (1919–1927) and his famous dispatches from the Scopes "monkey trial" at Dayton, Tennessee (1925). Mencken is once again at odds with a moral and intellectual tradition that stifles non-conformists.

The comic creedal statements (twelve of them claimed by *Smart Set* author F. Scott Fitzgerald in his copy of the book) together are meant to constitute proof of the credulity of "the national mind."

After the first edition, twenty-nine comically obscene articles were left over. Mencken knew that the "Comstocks" would not allow them in the book, so he had them privately printed for his friends in a four-page leaflet, now a collector's item.

In 1921, Knopf brought out the revised second edition reprinted here; it is enlarged to 869 items. Most of the new ones came from readers, so this was to some extent a national collaboration in the manner of Mencken's *The American Language,* which benefited from many specialist and nonspecialist contributions. (Six years later Nathan recycled the items and partially quoted Mencken's preface in *The New American Credo.*) The game continued when Mencken, Nathan, and Knopf founded *The American Mercury* in 1924. One department carried over from *The Smart Set* was "Americana," in which they quoted articles published throughout the nation to demonstrate the absurd doings and beliefs of the American people. If anything, the country came off worse than it did in *Credo,* because these were not imaginary (if often plausible) items of faith made up by the diabolical editors. Not everyone was amused: the editor of *The Saturday Evening Post* set up a department that offered contrary examples. Undaunted, Mencken and Nathan assembled two collections in book form (1925, 1926), and the composer Randall Thompson even selected five texts for *Americana: A Sequence of Choruses for Five Voices* (1932). Others were edited as *Mencken's Americana* (2002).

Mencken's first published books were *Ventures Into Verse* (1903) and the monographs on Shaw and Nietzsche. His other works in the years before *A Book of Prefaces* demonstrate the diversity of his interests, and they include a small Nietzsche anthology, a dialogue defending individualism over socialism, a ghost-written guide to baby care, a play, a travel book, and collections of his humor and satire from magazines and newspapers. After the amazing performance already noted in the years 1917–1920 (*Prefaces, Damn!, In Defense of Women, American Language, Prejudices: First Series,* and

American Credo, not to mention *Heliogabalus: A Buffoonery in Three Acts,* co-written with Nathan), he generally concentrated on literary and social criticism. Ahead lay self-compiled anthologies of his miscellaneous writing in the rest of the *Prejudices* series and in *A Mencken Chrestomathy* (1949). Less successful were treatises on democracy, religion, and morals. His strength lay in political commentary, including the matchless reports he sent from the quadrennial presidential nominating conventions (1904–1948). Several posthumous anthologies gather up these and other writings, as well as many of the estimated one hundred thousand letters that he wrote. Correspondence was his way of staying in touch with hundreds of writers and with those ordinary people who contributed to *The American Language.* He stipulated that three autobiographical works be kept sealed until after his death: his *Diary* (1989), *My Life as Author and Editor* (1993), and *Thirty-five Years of Newspaper Work* (1994). They exploded like time bombs on an America unused to his comic persona and trained to regard all satire as "mean-spirited." Thanks to a new kind of censorious Puritanism, now called "political correctness," the memoirs inspired the kind of controversy that Mencken provoked in his lifetime, as he once again "stirred up the animals." Readers of the three earlier works presented here will be better prepared to enjoy a master stylist, comedian, and cultural commentator.

Richard J. Schrader is a Professor of English at Boston College, where he specializes in medieval literature, bibliography and textual criticism, and H. L. Mencken. He has published extensively in these areas.

PREFACE TO THE FOURTH EDITION

THIS FOURTH PRINTING OF *A BOOK OF PREFACES* OFFERS ME temptation, as the third did, to revise the whole book, and particularly the chapters on Conrad, Dreiser and Huneker, all of whom have printed important new books since the text was completed. In addition, Huneker has died. But the changes that I'd make, after all, would be very slight, and so it seems better not to make them at all. From Conrad have come *The Arrow of Gold* and *The Rescue*, not to mention a large number of sumptuous reprints of old magazine articles, evidently put between covers for the sole purpose of entertaining collectors. From Dreiser have come *Free*, *Twelve Men*, *Hey, Rub-a-Dub-Dub* and some chapters of autobiography. From Huneker, before and after his death, have come *Unicorns*, *Bedouins*, *Steeple-Jack*, *Painted Veils* and *Variations*. But not one of these books materially modifies the position of its author. *The Arrow of Gold*, I suppose, has puzzled a good many of Conrad's admirers, but certainly *The Rescue* has offered ample proof that his old powers are not diminished. The Dreiser books, like their predecessors that I discuss here, reveal the curious unevenness of the author. Parts of *Free* are hollow and irritating, and nearly all of *Hey, Rub-a-Dub-Dub* is feeble, but in *Twelve Men* there are some chapters that rank with the very best of *The Titan* and *Jennie Gerhardt*. The place of Dreiser in our literature is frequently challenged, and often violently, but never successfully. As the years pass his solid dignity as an artist becomes more and more evident. Huneker's last five works changed his position very little. *Beduoins, Unicorns* and *Variations* belong mainly to his journalism, but into *Steeple-Jack*, and above all into *Painted Veils* he put his genuine self. I have discussed all of these books in other places, and paid my small tribute to the man himself, a light burning brightly through a dark night, and snuffed out only at the dawn.

I should add that the prices of Conrad first editions given on page 56 have been greatly exceeded during the past year or two. I should add also that the Comstockian imbecilities described in chapter 4 are still going on, and that the general trend of American legislation and jurisprudence is toward their indefinite continuance.

H. L. M.
Baltimore, January 1, 1922

A Book of Prefaces

→ CHAPTER ONE ←

JOSEPH CONRAD

§ 1

"UNDER ALL HIS STORIES THERE EBBS AND FLOWS A KIND OF tempered melancholy, a sense of seeking and not finding . . ." I take the words from a little book on Joseph Conrad by Wilson Follett, privately printed, and now, I believe, out of print.[1] They define both the mood of the stories as works of art and their burden and direction as criticisms of life. Like Dreiser, Conrad is forever fascinated by the "immense indifference of things," the tragic vanity of the blind groping that we call aspiration, the profound meaninglessness of life—fascinated, and left wondering. One looks in vain for an attempt at a solution of the riddle in the whole canon of his work. Dreiser, more than once, seems ready to take refuge behind an indeterminate sort of mysticism, even a facile supernaturalism, but Conrad, from first to last, faces squarely the massive and intolerable fact. His stories are not chronicles of men who conquer fate, nor of men who are unbent and undaunted by fate, but of men who are conquered and undone. Each protagonist is a new Prometheus, with a sardonic ignominy piled upon his helplessness. Each goes down a Greek route to defeat and disaster, leaving nothing behind him save an unanswered question. I can scarcely recall an exception. Kurtz, Lord Jim, Razumov, Nostromo, Captain

Whalley, Yanko Goorall, Verloc, Heyst, Gaspar Ruiz, Almayer: one and all they are destroyed and made a mock of by the blind, incomprehensible forces that beset them.

Even in *Youth, Typhoon,* and *The Shadow Line,* superficially stories of the indomitable, that same consuming melancholy, that same pressing sense of the irresistible and inexplicable, is always just beneath the surface. Captain Mac Whirr gets the *Nan-Shan* to port at last, but it is a victory that stands quite outside the man himself; he is no more than a marker in the unfathomable game; the elemental forces, fighting one another, almost disregard him; the view of him that we get is one of disdain, almost one of contempt. So, too, in *Youth.* A tale of the spirit's triumph, of youth besting destiny? I do not see it so. To me its significance, like that of *The Shadow Line,* is all subjective; it is an aging man's elegy upon the hope and high resolution that the years have blown away, a sentimental reminiscence of what the enigmatical gods have had their jest with, leaving only its gallant memory behind. The whole Conradean system sums itself up in the title of *Victory,* an incomparable piece of irony. Imagine a better label for that tragic record of heroic and yet bootless effort, that matchless picture, in microcosm, of the relentlessly cruel revolutions in the macrocosm!

Mr. Follett, perhaps with too much critical facility, finds the cause of Conrad's unyielding pessimism in the circumstances of his own life—his double exile, first from Poland, and then from the sea. But this is surely stretching the facts to fit an hypothesis. Neither exile, it must be plain, was enforced, nor is either irrevocable. Conrad has been back to Poland, and he is free to return to the ships whenever the spirit moves him. I see no reason for looking in such directions for his view of the world, nor even in the direction of his nationality. We detect certain curious qualities in every Slav simply because he is more given than we are to revealing the qualities that are in all of us. Introspection and self-revelation are his habit; he carries the study of man and fate to a point that seems morbid to westerners; he is forever gabbling about what he finds in his own soul. But in the last analysis his verdicts are the immemorial and almost universal ones. Surely his resignationism is not a Slavic copyright; all human philosophies and religions seem doomed to come to it at last. Once it takes shape as the concept of Nirvana, the desire for nothingness, the will to not-will. Again, it is fatalism in this form or that—Mohammedanism, Agnosticism . . . Calvinism! Yet again, it is the "Out, out, brief candle!" of Shakespeare, the *"Eheu fugaces"* of Horace, the *"Vanitas vanitatum; omnia vanitas!"* of the Preacher. Or, to make an end, it is millenarianism, the theory that the world is going to blow up tomorrow, or the day after, or two weeks hence, and that all sweating and striving are thus useless. Search where you will, near or far, in ancient or modern times, and you will never find a first-rate race or an enlightened age, in its moments of highest reflection, that ever gave more than a passing bow to optimism. Even Christianity, starting out as "glad tidings," has had to take on protective coloration to survive, and today its chief professors moan and blubber like Johann in Herod's rain-barrel. The sanctified are few and far between. The vast majority of us must suffer in hell, just as we suffer on earth. The divine grace, so omnipotent to save, is withheld from us. Why? There, alas, is your insoluble mystery, your riddle of the universe! . . .

This conviction that human life is a seeking without a finding, that its purpose is impenetrable, that joy and sorrow are alike meaningless, you will see written largely in the work of most great creative artists. It is obviously the final message, if any message is genuinely to be found there, of the nine symphonies of Ludwig van Beethoven, or, at any rate, of the three which show any intellectual content at all. Mark Twain, superficially a humourist and hence an optimist, was haunted by it in secret, as Nietzsche was by the idea of eternal recurrence: it forced itself through his guard in *The Mysterious Stranger* and *What is Man?* In Shakespeare, as Shaw has demonstrated, it amounts to a veritable obsession. And what else is there in Balzac, Goethe, Swift, Molière, Turgenev, Ibsen, Dostoyevsky, Romain Rolland, Anatole France? Or in the Zola of *L'Assomoir, Germinal, La Débâcle,* the whole Rougon-Macquart series? (The Zola of *Les Quatres Evangiles,* and particularly of *Fécondité,* turned meliorist and idealist, and became ludicrous.) Or in the Hauptmann of *Fuhrmann Henschel,* or in Hardy, or in Sudermann? (I mean, of course, Sudermann the novelist. Sudermann the dramatist is a mere mechanician.) . . . The younger men in all countries, insofar as they challenge the current sentimentality at all, seem to move irresistibly toward the same disdainful skepticism. Consider the last words of *Riders to the Sea.* Or Gorky's *Nachtasyl.* Or Frank Norris' *McTeague.* Or Stephen Crane's *The Blue Hotel.* Or the ironical fables of Dunsany. Or Dreiser's *Jennie Gerhardt.* Or George Moore's *Sister Teresa.*

Conrad, more than any of the other men I have mentioned, grounds his work firmly upon this sense of cosmic implacability, this confession of unintelligibility. The exact point of the story of Kurtz, in *Heart of Darkness,* is that it is pointless, that Kurtz's death is as meaningless as his life, that the moral of such a sordid tragedy is a wholesale negation of all morals. And this, no less, is the point of the story of Falk, and of that of Almayer, and of that of Jim. Mr. Follett (he must be a forward-looker in his heart!) finds himself, in the end, unable to accept so profound a determinism unadulterated, and so he injects a gratuitous and mythical romanticism into it, and hymns Conrad "as a comrade, one of a company gathered under the ensign of hope for common war on despair." With even greater error, William Lyon Phelps argues that his books "are based on the axiom of the moral law."[2] The one notion is as unsound as the other. Conrad makes war on nothing; he is preeminently *not* a moralist. He swings, indeed, as far from revolt and moralizing as is possible, for he does not even criticize God. His undoubted comradeship, his plain kindliness toward the soul he vivisects, is not the fruit of moral certainty, but of moral agnosticism.

He neither protests nor punishes; he merely smiles and pities. Like Mark Twain he might well say: "The more I see of men, the more they amuse me—and the more I pity them." He is *simpatico* precisely because of this ironical commiseration, this infinite disillusionment, this sharp understanding of the narrow limits of human volition and responsibility . . . I have said that he does not criticize God. One may even imagine him pitying God. . . .

§ 2

But in this pity, I need not add, there is no touch of sentimentality. No man could be less the romantic, blubbering over the sorrows of his own Werthers. No novelist could have smaller likeness to the brummagem emotion-squeezers of the Kipling type, with their playhouse fustian and their naïve ethical cocksureness. The thing that sets off Conrad from these facile fellows, and from the shallow pseudo-realists who so often coalesce with them and become indistinguishable from them, is precisely his quality of irony, and that irony is no more than a proof of the greater maturity of his personal culture, his essential superiority as a civilized man. It is the old difference between a Huxley and a Gladstone, a philosophy that is profound and a philosophy that is merely comfortable, "*Quid est veritas?*" and "Thus saith the Lord!" He brings into the English fiction of the day, not only an artistry that is vastly more fluent and delicate than the general, but also a highly unusual sophistication, a quite extraordinary detachment from all petty rages and puerile certainties. The winds of doctrine, howling all about him, leave him absolutely unmoved. He belongs to no party and has nothing to teach, save only a mystery as old as man. In the midst of the hysterical splutterings and battle cries of the Kiplings and Chestertons, the booming pedagogics of the Wellses and Shaws, and the smirking at keyholes of the Bennetts and de Morgans, he stands apart and almost alone, observing the sardonic comedy of man with an eye that sees every point and significance of it, but vouchsafing none of that sophomoric indignation, that Hyde Park wisdom, that flabby moralizing which freight and swamp the modern English novel. "At the centre of his web," says Arthur Symons, "sits an elemental sarcasm discussing human affairs with a calm and cynical ferocity. . . . He calls up all the dreams and illusions by which men have been destroyed and saved, and lays them mockingly naked. . . . He shows the bare side of every virtue, the hidden heroism of every vice and crime. He summons before him all the injustices that have come to birth out of ignorance and self-love. . . . And in all this there is no judgment, only an implacable comprehension, as of one outside nature, to whom joy and sorrow, right and wrong, savagery and civilization, are equal and indifferent. . . ."[3]

Obviously, no Englishman! No need to explain (with something akin to apology) that his name is really not Joseph Conrad at all, but Teodor Josef Konrad Karzeniowski, and that he is a Pole of noble lineage, with a vague touch of the Asiatic in him. The Anglo-Saxon mind, in these later days, becomes increasingly incapable of his whole point of view. Put into plain language, his doctrine can only fill it with wonder and fury. That mind is essentially moral in cut; it is believing, certain, indignant; it is as incapable of skepticism, save as a passing coryza of the spirit, as it is of wit, which is skepticism's daughter. Time was when this was not true, as Congreve, Pope, Wycherley and even Thackeray show, but that time was before the Reform Bill of 1832, the great intellectual levelling, the emancipation of the *chandala*. In these our days the Englishman is an incurable foe of distinction, and being so he must needs take in with his mother's milk the delusions which go with that enmity, and particularly the master delusion that all human problems, in the last analysis, are readily soluble, and that all that is required for their solution is to take counsel freely, to listen to wizards, to count votes, to agree upon legislation. This is the prime and immovable doctrine of the *mobile vulgus* set free; it is the loveliest of all the fruits of its defective powers of observation and reasoning, and above all, of its defective knowledge of demonstrated facts, especially in history. Take away this notion that there is some mysterious infallibility in the sense of the majority, this theory that the consensus of opinion is inspired, and the idea of equality begins to wither; in fact, it ceases to have any intelligibility at all. But the notion is not taken away; it is nourished; it flourishes on its own effluvia. And out of it spring the two rules which give direction to all popular thinking, the first being that no concept in politics or conduct is valid (or more accurately respectable), which rises above the comprehension of the great masses of men, or which violates any of their inherent prejudices or superstitions, and the second being that the articulate individual in the mob takes on some of the authority and inspiration of the mob itself, and that he is thus free to set himself up as a soothsayer, so long as he does not venture beyond the aforesaid bounds—in brief, that one man's opinion, provided it observe the current decorum, is as good as any other man's.

Practically, of course, this is simply an invitation to quackery. The man of genuine ideas is hedged in by taboos; the quack finds an audience already agape. The reply to the invitation, in the domain of applied ethics, is the revived and reinforced *Sklavenmoral* that besets all of us of English speech—the huggermugger morality of timorous, whining, unintelligent and unimaginative men—envy turned into law, cowardice sanctified, stupidity made noble, Puritanism. And in the theoretical field there is an even more luxuriant crop of bosh. Mountebanks almost innumerable tell us what we should believe and practice, in politics, religion, philosophy and the arts. England and the United States, between them, house more creeds than all the rest of the world together, and they are more absurd. They rise, they flame, they fall and go out, but always there are new ones, always the latest is worse than the last. What modern civilization save this of ours could have produced Christian Science, or the New Thought, or Billy Sundayism? What other could have yielded up the mawkish bumptiousness of the Uplift? What other could accept gravely the astounding imbecilities of English philanthropy and American law? The native output of fallacy and sentimentality, in fact, is not enough to satisfy the stupendous craving of the mob unleashed; there must needs be a constant importation of the aberrant fancies of other peoples. Let a new messiah leap up with a new message in any part of the world, and at once there is a response from the two great free nations. Once it was Tolstoi with a mouldy asceticism made of catacomb Christianity and senile soul-sickness; again it was Bergson, with a perfumed quasi-philosophy for the boudoirs of the faubourgs; yet again came Rudolf Eucken and Pastor Wagner, with their middle-class beeriness and banality. The list need go no further. It begins with preposterous Indian swamis and yoghis (most of them, to do them justice, diligent Jews from Grand street or the bagnios of Constantinople), and it ends with the fabulous Ibsen of the symbols (no more the real Ibsen than Christ was a prohibitionist), the Ellen Key of the new gyneolatry and the Signorina Montessori of the magical Method. It was a sure instinct that brought Eusapia Palladino to New York. It was the same sure instinct that brought Hall Caine.

I have mentioned Ibsen. A glance at the literature he has spawned in the vulgate is enough to show how much his falser aspects have intrigued the American mind and how little it has reacted to his shining skill as a dramatic craftsman—his one authentic claim upon fame. Read Jennette Lee's *The Ibsen Secret*,[4] perhaps the most successful of all the Ibsen gemaras in English, if you would know the virulence of the national appetite for bogus revelation. And so in all the arts. Whatever is profound and penetrating we stand off from; whatever is facile and shallow, particularly if it reveal a moral or mystical color, we embrace. Ibsen the first-rate dramatist was rejected with indignation precisely because of his merits—his sharp observation, his sardonic realism, his unsentimental logic. But the moment a meretricious and platitudinous ethical purpose began to be read into him—how he protested against it!—he was straightway adopted into our flabby culture. Compare Hauptmann and Brieux, the one a great artist, the other no more than a raucous journalist. Brieux's elaborate proofs that two and two are four have been hailed as epoch-making; one of his worst plays, indeed, has been presented with all the solemn hocus-pocus of a religious rite. But Hauptmann remains almost unknown; even the Nobel Prize did not give him a vogue. Run the roll: Maeterlinck and his languishing supernaturalism, Tagore and his Asiatic wind music, Selma Lagerlöf and her old maid's mooniness, Bernstein, Molnar and company and their out-worn tricks—but I pile up no more names. Consider one fact: the civilization that kissed Maeterlinck on both cheeks, and Tagore perhaps even more intimately, has yet to shake hands with Anatole France. . . .

This bemusement by superficial ideas, this neck-bending to quacks, this endless appetite for sesames and apocalypses, is depressingly visible in our native literature, as it is in our native theology, philosophy, and politics. "The British and American mind," says W. L. George,[5] "has been long honeycombed with moral impulse, at any rate since the Reformation; it is very much what the German mind was up to the middle of the Nineteenth Century." The artist, facing an audience which seems incapable of differentiating between aesthetic and ethical values, tends to become a preacher of sonorous nothings, and the actual moralist-propagandist finds his way into art well greased. No other people in Christendom produces so vast a crop of tin-horn haruspices. We have so many Orison Swett Mardens, Martin Tuppers, Edwin Markhams, Gerald Stanley Lees, Dr. Frank Cranes and Dr. Sylvanus

Stalls that their output is enough to supply the whole planet. We see, too, constantly, how thin is the barrier separating the chief Anglo-Saxon novelists and playwrights from the pasture of the platitudinarian. Jones and Pinero both made their first strikes, not as the artists they undoubtedly are, but as pinchbeck moralists, moaning over the sad fact that girls are seduced. Shaw, a highly dexterous dramaturgist, smothers his dramaturgy in a pifflish iconoclasm that is no more than a disguise for Puritanism. Bennett and Wells, competent novelists, turn easily from the novel to the volume of shoddy philosophizing. Kipling, with *Kim* behind him, becomes a vociferous leader-writer of the *Daily Mail* school, whooping a pothouse patriotism, hurling hysterical objurgations at the foe. Even W. L. George, potentially a novelist of sound consideration, drops his craft for the jehad of the suffragettes. Doyle, Barrie, Caine, Locke, Barker, Mrs. Ward, Beresford, Hewlett, Watson, Quiller-Couch—one and all, high and low, they are tempted by the public demand for sophistry, the ready market for pills. A Henry Bordeaux, in France, is an exception; in England he is the rule. The endless thirst to be soothed with cocksure asseverations, the great mob yearning to be dosed and comforted, is the undoing, over there, of three imaginative talents out of five.

And, in America, of nearly five out of five. Winston Churchill may serve as an example. He is a literary workman of very decent skill; the native critics speak of him with invariable respect; his standing within the craft was shown when he was unanimously chosen first president of the Authors' League of America. Examine his books in order. They proceed steadily from studies of human character and destiny, the proper business of the novelist, to mere outpourings of social and economic panaceas, the proper business of leader writers, chautauquas rabble-rousers and hedge politicians. *The Celebrity* and *Richard Carvel*, within their limits, are works of art; *The Inside of the Cup* is no more than a compendium of paralogy, as silly and smattering as a speech by William Jennings Bryan or a shocker by Jane Addams. Churchill, with the late Jack London to bear him company, may stand for a large class; in its lower ranks are such men as Reginald Wright Kauffman and Will Levington Comfort. Still more typical of the national taste for moral purpose and quack philosophy are the professional optimists and eye-dimmers, with their two grand divisions, the boarding-school romantics and the Christian Endeavor Society sentimentalists. Of the former I give you George Barr McCutcheon, Owen Wister, the late Richard Harding Davis, and a horde of women—most of them now humanely translated to the moving pictures. Of the latter I give you the fair authors of the "glad" books, so gigantically popular, so lavishly praised in the newspapers—with the wraith of the later Howells, the virtuous, kittenish Howells, floating about in the air above them. No other country can parallel this literature, either in its copiousness or in its banality. It is native and peculiar to a civilization which erects the unshakable certainties of the misinformed and quack-ridden into a national way of life. . . .

§ 3

My business, however, is not with the culture of Anglo-Saxondom, but only with Conrad's place therein. That place is isolated and remote; he is neither of it nor quite in it. In the midst of a futile meliorism which deceives the more, the more it soothes, he stands out like some sinister skeleton at the feast, regarding the festivities with a flickering and impenetrable grin. "To read him," says Arthur Symons, "is to shudder on the edge of a gulf, in a silent darkness." There is no need to be told that he is there almost by accident, that he came in a chance passerby, a bit uncertain of the door. It was not an artistic choice that made him write English instead of French; it was a choice with its roots in considerations far afield.

But once made, it concerned him no further. In his first book he was plainly a stranger, and all himself; in his last he is a stranger still—strange in his manner of speech, strange in his view of life, strange, above all, in his glowing and gorgeous artistry, his enthusiasm for beauty per se, his absolute detachment from that heresy which would make it no more than a servant to some bald and depressing theory of conduct, some axiom of the uncomprehending. He is, like Dunsany, a pure artist. His work, as he once explained, is not to edify, to console, to improve or to encourage, but simply to get upon paper some shadow of his own eager sense of the wonder and prodigality of life as men live it in the world, and of its unfathomable romance and mystery. *My task,* he went on, "is, by the power of the written word, to make you hear, to make you feel—it is, before all, to make you *see.* That—and no more, and it is everything." . . .[6]

This detachment from all infra-and-ultra-artistic purpose, this repudiation of the rôle of propagandist, this avowal of what Nietzsche was fond of calling innocence, explains the failure of Conrad to fit into the pigeonholes so laboriously prepared for him by critics who must shelve and label or be damned. He is too big for any of them, and of a shape too strange. He stands clear, not only of all the schools and factions that obtain in latter-day English fiction, but also of the whole stream of English literature since the Restoration. He is as isolated a figure as George Moore, and for much the same reason. Both are exotics, and both, in a very real sense, are public enemies, for both war upon the philosophies that caress the herd. Is Conrad the beyond-Kipling, as the early criticism of him sought to make him? Nonsense! As well speak of Mark Twain as the beyond-Petroleum V Nasby (as, indeed, was actually done). He is not only a finer artist than Kipling; he is a quite different kind of artist. Kipling, within his limits, shows a talent of a very high order. He is a craftsman of the utmost deftness. He gets his effects with almost perfect assurance.

Moreover, there is a poet in him; he knows how to reach the emotions. But once his stories are stripped down to the bare carcass their emptiness becomes immediately apparent. The ideas in them are not the ideas of a reflective and perspicacious man, but simply the ideas of a mobrator, a mouther of inanities, a bugler, a schoolgirl. Reduce any of them to a simple proposition, and that proposition, in so far as it is intelligible at all, will be ridiculous. It is precisely here that Conrad leaps immeasurably ahead. His ideas are not only sound; they are acute and unusual. They plough down into the substrata of human motive and act. They unearth conditions and considerations that lie concealed from the superficial glance. They get at the primary reactions. In particular and above all, they combat the conception of man as a pet and privy councillor of the gods, working out his own destiny in a sort of vacuum and constantly illumined by infallible revelations of his duty, and expose him as he is in fact: an organism infinitely more sensitive and responsive than other organisms, but still a mere organism in the end, a brother to the wild things and the protozoa, swayed by the same inscrutable fortunes, condemned to the same inchoate errors and irresolutions, and surrounded by the same terror and darkness. . . .

But is the Conrad I here describe simply a new variety of moralist, differing from the general only in the drift of the doctrine he preaches? Surely not. He is no more a moralist than an atheist is a theologian. His attitude toward all moral systems and axioms is that of a skeptic who rejects them unanimously, even including, and perhaps especially including, those to which, in moments of æsthetic detachment, he seems to give a formal and resigned sort of assent. It is this constant falling back upon "I do not know," this incessant conversion of the easy logic of romance into the harsh and dismaying logic of fact, that explains his failure to succeed as a popular novelist, despite his skill at evoking emotion, his towering artistic passion, his power to tell a thumping tale. He is talked of, he brings forth a mass of punditic criticism, he becomes in a sense the fashion; but it would be absurd to say that he has made the same profound impression upon the great class of normal novel-readers that Arnold Bennett once made, or H. G. Wells, or William de Morgan in his brief day, or even such cheap-jacks as Anthony Hope Hawkins and William J. Locke. His show fascinates, but his philosophy, in the last analysis, is unbearable. And in particular it is unbearable to women. One rarely meets a woman who, stripped of affection, shows any genuine enthusiasm for a Conrad book, or, indeed, any genuine comprehension of it. The feminine mind, which rules in English fiction, both as producer and as consumer, craves inevitably a more confident and comforting view of the world than Conrad has to offer. It seeks, not disillusion, but illusion. It protects itself against the disquieting questioning of life by pretending that all the riddles have been solved, that each new sage answers them afresh, that a few simple principles suffice to dispose of them. Women, one may say, have to subscribe to absurdities in order to account for themselves at all; it is the instinct of self-preservation which sends them to priests, as to other quacks. This is not because they are unintelligent, but rather because they have that sharp and sure sort of intelligence which is instinctive, and which passes under the name of intuition. It teaches them that the taboos which surround them, however absurd at bottom, nevertheless penalize their courage and curiosity with unescapable dudgeon, and so they become partisans of the existing order, and, per corollary, of the existing ethic. They may be menaced by phantoms, but at all events these phantoms really menace them. A woman who reacted otherwise than with distrust to such a book as *Victory* would be as abnormal as a woman who embraced *Jenseits von Gut und Böse* or *The Inestimable Life of the Great Gargantua.*

As for Conrad, he retaliates by approaching the sex somewhat gingerly. His women, in the main, are no more than soiled and tattered cards in a game played by the gods. The effort to erect them into the customary "sympathetic" heroines of fiction always breaks down under the drum fire of the plain facts. He sees quite accurately, it seems to me, how vastly the rôle of women has been exaggerated, how little they amount to in the authentic struggle of man. His heroes are moved by avarice, by ambition, by rebellion, by fear, by that "obscure inner necessity" which passes for nobility or the sense of duty—never by that puerile passion which is the mainspring of all masculine acts and aspirations in popular novels and on the stage. If they yield to amour at all, it is only at the urging of some more powerful and characteristic impulse, e.g., a fantastic notion of chivalry, as in the case of Heyst, or the thirst for dominion, as in the case of Kurtz. The one exception is offered by Razumov—and Razumov is Conrad's picture of a flabby fool, of a sentimentalist destroyed by his sentimentality. Dreiser has shown much the same process in Witla and Cowperwood, but he is less free from the conventional obsession than Conrad; he takes a love affair far more naïvely, and hence far more seriously.

I used to wonder why Conrad never tackled a straight-out story of adultery under Christianity, the standard matter of all our more pretentious fiction and drama. I was curious to see what his ethical agnosticism would make of it. The conclusion I came to at first was that his failure marked the limitations of his courage—in brief, that he hesitated to go against the orthodox axioms and assumptions in the department where they were most powerfully maintained. But it seems to me now that his abstinence has not been the fruit of timidity, but of disdain. He has shied at the hypothesis, not at its implications. His whole work, in truth, is a destructive criticism of the prevailing notion that such a story is momentous and worth telling. The current gyneolatry is as far outside his scheme of things as the current program of rewards and punishments, sins and virtues, causes and effects. He not only sees clearly that the destiny and soul of man are not moulded by petty jousts of sex, as the prophets of romantic love would have us believe; he is so impatient of the fallacy that he puts it as far behind him as possible, and sets his conflicts amid scenes that it cannot penetrate, save as a palpable absurdity. Love, in his stories, is either a feeble phosphorescence or a gigantic grotesquerie. In *Heart of Darkness*, perhaps, we get his typical view of it. Over all the frenzy and horror of the tale itself floats the irony of the trusting heart back in Brussels. Here we have his measure of the master sentimentality of them all. . . .

§ 4

As for Conrad the literary craftsman, opposing him for the moment to Conrad the showman of the human comedy, the quality that all who write about him seem chiefly to mark in him is his scorn of conventional form, his tendency to approach his story from two directions at once, his frequent involvement in apparently inextricable snarls of narrative, sub-narrative and sub-sub-narrative. *Lord Jim*, for example, starts out in the third person, presently swings into an exhaustive psychological discussion by the mythical Marlow, then goes into a brisk narrative at second (and sometimes at third) hand, and finally comes to a halt upon an unresolved dissonance, a half-heard chord of the ninth: "And that's the end. He passes away under a cloud, inscrutable at heart, forgotten, unforgiven, and excessively romantic." *Falk* is also a story within a story; this time the narrator is "one who had not spoken before, a man over fifty." In *Amy Foster* romance is filtered through the prosaic soul of a country doctor; it is almost as if a statistician told the tale of Horatius at the bridge. In *Under Western Eyes* the obfuscation is achieved by "a teacher of languages," endlessly lamenting his lack of the "high gifts of imagination and expression." In *Youth* and *Heart of Darkness* the chronicler and speculator is the shadowy Marlow, a "cloak to goe inbisabell" for Conrad himself. In *Chance* there are two separate stories, imperfectly welded together. Elsewhere there are hesitations, goings back, interpolations, interludes in the Socratic manner. And almost always there is heaviness in the getting under weigh. In *Heart of Darkness* we are on the twentieth page before we see the mouth of the great river, and in *Falk* we are on the twenty-fourth before we get a glimpse of Falk. *Chance* is nearly half done before the drift of the action is clearly apparent. In *Almayer's Folly* we are thrown into the middle of a story, and do not discover its beginning until we come to *An Outcast of the Islands*, a later book. As in structure, so in detail. Conrad pauses to explain, to speculate, to look about. Whole chapters concern themselves with detailed discussions of motives, with exchanges of views, with generalizations abandoned as soon as they are made. Even the author's own story, *A Personal Record* (in the English edition, *Some Reminiscences*) starts near the end, and then goes back, halting tortuously, to the beginning.

In the eyes of orthodox criticism, of course, this is a grave fault. The Kipling-Wells style of swift, shouldering, button-holing writing has accustomed readers and critics alike to a straight course and a rapid tempo. Moreover, it has accustomed them to a forthright certainty and directness of statement; they expect an author to account for his characters at once, and on grounds instantly comprehensible. This omniscience is a part of the prodigality of moral theory that I have been discussing. An author who knows just what is the matter with the world may be quite reasonably expected to know just what is the matter with his hero. Neither sort of assurance, I need not say, is to be found in Conrad. He is an inquirer, not a law-giver; an experimentalist, not a doctor. One constantly derives from his stories the notion that he is as much puzzled by his characters as the reader is—that he, too, is feeling his way among shadowy evidences. The discoveries that we make, about Lord Jim, about Nostromo or about Kurtz, come as fortuitously and as unexpectedly as the discoveries we make about the real figures of our world. The picture is built up bit by bit; it is never flashed suddenly and completely as by best-seller calciums; it remains a bit dim at the end. But in that very dimness, so tantalizing and yet so revealing, lies two-thirds of Conrad's art, or his craft, or his trick, or whatever you choose to call it. What he shows us is blurred at the edges, but so is life itself blurred at the edges. We see least clearly precisely what is nearest to us, and is hence most real to us. A man may profess to understand the President of the United States, but he seldom alleges, even to himself, that he understands his own wife.

In the character and in its reactions, in the act and in the motive: always that tremulousness, that groping, that confession of final bewilderment. "He passes away under a cloud, inscrutable at heart. . . ." And the cloud enshrouds the inner man as well as the outer, the secret springs of his being as well as the overt events of his life. "His meanest creatures," says Arthur Symons, "have in them a touch of honour, of honesty, or of heroism; his heroes have always some error, weakness, or mistake, some sin or crime, to redeem." What is Lord Jim, scoundrel and poltroon or gallant knight? What is Captain MacWhirr, hero or simply ass? What is Falk, beast or idealist? One leaves *Heart of Darkness* in that palpitating confusion which is shot through with intense curiosity. Kurtz is at once the most abominable of rogues and the most fantastic of dreamers. It is impossible to differentiate between his vision and his crimes, though all that we look upon as order in the universe stands between them. In Dreiser's novels there is the same anarchy of valuations, and it is chiefly responsible for the rage he excites in the unintelligent. The essential thing about Cowperwood is that he is two diverse beings at once; a puerile chaser of women and a great artist, a guinea pig and half a god. The essential thing about Carrie Meeber is that she remains innocent in the midst of her contaminations, that the virgin lives on in the kept woman. This is not the art of fiction as it is conventionally practised and understood. It is not explanation, labelling, assurance, moralizing. In the cant of newspaper criticism, it does not "satisfy." But the great artist is never one who satisfies in that feeble sense; he leaves the business to mountebanks who do it better. *My purpose,* said Ibsen, "is not to answer questions; it is to ask them." The spectator must bring something with him beyond the mere faculty of attention. If, coming to Conrad, he cannot, he is at the wrong door.

§ 5

Conrad's predilection for barbarous scenes and the more bald and shocking sort of drama has an obviously autobiographical basis. His own road ran into strange places in the days of his youth. He moved among men who were menaced by all the terrestrial cruelties, and by the almost unchecked rivalry and rapacity of their fellow men, without any appreciable barriers, whether of law, of convention or of sentimentality, to shield them. The struggle for existence, as he saw it, was well nigh as purely physical among human beings as among the carnivora of the jungle. Some of his stories, and among them his very best, are plainly little more than transcripts of his own experience. He himself is the enchanted boy of *Youth*; he is the ship-master of *Heart of Darkness*; he hovers in the background of all the island books and is visibly present in most of the tales of the sea.

And what he got out of that early experience was more than a mere body of reminiscence; it was a scheme of valuations. He came to his writing years with a sailor's disdain for the trifling hazards and emprises of market places and drawing rooms, and it shows itself whenever he sets pen to paper. A conflict, it would seem, can make no impression upon him save it be colossal. When his men combat, not nature, but other men, they carry over into the business the gigantic method of sailors battling with a tempest. *The Secret Agent* and *Under Western Eyes* fill the dull back streets of London and Geneva with pursuits, homicides and dynamitings. *Nostromo* is a long record of treacheries, butcheries and carnalities. *A Point of Honor* is coloured by the senseless, insatiable ferocity of Gobineau's *Renaissance. Victory* ends with a massacre of all the chief personages, a veritable catastrophe of blood. Whenever he turns from the starker lusts to the pale passions of man under civilization, Conrad fails. *The Return* is a thoroughly infirm piece of writing—a second rate magazine story. One concludes at once that the author himself does not believe in it. *The Inheritors* is worse; it becomes, after the first few pages, a flaccid artificiality, a bore. It is impossible to imagine the chief characters of the Conrad gallery in such scenes. Think of Captain MacWhirr reacting to social tradition, Lord Jim immersed in the class war, Lena Hermann seduced by the fashions, Almayer a candidate for office! As well think of Huckleberry Finn at Harvard, or Tom Jones practising law.

These things do not interest Conrad, chiefly, I suppose, because he does not understand them. His concern, one may say, is with the gross anatomy of passion, not with its histology. He seeks to depict emotion, not in its ultimate attenuation, but in its fundamental innocence and fury. Inevitably, his materials are those of what we call melodrama; he is at one, in the bare substance of his tales, with the manufacturers of the baldest shockers. But with a difference!—a difference, to wit, of approach and comprehension, a difference abysmal and revolutionary. He lifts melodrama to the dignity of an important business, and makes it a means to an end that the mere shock-monger never dreams of. In itself, remember, all this up-roar and blood-letting is not incredible, nor even improbable. The world, for all the pressure of order, is still full of savage and stupendous conflicts, of murders and debaucheries, of crimes indescribable and adventures almost unimaginable. One cannot reasonably ask a novelist to deny them or to gloss over them; all one may demand of him is that, if he make artistic use of them, he render them understandable—that he logically account for them, that he give them plausibility by showing their genesis in intelligible motives and colourable events.

The objection to the conventional melodramatist is that he fails to do this. It is not that his efforts are too florid, but that his causes are too puny. For all his exuberance of fancy, he seldom shows us a downright impossible event; what he does constantly show us is an inadequate and hence unconvincing motive. In a cheap theatre we see a bad actor, imperfectly disguised as a viscount, bind a shrieking young woman to the railroad tracks, with an express train approaching. Why does he do it? The melodramatist offers a double-headed reason, the first part being that the viscount is an amalgam of Satan and Don Juan and the second being that the young woman prefers death to dishonour. Both parts are absurd. Our eyes show us at once that the fellow is far more the floorwalker, the head barber, the Knight of Pythias than either the Satan or the Don Juan, and our experience of life tells us that young women in yellow wigs do not actually rate their virginity so dearly. But women are undoubtedly done to death in this way—not every day, perhaps, but now and then. Men bind them, trains run over them, the newspapers discuss the crime, the pursuit of the felon, the ensuing jousting of the jurisconsults. Why, then? The true answer, when it is forthcoming at all, is always much more complex than the melodramatist's answer. It may be so enormously complex, indeed, as to transcend all the normal laws of cause and effect. It may be an answer made up largely, or even wholly, of the fantastic, the astounding, the unearthly reasons of lunacy. That is the chief, if not the only difference between melodrama and reality. The events of the two may be, and often are identical. It is only in their underlying network of causes that they are dissimilar and incommensurate.

Here, in brief, you have the point of essential distinction between the stories of Conrad, a supreme artist in fiction, and the trashy confections of the literary artisans—e.g., Sienkiewicz,

Dumas, Lew Wallace, and their kind. Conrad's materials, at bottom, are almost identical with those of the artisans. He, too, has his chariot races, his castaways, his carnivals of blood in the arena. He, too, takes us through shipwrecks, revolutions, assassinations, gaudy heroisms, abominable treacheries. But always he illuminates the nude and amazing event with shafts of light which reveal not only the last detail of its workings, but also the complex of origins and inducements behind it. Always, he throws about it a probability which, in the end, becomes almost inevitability. His *Nostromo,* for example, in its externals, is a mere tale of South American turmoil; its materials are those of *Soldiers of Fortune.* But what a difference in method, in point of approach, in inner content! Davis was content to show the overt act, scarcely accounting for it at all, and then only in terms of conventional romance. Conrad penetrates to the motive concealed in it, the psychological spring and basis of it, the whole fabric of weakness, habit and aberration underlying it. The one achieved an agreeable romance, and an agreeable romance only. The other achieves an extraordinarily brilliant and incisive study of the Latin-American temperament—a full length exposure of the perverse passions and incomprehensible ideals which provoke presumably sane men to pursue one another like wolves, and of the reactions of that incessant pursuit upon the men themselves, and upon their primary ideas, and upon the institutions under which they live. I do not say that Conrad is always exhaustive in his explanations, or that he is accurate. In the first case I know that he often is not, in the second case I do not know whether he is or he isn't. But I do say that, within the scope of his vision, he is wholly convincing; that the men and women he sets into his scene show ineluctably vivid and persuasive personality; that the theories he brings forward to account for their acts are intelligible; that the effects of those acts, upon actors and immediate spectators alike, are such as might be reasonably expected to issue; that the final impression is one of searching and indubitable veracity. One leaves *Nostromo* with a memory as intense and lucid as that of a real experience. The thing is not mere photography. It is interpretative painting at its highest.

In all his stories you will find this same concern with the inextricable movement of phenomena and noumena between event and event, this same curiosity as to first causes and ultimate effects. Sometimes, as in *The Point of Honor* and *The End of the Tether*, he attempts to work out the obscure genesis, in some chance emotion or experience, of an extraordinary series of transactions. At other times, as in *Typhoon, Youth, Falk* and *The Shadow Line*, his endeavour is to determine the effect of some gigantic and fortuitous event upon the mind and soul of a given man. At yet other times, as in *Almayer's Folly, Lord Jim* and *Under Western Eyes*, it is his aim to show how cause and effect are intricately commingled, so that it is difficult to separate motive from consequence, and consequence from motive. But always it is the process of mind rather than the actual act that interests him. Always he is trying to penetrate the actor's mask and interpret the actor's frenzy. It is this concern with the profounder aspects of human nature, this bold grappling with the deeper and more recondite problems of his art, that gives him consideration as a first-rate artist. He differs from the common novelists of his time as a Beethoven differs from a Mendelssohn. Some of them are quite his equals in technical skill, and a few of them, notably Bennett and Wells, often show an actual superiority, but when it comes to that graver business which underlies all mere virtuosity, he is unmistakably the superior of the whole corps of them.

This superiority is only the more vividly revealed by the shopworn shoddiness of most of his materials. He takes whatever is nearest to hand, out of his own rich experience or out of the common store of romance. He seems to disdain the petty advantages which go with the invention of novel plots, extravagant characters and unprecedented snarls of circumstance. All the classical doings of anarchists are to be found in *The Secret Agent*; one has heard them copiously credited, of late, to so-called Reds. *Youth*, as a story, is no more than an orthodox sea story, and W. Clark Russell contrived better ones. In *Chance* we have a stern father at his immemorial tricks. In *Victory* there are villains worthy of Jack B. Yeats' melodramas of the Spanish Main. In *Nostromo* we encounter the whole stock company of Richard Harding Davis and O. Henry. And in *Under Western Eyes* the protagonist is one who finds his love among the women of his enemies—a situation at the heart of all the military melodramas ever written.

But what Conrad makes of that ancient and flyblown stuff, that rubbish from the lumber room of the imagination! Consider, for example, *Under Western Eyes*, by no means the best of his stories. The plot is that of *Shenandoah* and *Held by the Enemy*—but how brilliantly it is endowed with a new significance, how penetratingly its remotest currents are followed out, how magnificently it is made to fit into that colossal panorama of Holy Russia! It is always this background, this complex of obscure and baffling influences, this drama under the drama, that Conrad spends his skill upon, and not the obvious commerce of the actual stage. It is not the special effect that he seeks, but the general effect. It is not so much man the individual that interests him, as the shadowy accumulation of traditions, instincts and blind chances which shapes the individual's destiny. Here, true enough, we have a full-length portrait of Razumov, glowing with life. But here, far more importantly, we also have an amazingly meticulous and illuminating study of the Russian character, with all its confused mingling of Western realism and Oriental fogginess, its crazy tendency to go shooting off into the spaces of an incomprehensible metaphysic, its general transcendence of all that we Celts and Saxons and Latins hold to be true of human motive and human act. Russia is a world apart: that is the sum and substance of the tale. In the island stories we have the same elaborate projection of the East, of its fantastic barbarism, of brooding Asia. And in the sea stories we have, perhaps for the first time in English fiction, a vast and adequate picture of the sea, the symbol at once of man's eternal striving and of his eternal impotence. Here, at last, the colossus has found its interpreter. There is in *Typhoon* and *The Nigger of the Narcissus,* and, above all, in *The Mirror of the Sea,* a poetic evocation of the sea's stupendous majesty that is unparalleled outside the ancient sagas. Conrad describes it with a degree of graphic skill that is superb and incomparable. He challenges at once the pictorial vigour of Hugo and the aesthetic sensitiveness of Lafcadio Hearn, and surpasses them both. And beyond this mere dazzling visualization, he gets into his pictures an overwhelming sense of that vast drama of which they are no more than the flat, lifeless representation—of that inexorable and uncompassionate struggle which is life itself. The sea to him is a living thing, an omnipotent and unfathomable thing, almost a god. He sees it as the Eternal Enemy, deceitful in its caresses, sudden in its rages, relentless in its enmities, and forever a mystery.

§ 6

Conrad's first novel, *Almayer's Folly,* was printed in 1895. He tells us in *A Personal Record* that it took him seven years to write it—seven years of pertinacious effort, of trial and error, of learning how to write. He was, at this time thirty-eight years old. Seventeen years before, landing in England to fit himself for the British merchant service, he had made his first acquaintance with the English language. The interval had been spent almost continuously at sea—in the Eastern islands, along the China coast, on the Congo and in the South Atlantic. That he hesitated between French and English is a story often told, but he himself is authority for the statement that it is more symbolical than true. Flaubert, in those days, was his idol, as we know, but the speech of his daily business won, and English literature reaped the greatest of all its usufructs from English sea power. To this day there are marks of his origins in his style. His periods, more than once, have an inept and foreign smack. In fishing for the right phrase one sometimes feels that he finds a French phrase, or even a Polish phrase, and that it loses something by being done into English.

The credit for discovering *Almayer's Folly*, as the publishers say, belongs to Edward Garnett, then a reader for T. Fisher Unwin. The book was brought out modestly and seems to have received little attention. The first edition, it would appear, ran to no more than a thousand copies; at all events, specimens of it are now very hard to find, and collectors pay high prices for them. When *An Outcast of the Islands* followed, a year later, a few alert readers began to take notice of the author, and one of them was Sir (then Mr.) Hugh Clifford, a former Governor of the Federated Malay States and himself the author of several excellent books upon the Malay. Clifford gave Conrad encouragement privately and talked him up in literary circles, but the majority of English critics remained unaware of him. After an interval of two years, during which he struggled between his desire to write and the temptation to return to the sea, he published *The Nigger of the Narcissus.*[7] It made a fair success of esteem, but still there was no recognition of the author's true stature. Then followed *Tales of Unrest* and *Lord Jim,* and after them the feeblest of all the Conrad books, *The Inheritors,* written in collaboration with Ford Madox Hueffer. It is easy to see in this collaboration, and no less in the character of the book, an indication of irresolution, and perhaps even of downright loss of hope. But success, in fact, was just around the corner. In 1902 came *Youth,* and straightway Conrad was the lion of literary London. The chorus of approval that greeted it was almost a roar; all sorts of critics and reviewers, from H. G. Wells to W. L. Courtney, and from John Galsworthy to W. Robertson Nicoll, took a hand. Writing home to the New York *Times,* W. L. Alden reported that he had "not heard one dissenting voice in regard to the book," but that the praise it received "was unanimous," and that the newspapers and literary weeklies rivalled one another "in their efforts to express their admiration for it."

This benign whooping, however, failed to awaken the enthusiasm of the mass of novel-readers and brought but meagre orders from the circulating libraries. *Typhoon* came upon the heels of *Youth*, but still the sales of the Conrad books continued small and the author remained in very uncomfortable circumstances. Even after four or five years he was still so poor that he was glad to accept a modest pension from the British Civil List. This official recognition of his genius, when it came at last, seems to have impressed the public, characteristically enough, far more than his books themselves had done, and the foundations were thus laid for that wider recognition of his genius which now prevails. But getting him on his legs was slow work, and such friends as Hueffer, Clifford and Galsworthy had to do a lot of arduous logrolling. Even after the splash made by *Youth* his publishing arrangements seem to have remained somewhat insecure. His first eleven books show six different imprints; it was not until his twelfth that he settled down to a publisher. His American editions tell an even stranger story. The first six of them were brought out by six different publishers; the first eight by no less than seven. But today he has a regular American publisher at last, and in England a complete edition of his works is in progress.

Thanks to the indefatigable efforts of that American publisher (who labours for Gene Stratton-Porter and Gerald Stanley Lee in the same manner) Conrad has been forced upon the public notice in the United States, and it is the fashion among all who pretend to aesthetic consciousness to read him, or, at all events, to talk about him. His books have been brought together in a uniform edition for the newly intellectual, bound in blue leather, like the "complete library sets" of Kipling, O. Henry, Guy de Maupassant, and Paul de Kock. The more literary newspapers print his praises; he is hymned by professorial critics as a prophet of virtue; his genius is certificated by such diverse authorities as Hildegarde Hawthorne and Louis Joseph Vance; I myself lately sat on a Conrad Committee, along with Booth Tarkington, David Belasco, Irvin Cobb, Walter Pritchard Eaton and Hamlin Garland—surely an astounding posse of *literati!* Moreover, Conrad himself shows a disposition to reach out for a wider audience. His *Victory,* first published in *Munsey's Magazine,* revealed obvious efforts to be intelligible to the general. A few more turns of the screw and it might have gone into the *Saturday Evening Post,* between serials by Harris Dickson and Rex Beach.

Meanwhile, in the shadow of this painfully growing celebrity as a novelist, Conrad takes on conderation as a bibelot, and the dealers in first editions probably make more profit out of some of his books than ever he has made himself. His manuscripts are cornered, I believe, by an eminent collector of literary curiosities in New York, who seems to have a contract with the novelist to take them as fast as they are produced—perhaps the only arrangement of the sort in literary history. His first editions begin to bring higher premiums than those of any other living author. Considering the fact that the oldest of them is less than twenty-five years old, they probably set new records for the trade. Even the latest in date are eagerly sought, and it is not uncommon to see an English edition of a Conrad book sold at an advance in New York within a month of its publication.[8]

As I hint, however, there is not much reason to believe that this somewhat extravagant fashion is based upon any genuine liking, or any very widespread understanding. The truth is that, for all the adept tub-thumping of publishers, Conrad's sales still fall a good deal behind those of even the most modest of best-seller manufacturers, and that the respect with which his successive volumes are received is accompanied by enthusiasm in a relatively narrow circle only. A clan of Conrad fanatics exists, and surrounding it there is a body of readers who read him because it is the intellectual thing to do, and who talk of him because talking of him is expected. But beyond that he seems to make little impression. When *Victory* was printed in *Munsey's Magazine* it was a failure; no other single novel, indeed, contributed more toward the abandonment of the policy of printing a complete novel in each issue. The other popular magazines show but small inclination for Conrad manuscripts. Some time ago his account of a visit to Poland in wartime was offered on the American market by an English author's agent. At the start a price of $2,500 was put upon it, but after vainly inviting buyers for a couple of months it was finally disposed of to a literary newspaper which seldom spends so much as $2,500, I daresay, for a whole month's supply of copy.

In the United States, at least, novelists are made and unmade, not by critical majorities, but by women, male and female. The art of fiction among us, as Henry James once said, "is almost exclusively feminine." In the books of such a man as William Dean Howells it is difficult to find a single line that is typically and exclusively masculine. One could easily imagine Edith Wharton, or Mrs. Watts, or even Agnes Repplier, writing all of them. When a first-rate novelist emerges from obscurity it is almost always by some fortuitous plucking of the dexter string. *Sister Carrie,* for example, has made a belated commercial success, not because its dignity as a human document is understood, but because it is mistaken for a sad tale of amour, not unrelated to *The Woman Thou Gavest Me* and *Dora Thorne.* In Conrad there is no such sweet bait for the fair and sentimental. The sedentary multipara, curled up in her boudoir on a rainy afternoon, finds nothing to her taste in his grim tales. The Conrad philosophy is harsh, unyielding, repellent. The Conrad heroes are nearly all boors and ruffians. Their very love-making has something sinister and abhorrent in it; one cannot imagine them in the moving pictures, played by tailored beauties with long eyelashes. More, I venture that the censors would object to them, even disguised as floor-walkers. Surely that would be a besotted board which would pass the irregular amours of Lord Jim, the domestic brawls of Almayer, the revolting devil's mass of Kurtz, Falk's disgusting feeding in the Southern Ocean, or the butchery on Heyst's island. Stevenson's *Treasure Island* has been put upon the stage, but *An Outcast of the Islands* would be as impossible there as *Barry Lyndon* or *La Terre.* The world fails to breed actors for such rôles, or stage managers to penetrate such travails of the spirit, or audiences for the revelation thereof.

With the Conrad cult, so discreetly nurtured out of a Barabbasian silo, there arises a considerable Conrad literature, most of it quite valueless. Huneker's essay, in *Ivory, Apes and Peacocks,*[9] gets little beyond the obvious; William Lyon Phelps, in *The Advance of the English Novel,* achieves only a meagre judgment;[10] Frederic Taber Cooper tries to estimate such things as *The Secret Agent* and *Under Western Eye* in terms of the Harvard enlightenment;[11] John Galsworthy wastes himself upon futile comparisons;[12] even Sir Hugh Clifford, for all his quick insight, makes irrelevant objections to Conrad's principles of Malay psychology.[13] Who cares? Conrad is his own God, and creates his own Malay! The best of the existing studies of Conrad, despite certain sentimentalities arising out of youth and schooling, is in the book of Wilson Follett, before mentioned. The worst is in the official biography by Richard Curie,[14] for which Conrad himself obtained a publisher and upon which his *imprimatur* may be thus assumed to lie. If it does, then its absurdities are nothing new, for we all know what a botch Ibsen made of accounting for himself. But, even so, the assumption stretches the probabilities more than once. Surely it is hard to think of Conrad putting *Lord Jim* below *Chance* and *The Secret Agent* on the ground that it "raises a fierce moral issue." Nothing, indeed, could be worse nonsense—save it be an American critic's doctrine that "Conrad denounces pessimism."

Lord Jim no more raises a moral issue than *The Titan.* It is, if anything, a devastating exposure of a moral issue. Its villain is almost heroic; its hero, judged by his peers, is a scoundrel. . . .

Hugh Walpole, himself a competent novelist, does far better in his little volume, *Joseph Conrad.*[15] In its brief space he is unable to examine all of the books in detail, but he at least manages to get through a careful study of Conrad's method, and his professional skill and interest make it valuable.

§ 7

There is a notion that judgments of living artists are impossible. They are bound to be corrupted, we are told, by prejudice, false perspective, mob emotion, error. The question whether this or that man is great or small is one which only posterity can answer. A silly begging of the question, for doesn't posterity also make mistakes? Shakespeare's ghost has seen two or three posterities, beautifully at odds. Even today, it must notice a difference in flitting from London to Berlin. The shade of Milton has been tricked in the same way. So, also, has Johann Sebastian Bach's. It needed a Mendelssohn to rescue it from Coventry—and now Mendelssohn himself, once so shining a light, is condemned to the shadows in his turn. We are not dead yet; we are here, and it is now. Therefore, let us at least venture, guess, opine.

My own conviction, sweeping all those reaches of living fiction that I know, is that Conrad's figure stands out from the field like the Alps from the Piedmont plain. He not only has no masters in the novel; he has scarcely a colourable peer. Perhaps Thomas Hardy and Anatole France—old men both, their work behind them. But who else? James is dead. Meredith is dead. So is George Moore, though he lingers on. So are all the Russians of the first rank; Andrieff, Gorki and their like are light cavalry. In Sudermann,

Germany has a writer of short stories of very high calibre, but where is the German novelist to match Conrad? Clara Viebig? Thomas Mann? Gustav Frenssen? Arthur Schnitzler?, Surely not! As for the Italians, they are either absurd tear-squeezers or more absurd harlequins. As for the Spaniards and the Scandinavians, they would pass for geniuses only in Suburbia. In America, setting aside an odd volume here and there, one can discern only Dreiser—and of Dreiser's limitations I shall discourse anon. There remains England. England has the best second-raters in the world; nowhere else is the general level of novel writing so high; nowhere else is there a corps of journeyman novelists comparable to Wells, Bennett, Benson, Walpole, Beresford, George, Galsworthy, Hichens, De Morgan, Miss Sinclair, Hewlett and company. They have a prodigious facility; they know how to write; even the least of them is, at all events, a more competent artisan than, say, Dickens, or Bulwer-Lytton, or Sienkiewicz, or Zola. But the literary *grande passion* is simply not in them. They get nowhere with their suave and interminable volumes. Their view of the world and its wonders is narrow and superficial. They are, at bottom, no more than clever mechanicians.

As Galsworthy has said, Conrad lifts himself immeasurably above them all. One might well call him, if the term had not been cheapened into cant, a cosmic artist. His mind works upon a colossal scale; he conjures up the general out of the particular. What he sees and describes in his books is not merely this man's aspiration or that woman's destiny, but the overwhelming sweep and devastation of universal forces, the great central drama that is at the heart of all other dramas, the tragic struggles of the soul of man under the gross stupidity and obscene joking of the gods. "In the novels of Conrad," says Galsworthy, "nature is first, man is second." But not a mute, a docile second! He may think, as Walpole argues, that "life is too strong, too clever and too remorseless for the sons of men," but he does not think that they are too weak and poor in spirit to challenge it. It is the challenging that engrosses him, and enchants him, and raises up the magic of his wonder. It is as futile, in the end, as Hamlet's or Faust's—but still a gallant and a gorgeous adventure, a game uproariously worth the playing, an enterprise "inscrutable . . . and excessively romantic." . . .

If you want to get his measure, read *Youth* or *Falk* or *Heart of Darkness,* and then try to read the best of Kipling. I think you will come to some understanding, by that simple experiment, of the difference between an adroit artisan's bag of tricks and the lofty sincerity and passion of a first-rate artist.

→ CHAPTER TWO ←

THEODORE DREISER

§ 1

OUT OF THE DESERT OF AMERICAN FICTIONEERING, SO POPULOUS and yet so dreary, Dreiser stands up—a phenomenon unescapably visible, but disconcertingly hard to explain. What forces combined to produce him in the first place, and how has he managed to hold out so long against the prevailing blasts—of disheartening misunderstanding and misrepresentation, of Puritan suspicion and opposition, of artistic isolation, of commercial seduction? There is something downright heroic in the way the man has held his narrow and perilous ground, disdaining all compromise, unmoved by the cheap success that lies so inviting around the corner. He has faced, in his day, almost every form of attack that a serious artist can conceivably encounter, and yet all of them together have scarcely budged him an inch. He still plods along in the laborious, cheerless way he first marked out for himself; he is quite as undaunted by baited praise as by bludgeoning, malignant abuse; his later novels are, if anything, more unyieldingly dreiserian than his earliest. As one who has long sought to entice him in this direction or that, fatuously presuming to instruct him in what would improve him and profit him, I may well hear a reluctant and resigned sort of testimony to his gigantic steadfastness. It is almost as if any change in his manner, any concession to what is usual and esteemed, any amelioration of his blind, relentless exercises of *force majeure,* were a physical impossibility. One feels him at last to be authentically no more than a helpless instrument (or victim) of that inchoate flow of forces which he himself is so fond of depicting as at once the answer to the riddle of life, and a riddle ten times more vexing and accursed.

And his origins, as I say, are quite as mysterious as his motive power. To fit him into the unrolling chart of American, or even of English fiction is extremely difficult. Save one thinks of H. B. Fuller (whose *With the Procession* and *The Cliff-Dwellers* are still remembered by Huneker, but by whom else?[1]), he seems to have had no fore-runner among us, and for all the discussion of him that goes on, he has few avowed disciples, and none of them gets within miles of him. One catches echoes of him, perhaps, in Willa Sibert Cather, in Mary S. Watts, in David Graham Phillips, in Sherwood Anderson and in Joseph Medill Patterson, but, after all, they are no more than echoes. In Robert Herrick the thing descends to a feeble parody; in imitators further removed to sheer burlesque. All the latter-day American novelists of consideration are vastly more facile than Dreiser in their philosophy, as they are in their style. In the fact, perhaps, lies the measure of their difference. What they lack, great and small, is the gesture of pity, the note of awe, the profound sense of wonder—in a phrase, that "soberness of mind" which William Lyon Phelps sees as the hallmark of Conrad and Hardy, and which even the most stupid cannot escape in Dreiser. The normal American novel, even in its most serious forms, takes colour from the national cocksureness and superficiality. It runs monotonously to ready explanations, a somewhat infantile smugness and hopefulness, a habit of reducing the unknowable to terms of the not worth knowing. What it cannot explain away with ready formulae, as in the later Winston Churchill, it snickers over as scarcely worth explaining at all, as in the later Howells. Such a brave and tragic book as *Ethan Frome* is so rare as to be almost singular, even with Mrs. Wharton. There is, I daresay, not much market for that sort of thing. In the arts, as in the concerns of everyday, the American seeks escape from the insoluble by pretending that it is solved. A comfortable phrase is what he craves beyond all things—and comfortable phrases are surely not to be sought in Dreiser's stock.

I have heard argument that he is a follower of Frank Norris, and two or three facts lend it a specious probability. *McTeague* was printed in 1899; *Sister Carrie* a year later. Moreover, Norris was the first to see the merit of the latter book, and he fought a gallant fight, as literary advisor to Doubleday, Page & Co., against its suppression after it was in type. But this theory runs aground upon two circumstances, the first being that Dreiser did not actually read *McTeague,* nor, indeed, grow aware of Norris, until after *Sister Carrie* was completed, and the other being that his development, once he began to write other books, was along paths far distant from those pursued by Norris himself. Dreiser, in truth, was a bigger man than Norris from the start; it is to the latter's unending honour that he recognized the fact instanter, and yet did all he could to help his rival. It is imaginable, of course, that Norris, living fifteen years longer, might have overtaken Dreiser, and even surpassed him; one finds an arrow pointing that way in *Vandover and the Brute* (not printed until 1914). But it swings sharply around in *The Epic of the Wheat.* In the second volume of that incomplete trilogy, *The Pit,* there is an obvious concession to the popular taste in romance; the thing is so frankly written down, indeed, that a play has been made of it, and Broadway has applauded it. And in *The Octopus,* despite some excellent writing, there is a descent to a mysticism so fantastic and preposterous that it quickly passes beyond serious consideration. Norris, in his day, swung even lower—for example, in *A Man's*

Woman and in some of his short stories. He was a pioneer, perhaps only half sure of the way he wanted to go, and the evil lures of popular success lay all about him. It is no wonder that he sometimes seemed to lose his direction.

Émile Zola is another literary father whose paternity grows dubious on examination. I once printed an article exposing what seemed to me to be a Zolaesque attitude of mind, and even some trace of the actual Zola manner, in *Jennie Gerhardt*; there came from Dreiser the news that he had never read a line of Zola, and knew nothing about his novels. Not a complete answer, of course; the influence might have been exerted at second hand. But through whom? I confess that I am unable to name a likely medium. The effects of Zola upon Anglo-Saxon fiction have been almost *nil;* his only avowed disciple, George Moore, has long since recanted and reformed; he has scarcely rippled the prevailing romanticism. . . . Thomas Hardy? Here, I daresay, we strike a better scent. There are many obvious likenesses between *Tess of the D'Urbervilles* and *Jennie Gerhardt* and again between *Jude the Obscure* and *Sister Carrie.* All four stories deal penetratingly and poignantly with the essential tragedy of women; all disdain the petty, specious explanations of popular fiction; in each one finds a poetical and melancholy beauty. Moreover, Dreiser himself confesses to an enchanted discovery of Hardy in 1896, three years before *Sister Carrie* was begun. But it is easy to push such a fact too hard, and to search for likenesses and parallels that are really not there. The truth is that Dreiser's points of contact with Hardy might be easily matched by many striking points of difference, and that the fundamental ideas in their novels, despite a common sympathy, are anything but identical. Nor does one apprehend any ponderable result of Dreiser's youthful enthusiasm for Balzac, which antedated his discovery of Hardy by two years. He got from both men a sense of the scope and dignity of the novel; they taught him that a story might be a good one, and yet considerably more than a story; they showed him the essential drama of the commonplace. But that they had more influence in forming his point of view, or even in shaping his technique, than any one of half a dozen other gods of those young days—this I scarcely find. In the structure of his novels, and in their manner of approach to life no less, they call up the work of Dostoyevsky and Turgenev far more than the work of either of these men—but of all the Russians save Tolstoi (as of Flaubert) Dreiser himself tells us that he was ignorant until ten years after *Sister Carrie.* In his days of preparation, indeed, his reading was so copious and so disorderly that antagonistic influences must have well-nigh neutralized one another, and so left the curious youngster to work out his own method and his own philosophy. Stevenson went down with Balzac, Poe with Hardy, Dumas *fils* with Tolstoi. There were even months of delight in Sienkiewicz, Lew Wallace and E. P. Roe! The whole repertory of the pedagogues had been fought through in school and college: Dickens, Thackeray, Hawthorne, Washington Irving, Kingsley, Scott, Only Irving and Hawthorne seem to have made deep impressions. "I used to lie under a tree," says Dreiser, "and read *Twice Told Tales* by the hour. I thought *The Alhambra* was a perfect creation, and I still have a lingering affection for it." Add Bret Harte, George Ebers, William Dean Howells, Oliver Wendell Holmes, and you have a literary stew indeed! . . . But for all its bubbling I see a far more potent influence in the chance discovery of Spencer and Huxley at twenty-three—the year of choosing! Who, indeed, will ever measure the effect of those two giants upon the young men of that era—Spencer with his inordinate meticulousness, his relentless pursuit of facts, his overpowering syllogisms, and Huxley with his devastating agnosticism, his insatiable questionings of the old axioms, above all, his brilliant style? Huxley, it would appear, has been condemned to the scientific hulks, along with bores innumerable and unspeakable; one looks in vain for any appreciation of him in treatises on beautiful letters.[2] And yet the man was a superb artist in works, a master-writer even more than a master-biologist, one of the few truly great stylists that England has produced since the time of Anne. One can easily imagine the effect of two such vigorous and intriguing minds upon a youth groping about for self-understanding and self-expression. They swept him clean, he tells us, of the lingering faith of his boyhood—a mediaeval, Rhenish Catholicism;—more, they filled him with a new and eager curiosity, an intense interest in the life that lay about him, a desire to seek out its hidden workings and underlying causes. A young man set afire by Huxley might perhaps make a very bad novelist, but it is a certainty that he could never make a sentimental and superficial one. There is no need to go further than this single moving adventure to find the genesis of Dreiser's disdain of the current platitudes, his sense of life as a complex biological phenomenon, only dimly comprehended, and his tenacious way of thinking things out, and of holding to what he finds good. Ah, that he had learned from Huxley, not only how to inquire, but also how to report! That he had picked up a talent for that dazzling style, so sweet to the ear, so damnably persuasive, so crystal-clear!

But the more one examines Dreiser, either as writer or as theorist of man, the more his essential isolation becomes apparent. He got a habit of mind from Huxley, but he completely missed Huxley's habit of writing. He got a view of woman from Hardy, but he soon changed it out of all resemblance. He got a certain fine ambition and gusto out of Balzac, but all that was French and characteristic he left behind. So with Zola, Howells, Tolstoi and the rest. The tracing of likenesses quickly becomes rabbinism, almost cabalism. The differences are huge and sprout up in all directions. Nor do I see anything save a flaming up of colonial passion in the current efforts to fit him into a German frame, and make him an agent of Prussian frightfulness in letters. Such childish gabble one looks for in the *New York Times,* and there is where one actually finds it. Even the literary monthlies have stood clear of it; it is important only as material for that treatise upon the patrioteer and his bawling which remains to be written. The name of the man, true enough, is obviously Germanic, and he has told us himself, in *A Traveler at Forty,* how he sought out and found the tombs of his ancestors in some little town of the Rhine country. There are more of these genealogical revelations in *A Hoosier Holiday,* but they show a Rhenish strain that was already running thin in boyhood. No one, indeed, who reads a Dreiser novel can fail to see the gap separating the author from these half-forgotten forbears. He shows even less of German influence than of English influence.

There is, as a matter of fact, little in modern German fiction that is intelligibly comparable to *Jennie Gerhardt* and *The Titan,* either as a study of man or as a work of art. The naturalistic movement of the eighties was launched by men whose eyes were upon the theatre, and it is in that field that nine-tenths of its force has been spent. "German naturalism," says George Madison Priest, quoting Gotthold Klee's "Grunzüge der deutschen Literaturgeschichte" "created a new type only in the drama."[3] True enough, it has also produced occasional novels, and some of them are respectable. Gustav Frenssen's *Jörn Uhl* is a specimen: it has been done into English. Another is Clara Viebig's *Das tägliche Brot,* which Ludwig Lewisohn compares to George Moore's *Esther Waters.* Yet another is Thomas Mann's *Buddenbrooks.* But it would be absurd to cite these works as evidences of a national quality, and doubly absurd to think of them as inspiring such books as *Jennie Gerhardt* and *The Titan,* which excel them in everything save workmanship. The case of Mann reveals a tendency that is visible in nearly all of his contemporaries. Starting out as an agnostic realist not unlike the Arnold Bennett of *The Old Wives' Tale,* he has gradually taken on a hesitating sort of romanticism, and in one of his later books, *Königliche Hoheit* (in English, *Royal Highness*) he ends upon a note of sentimentalism borrowed from Wagner's *Ring.* Fräulein Viebig has also succumbed to banal and extra-artistic purposes. Her *Die Wacht am Rhein,* for all its merits in detail, is, at bottom, no more than an eloquent hymn to patriotism—a theme which almost always baffles novelists. As for Frenssen, he is a parson by trade, and carries over into the novel a good deal of the windy moralizing of the pulpit. All of these German naturalists—and they are the only German novelists worth considering—share the weakness of Zola, their *Stammvater*. They, too, fall into the morass that engulfed *Fécondité*, and make sentimental propaganda.

I go into this matter in detail, not because it is intrinsically of any moment, but because the effort to depict Dreiser as a secret agent of the Wilhelmstrasse, told off to inject subtle doses of *Kultur* into a naïve and pious people, has taken on the proportions of an organized movement. The same critical imbecility which detects naught save a Tom cat in Frank Cowperwood can find naught save an abhorrent foreigner in Cowperwood's creator. The truth is that the trembling patriots of letters, male and female, are simply at their old game of seeing a man under the bed. Dreiser, in fact, is densely ignorant of German literature, as he is of the better part of French literature, and of much of English literature. He did not even read Hauptmann until after *Jennie Gerhardt* had been written, and such typical German moderns as Ludwig Thoma, Otto Julius Bierbaum and Richard Dehmel remain as strange to him as Heliogabalus.

§ 2

In his manner, as opposed to his matter, he is more the Teuton, for he shows all of the racial patience and pertinacity and all of the racial lack of humour. Writing a novel is as solemn a business to him as trimming a beard is to a German barber. He blasts his way through his interminable stories by something not unlike main strength; his writing, one feels, often takes on the character of an actual siege operation, with tunnellings, drum fire, assaults in close order and hand-to-hand fighting. Once, seeking an analogy, I called him the Hindenburg of the novel. If it holds, then *The 'Genius'* is his Poland. The field of action bears the aspect, at the end, of a hostile province meticulously brought under the yoke, with every road and lane explored to its beginning, and every crossroads village laboriously taken, inventoried and policed. Here is the very negation of Gallic lightness and intuition, and of all other forms of impressionism as well. Here is no series of illuminating flashes, but a gradual bathing of the whole scene with white light, so that every detail stands out.

And many of those details, of course, are trivial; even irritating. They do not help the picture; they muddle and obscure it; one wonders impatiently what their meaning is, and what the purpose may be of revealing them with such a precise, portentous air. . . . Turn to page 703 of *The 'Genius.'* By the time one gets there, one has hewn and hacked one's way through 702 large pages of fine print—97 long chapters, more than 250,000 words. And yet, at this hurried and impatient point, with the *coda* already begun, Dreiser halts the whole narrative to explain the origin, nature and inner meaning of Christian Science, and to make us privy to a lot of chatty stuff about Mrs. Althea Jones, a professional healer, and to supply us with detailed plans and specifications of the apartment house in which she lives, works her tawdry miracles, and has her being. Here, in sober summary, are the particulars:

1. That the house is "of conventional design."
2. That there is "a spacious areaway" between its two wings.
3. That these wings are "of cream-coloured pressed brick."
4. That the entrance between them is "protected by a handsome wrought-iron door."
5. That to either side of this door is "an electric lamp support of handsome design."
6. That in each of these lamp supports there are "lovely cream-coloured globes, shedding a soft lustre."

7. That inside is "the usual lobby."
8. That in the lobby is "the usual elevator."
9. That in the elevator is the usual "uniformed negro elevator man."
10. That this negro elevator man (name not given) is "indifferent and impertinent."
11. That a telephone switchboard is also in the lobby.
12. That the building is seven stories in height.

In *The Financier* there is the same exasperating rolling up of irrelevant facts. The court proceedings in the trial of Cowperwood are given with all the exactness of a parliamentary report in the London *Times*. The speeches of the opposing counsel are set down nearly in full, and with them the remarks of the judge, and after that the opinion of the Appellate Court on appeal, with the dissenting opinions as a sort of appendix. In *Sister Carrie* the thing is less savagely carried out, but that is not Dreiser's fault, for the manuscript was revised by some anonymous hand, and the printed version is but little more than half the length of the original. In *The Titan* and *Jennie Gerhardt* no such brake upon exuberance is visible; both books are crammed with details that serve no purpose, and are as flat as ditch-water. Even in the two volumes of personal record, *A Traveler at Forty* and *A Hoosier Holiday*, there is the same furious accumulation of trivialities. Consider the former. It is without structure, without selection, without reticence. One arises from it as from a great babbling, half drunken. On the one hand the author fills a long and gloomy chapter with the story of the Borgias, apparently under the impression that it is news, and on the other hand he enters into intimate and inconsequential confidences about all the persons he meets en route, sparing neither the innocent nor the obscure. The children of his English host at Bridgely Level strike him as fantastic little creatures, even as a bit uncanny—and he duly sets it down. He meets an Englishman on a French train who pleases him much, and the two become good friends and see Rome together, but the fellow's wife is "obstreperous" and "haughty in her manner" and so "loud-spoken in her opinions" that she is "really offensive"—and down it goes. He makes an impression on a Mlle. Marcelle in Paris, and she accompanies him from Monte Carlo to Ventimiglia, and there gives him a parting kiss and whispers, *"Avril-Fontainebleau"*—and lo, this sweet one is duly spread upon the minutes. He permits himself to be arrested by a fair privateer in Piccadilly, and goes with her to one of the dens of sin that suffragettes see in their nightmares, and cross-examines her at length regarding her ancestry, her professional ethics and ideals, and her earnings at her dismal craft—and into the book goes a full report of the proceedings. He is entertained by an eminent Dutch jurist in Amsterdam—and upon the pages of the chronicle it appears that the gentleman is "waxy" and "a little pedantic," and that he is probably the sort of "thin, delicate, well barbered" professor that Ibsen had in mind when he cast about for a husband for the daughter of General Gabler.

Such is the art of writing as Dreiser understands it and practises it—an endless piling up of minutiae, an almost ferocious tracking down of ions, electrons and molecules, an unshakable determination to tell it all. One is amazed by the mole-like diligence of the man, and no less by his exasperating disregard for the ease of his readers. A Dreiser novel, at least of the later canon, cannot be read as other novels are read—on a winter evening or summer afternoon, between meal and meal, travelling from New York to Boston. It demands the attention for almost a week, and uses up the faculties for a month. If, reading *The 'Genius,'* one were to become engrossed in the fabulous manner described in the publishers' advertisements, and so find oneself unable to put it down and go to bed before the end, one would get no sleep for three days and three nights.

Worse, there are no charms of style to mitigate the rigours of these vast steppes and pampas of narration. Joseph Joubert's saying that "words should stand out well from the paper" is quite incomprehensible to Dreiser; he never imitates Flaubert by writing for *"la respiration et l'oreille."* There is no painful groping for the inevitable word, or for what Walter Pater called "the gipsy phrase"; the common, even the commonplace, coin of speech is good enough. On the first page of *Jennie Gerhardt* one encounters "frank, open countenance," "diffident manner," "helpless poor," "untutored mind," "honest necessity," and half a dozen other stand-bys of the second-rate newspaper reporter. In *Sister Carrie* one finds "high noon," "hurrying throng," "unassuming restaurant," "dainty slippers," "high-strung nature," and "cool, calculating world"—all on a few pages. Carrie's sister, Minnie Hanson, "gets" the supper. Hanson himself is "wrapped up" in his child. Carrie decides to enter Storm and King's office, "no matter what." In *The Titan* the word "trig" is worked to death; it takes on, toward the end, the character of a banal and preposterous refrain. In the other books one encounters mates for it—words made to do duty in as many senses as the American verb "to fix" or the journalistic "to secure." . . .

I often wonder if Dreiser gets anything properly describable as pleasure out of this dogged accumulation of threadbare, undistinguished, uninspiring nouns, adjectives, verbs, adverbs, pronouns, participles and conjunctions. To the man with an ear for verbal delicacies—the man who searches painfully for the perfect word, and puts the way of saying a thing above the thing said—there is in writing the constant joy of sudden discovery, of happy accident. A phrase springs up full blown, sweet and caressing. But what joy can there be in rolling up sentences that have no more life and beauty in them, intrinsically, than so many election bulletins? Where is the thrill in the manufacture of such a paragraph as that in which Mrs.

Althea Jones' sordid habitat is described with such inexorable particularity? Or in the laborious confection of such stuff as this, from Book I, Chapter IV, of *The 'Genius'*?:

The city of Chicago—who shall portray it! This vast ruck of life that had sprung suddenly into existence upon the dank marshes of a lake shore!

Or this from the epilogue to *The Financier*;

There is a certain fish whose scientific name is Mycteroperca Bonaci, and whose common name is Black Grouper, which is of considerable value as an afterthought in this connection, and which deserves much to be better known. It is a healthy creature, growing quite regularly to a weight of two hundred and fifty pounds, and living a comfortable, lengthy existence because of its very remarkable ability to adapt itself to conditions. . . .

Or this from his pamphlet, *Life, Art and America*:[4]

Alas, alas! for art in America. It has a hard stubby row to hoe.

But I offer no more examples. Every reader of the Dreiser novels must cherish astounding specimens—of awkward, platitudinous marginalia, of whole scenes spoiled by bad writing, of phrases as brackish as so many lumps of sodium hyposulphite. Here and there, as in parts of *The Titan* and again in parts of *A Hoosier Holiday*, an evil conscience seems to haunt him and he gives hard striving to his manner, and more than once there emerges something that is almost graceful. But a backsliding always follows this phosphorescence of reform. *The 'Genius,'* coming after *The Titan,* marks the high tide of his bad writing. There are passages in it so clumsy, so inept, so irritating that they seem almost unbelievable; nothing worse is to be found in the newspapers. Nor is there any compensatory deftness in structure, or solidity of design, to make up for this carelessness in detail. The well-made novel, of course, can be as hollow as the well-made play of Scribe—but let us at least have a beginning, a middle and an end! Such a story as *The 'Genius'* is as gross and shapeless as Brünnhilde. It billows and bulges out like a cloud of smoke, and its internal organization is almost as vague. There are episodes that, with a few chapters added, would make very respectable novels. There are chapters that need but a touch or two to be excellent short stories. The thing rambles, staggers, trips, heaves, pitches, struggles, totters, wavers, halts, turns aside, trembles on the edge of collapse. More than once it seems to be foundering, both in the equine and in the maritime senses. The tale has been heard of a tree so tall that it took two men to see to the top of it. Here is a novel so brobdingnagian that a single reader can scarcely read his way through it. . . .

§ 3

Of the general ideas which lie at the bottom of all of Dreiser's work it is impossible to be in ignorance, for he has exposed them at length in *A Hoosier Holiday* and summarized them in *Life, Art and America*. In their main outlines they are not unlike the fundamental assumptions of Joseph Conrad. Both novelists see human existence as a seeking without a finding; both reject the prevailing interpretations of its meaning and mechanism; both take refuge in "I do not know." Put *A Hoosier Holiday* beside Conrad's *A Personal Record,* and you will come upon parallels from end to end. Or better still, put it beside Hugh Walpole's *Joseph Conrad,* in which the Conradean metaphysic is condensed from the novels even better than Conrad has done it himself: at once you will see how the two novelists, each a worker in the elemental emotions, each a rebel against the current assurance and superficiality, each an alien to his place and time, touch each other in a hundred ways.

Conrad, says Walpole, "is of the firm and resolute conviction that life is too strong, too clever and too remorseless for the sons of men." And then, in amplification: "It is as though, from some high window, looking down, he were able to watch some shore, from whose security men were forever launching little cockleshell boats upon a limitless and angry sea. . . . From his height he can follow their fortunes, their brave struggles, their fortitude to the very end. He admires their courage, the simplicity of their faith, but his irony springs from his knowledge of the inevitable end." . . .

Substitute the name of Dreiser for that of Conrad, and you will have to change scarcely a word. Perhaps one, to wit, "clever." I suspect that Dreiser, writing so of his own creed, would be tempted to make it "stupid," or, at all events, "unintelligible." The struggle of man, as he sees it, is more than impotent; it is gratuitous and purposeless. There is, to his eye, no grand ingenuity, no skilful adaptation of means to end, no moral (or even dramatic) plan in the order of the universe. He can get out of it only a sense of profound and inexplicable *dis*order. The waves which batter the cockleshells change their direction at every instant. Their navigation is a vast adventure, but intolerably fortuitous and inept—a voyage without chart, compass, sun or stars. . . .

So at bottom. But to look into the blackness steadily, of course, is almost beyond the endurance of man. In the very moment that its impenetrability is grasped the imagination begins attacking it with pale beams of false light. All religions, I daresay, are thus projected from the questioning soul of man, and not only all religious, but also all great agnosticisms. Nietzsche, shrinking from the horror of that abyss of negation, revived the Pythagorean concept of *der ewigen Wiederkunft*—a vain and blood-curdling sort of comfort. To it, after a while, he added explanations almost Christian—a whole repertoire of whys and wherefores, aims and goals, aspirations and significances. The late Mark Twain, in an unpublished work, toyed with a equally daring idea: that men are to some unimaginably vast and incomprehensible Being what the unicellular organisms of his body are to man, and so on *ad infinitum.* Dreiser occasionally inclines to much the same hypothesis; he likens the endless reactions going on in the world we know, the myriadal creation, collision and destruction of entities, to the slow accumulation and organization of cells *in utero.* He would make us specks in the insentient embryo of some gigantic Presence whose form is still unimaginable and whose birth must wait for Eons and Eons. Again, he turns to something not easily distinguishable from philosophical idealism, whether out of Berkeley or Fichte it is hard to make out—that is, he would interpret the whole phenomenon of life as no more than an appearance, a nightmare of some unseen sleeper or of men themselves, an "uncanny blur of nothingness"—in Euripides' phrase, "a song sung by an idiot, dancing down the wind." Yet again, he talks vaguely of the intricate polyphony of a cosmic orchestra, cacophonous to our dull ears. Finally, he puts the observed into the ordered, reading a purpose in the displayed event: "life was intended to sting and hurt". . . . But these are only gropings, and not to be read too critically. From speculations and explanations he always returns, Conrad-like, to the bald fact: to "the spectacle and stress of life." All he can make out clearly is "a vast compulsion which has nothing to do with the individual desires or tastes or impulses of individuals." That compulsion springs "from the settling processes of forces which we do not in the least understand, over which we have no control, and in whose grip we are as grains of dust or sand, blown hither and thither, for what purpose we cannot even suspect."[5] Man is not only doomed to defeat, but denied any glimpse or understanding of his antagonist. Here we come upon an agnosticism that has almost got beyond curiosity. What good would it do us, asks Dreiser, to know? In our ignorance and helplessness, we may at least get a slave's consolation out of cursing the unknown gods. Suppose we saw them striving blindly, too, and pitied them? . . .

But, as I say, this scepticism is often tempered by guesses at a possibly hidden truth, and the confession that this truth may exist reveals the practical unworkableness of the unconditioned system, at least for Dreiser. Conrad is far more resolute, and it is easy to see why. He is, by birth and training, an aristocrat. He has the gift of emotional detachment. The lures of facile doctrine do not move him. In his irony there is a disdain which plays about even the ironist himself. Dreiser is a product of far different forces and traditions, and is capable of no such escapement. Struggle as he may, and fume and protest as he may, he can no more shake off the chains of his intellectual and cultural heritage than he can change the shape of his nose. What that heritage is you may find out in detail by reading *A Hoosier Holiday*, or in summary by glancing at the first few pages of *Life, Art and America*. Briefly described, it is the burden of a believing mind, a moral attitude, a lingering superstition. One-half of the man's brain, so to speak, wars with the other half. He is intelligent, he is thoughtful, he is a sound artist—but there come moments when a dead hand falls upon him, and he is once more the Indiana peasant, snuffing absurdly over imbecile sentimentalities, giving a grave ear to quackeries, snorting and eye-rolling with the best of them. One generation spans too short a time to free the soul of man. Nietzsche, to the end of his days, remained a Prussian pastor's son, and hence two-thirds a Puritan; he erected his war upon holiness, toward the end, into a sort of holy war. Kipling, the grandson of a Methodist preacher, reveals the tin-pot evangelist with increasing clarity as youth and its ribaldries pass away and he falls back upon his fundamentals. And that other English novelist who springs from the servants' hall—let us not be surprised or blame him if he sometimes writes like a bounder.

The truth about Dreiser is that he is still in the transition stage between Christian Endeavour and civilization, between Warsaw, Indiana and the Socratic grove, between being a good American and being a free man, and so he sometimes vacillates perilously between a moral sentimentalism and a somewhat extravagant revolt. *The 'Genius,'* on the one hand, is almost a tract for rectitude, a Warning to the Young; its motto might be *Scheut die Dirnen!* And on the other hand, it is full of a laborious truculence that can only be explained by imagining the author as heroically determined to prove that he is a plain-spoken fellow and his own man, let the chips fall where they may. So, in spots, in *The Financier* and *The Titan,* both of them far better books. There is an almost moral frenzy to expose and riddle what passes for morality among the stupid. The isolation of irony is never reached; the man is still evangelical; his ideas are still novelties to him; he is as solemnly absurd in some of his floutings of the *Code Américain* as he is in his respect for Bouguereau, or in his flirtings with the New Thought, or in his naïve belief in the importance of novel-writing. Somewhere or other I have called all this the Greenwich Village complex. It is not genuine artists, serving beauty reverently and proudly, who herd in those cockroached cellars and bawl for art; it is a mob of half-educated yokels and cockneys to whom the very idea of art is still novel, and intoxicating—and more than a little bawdy.

Not that Dreiser actually belongs to this ragamuffin company. Far from it, indeed. There is in him, hidden deep-down, a great instinctive artist, and hence the makings of an aristocrat. In his muddled way, held back by the manacles of his race and time, and his steps made uncertain by a guiding theory which too often eludes his own comprehension, he yet manages to produce works of art of unquestionable beauty and authority, and to interpret life in a manner that is poignant and illuminating. There is vastly more intuition in him than intellectualism; his talent is essentially feminine, as Conrad's is masculine; his ideas always seem to be deduced from his feelings. The view of life that got into *Sister Carrie,* his first book, was not the product of a conscious thinking out of Carrie's problems. It simply got itself there by the force of the artistic passion behind it; its coherent statement had to wait for other and more reflective days. The thing began as a vision, not as a syllogism. Here the name of Franz Schubert inevitably comes up. Schubert was an ignoramus, even in music; he knew less about polyphony, which is the mother of harmony, which is the mother of music, than the average conservatory professor. But nevertheless he had such a vast instinctive sensitiveness to musical values, such a profound and accurate feeling for beauty in tone, that he not only arrived at the truth in tonal relations, but even went beyond what, in his day, was known to be the truth, and so led an advance. Likewise, Giorgione da Castelfranco and Masaccio come to mind: painters of the first rank, but untutored, unsophisticated, uncouth. Dreiser, within his limits, belongs to this cabot-shod company of the elect. One thinks of Conrad, not as artist first, but as savant. There is something of the icy aloofness of the laboratory in him, even when the images he conjures up pulsate with the very glow of life. He is almost as self-conscious as the Beethoven of the last quartets. In Dreiser the thing is more intimate, more disorderly, more a matter of pure feeling. He gets his effects, one might almost say, not by designing them, but by living them.

But whatever the process, the power of the image evoked is not to be gainsaid. It is not only brilliant on the surface, but mysterious and appealing in its depths. One swiftly forgets his intolerable writing, his mirthless, sedulous, repellent manner, in the face of the Athenian tragedy he instils into his seduced and soul-sick servant girls, his barbaric pirates of finances, his conquered and hamstrung supermen, his wives who sit and wait. He has, like Conrad, a sure talent for depicting the spirit in disintegration. Old Gerhardt, in *Jennie Gerhardt*, is alone worth all the *dramatis personae* of popular American fiction since the days of *Rob o' the Bowl*; Howells could no more have created him, in his Rodinesque impudence of outline, than he could have created Tartuffe or Gargantua. Such a novel as *Sister Carrie* stands quite outside the brief traffic of the customary stage. It leaves behind it an unescapable impression of bigness, of epic sweep and dignity. It is not a mere story, not a novel in the customary American meaning of the word; it is at once a psalm of life and a criticism of life—and that criticism loses nothing by the fact that its burden is despair. Here, precisely, is the point of Dreiser's departure from his fellows. He puts into his novels a touch of the eternal *Weltschmerz*. They get below the drama that is of the moment and reveal the greater drama that is without end. They arouse those deep and lasting emotions which grow out of the recognition of elemental and universal tragedy. His aim is not merely to tell a tale; his aim is to show the vast ebb and flow of forces which sway and condition human destiny. One cannot imagine him consenting to Conan Doyle's statement of the purpose of fiction, quoted with characteristic approval by the New York *Times*: "to amuse mankind, to help the sick and the dull and the weary." Nor is his purpose to instruct; if he is a pedagogue it is only incidentally and as a weakness. The thing he seeks to do is to stir, to awaken, to move. One does not arise from such a book as *Sister Carrie* with a smirk of satisfaction; one leaves it infinitely touched.

§ 4

It is, indeed, a truly amazing first book, and one marvels to hear that it was begun lightly. Dreiser in those days *(circa* 1899), had seven or eight years of newspaper work behind him, in Chicago, St. Louis, Toledo, Cleveland, Buffalo, Pittsburgh and New York, and was beginning to feel that reaction of disgust which attacks all newspaper men when the enthusiasm of youth wears out. He had been successful, but he saw how hollow that success was, and how little surety it held out for the future. The theatre was what chiefly lured him; he had written plays in his nonage, and he now proposed to do them on a large scale, and so get some of the easy dollars of Broadway. It was an old friend from Toledo, Arthur Henry, who turned him toward story-writing. The two had met while Henry was city editor of the *Blade,* and Dreiser a reporter looking for a job.[6] A firm friendship sprang up, and Henry conceived a high opinion of Dreiser's ability, and urged him to try a short story. Dreiser was distrustful of his own skill, but Henry kept at him, and finally, during a holiday the two spent together at Maumee, Ohio, he made the attempt. Henry had the manuscript typewritten and sent it to *Ainslee's Magazine.* A week or so later there came a cheque for $75.

This was in 1898. Dreiser wrote four more stories during the year following, and sold them all. Henry now urged him to attempt a novel, but again his distrust of himself held him back. Henry finally tried a rather unusual argument: he had a novel of his own on the stocks,[7] and he represented that he was in difficulties with it and in need of company. One day, in September, 1899, Dreiser took a sheet of yellow paper and wrote a title at random. That title was *Sister Carrie,* and with no more definite plan than the mere name offered the book began. It went ahead steadily enough until the middle of October, and had come by then to the place where Carrie meets Hurstwood. At that point Dreiser left it in disgust. It seemed pitifully dull and inconsequential, and for two months he put the manuscript away. Then, under renewed urgings by Henry, he resumed the writing, and kept on to the place where Hurstwood steals the money. Here he went aground upon a comparatively simple problem; he couldn't devise a way to manage the robbery. Late in January he gave it up. But the faithful Henry kept urging him, and in March he resumed work, and soon had the story finished. The latter part, despite many distractions, went quickly. Once the manuscript was complete, Henry suggested various cuts, and in all about 40,000 words came out. The fair copy went to the Harpers. They refused it without ceremony and soon afterward Dreiser carried the manuscript to Doubleday, Page & Co. He left it with Frank Doubleday, and before long there came notice of its acceptance, and, what is more, a contract. But after the story was in type it fell into the hands of the wife of one of the members of the firm, and she conceived so strong a notion of its immorality that she soon convinced her husband and his associates. There followed a series of acrimonious negotiations, with Dreiser holding resolutely to the letter of his contract. It was at this point that Frank Norris entered the combat—bravely but in vain. The pious Barabbases, confronted by their signature, found it impossible to throw up the book entirely, but there was no nomination in the bond regarding either the style of binding or the number of copies to be issued, and so they evaded further dispute by bringing out the book in a very small edition and with modest unstamped covers. Copies of this edition are now eagerly sought by book-collectors, and one in good condition fetches $25 or more in the auction rooms. Even the second edition (1907), bearing the imprint of B. W. Dodge & Co., carries an increasing premium.

The passing years work strange farces. The Harpers, who had refused *Sister Carrie* with a spirit bordering upon indignation in 1900, took over the rights of publication from B. W. Dodge & Co., in 1912, and reissued the book in a new (and extremely hideous) format, with a publisher's note containing smug quotations from the encomiums of the *Fortnightly Review,* the *Athenaeum,* the *Spectator,* the *Academy* and other London critical journals. More, they contrived humorously to push the date of their copyright back to 1900. But this new enthusiasm for artistic freedom did not last long. They had published *Jennie Gerhardt* in 1911 and they did *The Financier* in 1912, but when *The Titan* followed, in 1914, they were seized with qualms, and suppressed the book after it had got into type. In this emergency the English firm of John Lane came to the rescue, only to seek cover itself when the Comstocks attacked *The 'Genius,'* two years later. . . . For his high services to American letters, Walter H. Page, of Doubleday, Page & Co., was made ambassador to England, where *Sister Carrie* is regarded (according to the Harpers), as "the best story, on the whole, that has yet come out of America." A curious series of episodes. Another proof, perhaps, of that cosmic imbecility upon which Dreiser is so fond of discoursing. . . .

But of all this I shall say more later on, when I come to discuss the critical reception of the Dreiser novels, and the efforts made by the New York Society for the Suppression of Vice to stop their sale. The thing to notice here is that the author's difficulties with *Sister Carrie* came within an ace of turning him from novel-writing completely. Stray copies of the suppressed first edition, true enough, fell into the hands of critics who saw the story's value, and during the first year or two of the century it enjoyed a sort of esoteric vogue, and encouragement came from unexpected sources. Moreover, a somewhat bowdlerized English edition, published by William Heinemann in 1901, made a fair success, and even provoked a certain mild controversy. But the author's income from the book remained almost *nil,* and so he was forced to seek a livelihood in other directions. His history during the next ten years belongs to the tragicomedy of letters. For five of them he was a Grub Street hack, turning his hand to any literary job that offered. He wrote short stories for the popular magazines, or special articles, or poems, according as their needs varied. He concocted fabulous tales for the illustrated supplements of the Sunday newspapers. He rewrote the bad stuff of other men. He returned to reporting. He did odd pieces of editing. He tried his hand at one-act plays. He even ventured upon advertisement writing. And all the while, the best that he could get out of his industry was a meagre living.

In 1905, tiring of the uncertainties of this life, he accepted a post on the staff of Street & Smith, the millionaire publishers of cheap magazines, servant-girl romances and dime-novels, and here, in the very slums of letters, he laboured with tongue in cheek until the next year. The tale of his duties will fill, I daresay, a volume or two in the autobiography on which he is said to be working; it is a chronicle full of achieved impossibilities. One of his jobs, for example, was to reduce a whole series of dime-novels, each 60,000 words in length, to 30,000 words apiece. He accomplished it by cutting each one into halves, and writing a new ending for the first half and a new beginning for the second, with new titles for both. This doubling of their property aroused the admiration of his employers; they promised him an assured and easy future in the dime-novel business. But he tired of it, despite this revelation of a gift for it, and in 1906 he became managing editor of the *Broadway Magazine,* then struggling into public notice. A year later he transferred his flag to the Butterick Building, and became chief editor of the *Delineator,* the *Designer* and other such gospels for the fair. Here, of course, he was as much out of water as in the dime-novel foundry of Street & Smith, but at all events the pay was good, and there was a certain leisure at the end of the day's work. In 1907, as part of his duties, he organized the National Child Rescue Campaign, which still rages as the *Delineator's* contribution to the Uplift. At about the same time he began *Jennie Gerhardt.* It is curious to note that, during these same years, Arnold Bennett was slaving in London as the editor of *Woman.*

Dreiser left the *Delineator* in 1910, and for the next half year or so endeavoured to pump vitality into the *Bohemian Magazine,* in which he had acquired a proprietary interest. But the *Bohemian* soon departed this life, carrying some of his savings with it, and he gave over his enforced leisure to *Jennie Gerhardt,* completing the book in 1911. Its publication by the Harpers during the same year worked his final emancipation from the editorial desk. It was praised, and what is more, it sold, and royalties began to come in. A new edition of *Sister Carrie* followed in 1912, with *The Financier* hard upon its heels. Since then Dreiser has devoted himself wholly to serious work. *The Financier* was put forth as the first volume of "a trilogy of desire"; the second volume, *The Titan,* was published in 1914; the third is yet to come. *The 'Genius'* appeared in 1915; *The Bulwark* is just announced. In 1912, accompanied by Grant

Richards, the London publisher, Dreiser made his first trip abroad, visiting England, France, Italy and Germany. His impressions were recorded in *A Traveler at Forty,* published in 1913. In the summer of 1915, accompanied by Franklin Booth, the illustrator, he made an automobile journey to his old haunts in Indiana, and the record is in *A Hoosier Holiday,* published in 1916. His other writings include a volume of *Plays of the Natural and the Supernatural* (1916); *Life, Art and America,* a pamphlet against Puritanism in letters (1917); a dozen or more short stories and novelettes, a few poems, and a three-act drama, *The Hand of the Potter.*

Dreiser was born at Terre Haute, Indiana, on August 27, 1871, and, like most of us, is of mongrel blood, with the German, perhaps, predominating. He is a tall man, awkward in movement and nervous in habit; the boon of beauty has been denied him. The history of his youth is set forth in full in *A Hoosier Holiday.* It is curious to note that he is a brother to the late Paul Dresser, author of "The Banks of the Wabash" and other popular songs, and that he himself, helping Paul over a hard place, wrote the affecting chorus:

Oh, the moon is fair tonight along the Wabash,
From the fields there comes the breath of new-mown hay;
Through the sycamores the candle lights are gleaming. . . .

But no doubt you know it.

§ 5

The work of Dreiser, considered as craftsmanship pure and simple, is extremely uneven, and the distance separating his best from his worst is almost infinite. It is difficult to believe that the novelist who wrote certain extraordinarily vivid chapters in *Jennie Gerhardt,* and *A Hoosier Holiday,* and, above all, in *The Titan,* is the same who achieved the unescapable dulness of parts of *The Financier* and the general stupidity and stodginess of *The 'Genius.'* Moreover, the tide of his writing does not rise or fall with any regularity; he neither improves steadily nor grows worse steadily. Only half an eye is needed to see the superiority of *Jennie Gerhardt,* as a sheer piece of writing, to *Sister Carrie,* but on turning to *The Financier,* which followed *Jennie Gerhardt* by an interval of but one year, one observes a falling off which, at its greatest, is almost indistinguishable from a collapse. *Jennie Gerhardt* is suave, persuasive, well-ordered, solid in structure, instinct with life. *The Financier,* for all its merits in detail, is loose, tedious, vapid, exasperating. But had any critic, in the autumn of 1912, argued thereby that Dreiser was finished, that he had shot his bolt, his discomfiture would have come swiftly, for *The Titan,* which followed in 1914, was almost as well done as *The Financier* had been ill done, and there are parts of it which remain, to this day, the very best writing that Dreiser has ever achieved. But *The 'Genius'*? Ay, in *The 'Genius'* the pendulum swings back again! It is flaccid, elephantine, doltish, coarse, dismal, flatulent, sophomoric, ignorant, unconvincing, wearisome. One pities the jurisconsult who is condemned, by Comstockian clamour, to plough through such a novel. In it there is a sort of humourless *reductio ad absurdum,* not only of the Dreiser manner, but even of certain salient tenets of the Dreiser philosophy. At its best it has a moral flavour. At its worst it is almost maudlin. . . .

The most successful of the Dreiser novels, judged by sales, is *Sister Carrie,* and the causes thereof are not far to seek. On the one hand, its suppression in 1900 gave it a whispered fame that was converted into a public celebrity when it was republished in 1907, and on the other hand it shares with *Jennie Gerhardt* the capital advantage of having a young and appealing woman for its chief figure. The sentimentalists thus have a heroine to cry over, and to put into a familiar pigeonhole; Carrie becomes a sort of Pollyanna. More, it is, at bottom, a tale of love—the one theme of permanent interest to the average American novel-reader, the chief stuffing of all our best-selling romances. True enough, it is vastly more than this—there is in it, for example, the astounding portrait of Hurstwood—but it seems to me plain that its relative popularity is by no means a test of its relative merit, and that the causes of that popularity must be sought in other directions. Its defect, as a work of art, is a defect of structure. Like Norris' *McTeague* it has a broken back. In the midst of the story of Carrie, Dreiser pauses to tell the story of Hurstwood—a memorably vivid and tragic story, to be sure, but still one that, considering artistic form and organization, does damage to the main business of the book. Its outstanding merit is its simplicity, its unaffected seriousness and fervour, the spirit of youth that is in it. One feels that it was written, not by a novelist conscious of his tricks, but by a novice carried away by his own flaming eagerness, his own high sense of the interest of what he was doing. In this aspect, it is perhaps more typically Dreiserian than any of its successors. And maybe we may seek here for a good deal of its popular appeal, for there is a contagion in naivete as in enthusiasm, and the simple novel-reader may recognize the kinship of a simple mind in the novelist.

But it is in *Jennie Gerhardt* that Dreiser first shows his true mettle. . . . "The power to tell the same story in two forms," said George Moore, "is the sign of the true artist." Here Dreiser sets himself that difficult task, and here he carries it off with almost complete success. Reduce the story to a hundred words, and the same words would also describe *Sister Carrie.* Jennie, like Carrie, is a rose grown from turnip-seed. Over each, at the start, hangs poverty, ignorance, the dumb helplessness of the Shudra, and yet in each there is that indescribable something, that element of essential gentleness, that innate inward beauty which levels all barriers of caste, and makes Esther a fit queen for Ahasuerus. Some Frenchman has put it into a phrase: *"Une âme grande dans un petit destin"*—a great soul in a small destiny. Jennie has some touch of that greatness; Dreiser is forever calling her "a big woman"; it is a refrain almost as irritating as the "trig" of *The Titan*. Carrie, one feels, is of baser metal; her dignity never rises to anything approaching nobility. But the history of each is the history of the other. Jennie, like Carrie, escapes from the physical miseries of the struggle for existence only to taste the worse miseries of the struggle for happiness. Don't mistake me; we have here no maudlin tales of seduced maidens. Seduction, in truth, is far from tragedy for either Jennie or Carrie. The gain of each, until the actual event has been left behind and obliterated by experiences more salient and poignant, is greater than her loss, and that gain is to the soul as well as to the creature. With the rise from want to security, from fear to ease, comes an awakening of the finer perceptions, a widening of the sympathies, a gradual unfolding of the delicate flower called personality, an increased capacity for loving and living. But with all this, and as a part of it, there comes, too, an increased capacity for suffering—and so in the end, when love slips away and the empty years stretch before, it is the awakened and supersentient woman that pays for the folly of the groping, bewildered girl. The tragedy of Carrie and Jennie, in brief, is not that they are degraded, but that they are lifted up, not that they go to the gutter, but that they escape the gutter and glimpse the stars.

But if the two stories are thus variations upon the same sombre theme, if each starts from the same place and arrives at the same dark goal, if each shows a woman heartened by the same hopes and tortured by the same agonies, there is still a vast difference between them, and that difference is the measure of the author's progress in his craft during the eleven years between 1900 and 1911. *Sister Carrie*, at bottom, is no more than a first sketch, a rough piling up of observations and ideas, disordered and often incoherent. In the midst of the story, as I have said, the author forgets it, and starts off upon another. In *Jennie Gerhardt* there is no such flaccidity of structure, no such vacillation in aim, no such proliferation of episode. Considering that it is by Dreiser, it is extraordinarily adept and intelligent in design; only in *The Titan* has he ever done so well. From beginning to end the narrative flows logically, steadily, congruously. Episodes there are, of course, but they keep their proper place and bulk. It is always Jennie that stands at the centre of the traffic; it is in Jennie's soul that every scene is ultimately played out. Her father and mother; Senator Brander, the god of her first worship; her daughter Vesta, and Lester Kane, the man who makes and mars her—all these are drawn with infinite painstaking, and in every one of them there is the blood of life. But it is Jennie that dominates the drama from curtain to curtain. Not an event is unrelated to her; not a climax fails to make clearer the struggles going on in her mind and heart.

It is in *Jennie Gerhardt* that Dreiser's view of life begins to take on coherence and to show a general tendency. In *Sister Carrie* the thing is still chiefly representation and no more; the image is undoubtedly vivid, but its significance, in the main, is left undisplayed. In Jennie Gerhardt this pictorial achievement is reinforced by interpretation; one carries away an impression that something has been said; it is not so much a visual image of Jennie that remains as a sense of the implacable tragedy that engulfs her. The book is full of artistic passion. It lives and glows. It awakens recognition and feeling. Its lucid ideational structure, even more than the artless gusto of *Sister Carrie,* produces a penetrating and powerful effect. Jennie is no mere individual; she is a type of the national character, almost the archetype of the muddled, aspiring, tragic, fate-flogged mass. And the scene in which she is set is brilliantly national too. The Chicago of those great days of feverish money-grabbing and crazy aspiration may well stand as the epitome of America, and it is made clearer here than in any other American novel—clearer than in *The Pit* or *The Cliff-Dwellers*—clearer than in any book by an Easterner—almost as clear as the Paris of Balzac and Zola. Finally, the style of the story is indissolubly wedded to its matter. The narrative, in places, has an almost scriptural solemnity; in its very harshness and baldness there is something subtly meet and fitting. One cannot imagine such a history done in the strained phrases of Meredith or the fugal manner of Henry James. One cannot imagine that stark, stenographic dialogue adorned with the tinsel of pretty words. The thing, to reach the heights it touches, could have been done only in the way it has been done. As it stands, I would not take anything away from it, not even its journalistic banalities, its lack of humour, its incessant returns to C major. A primitive and touching poetry is in it. It is a novel, I am convinced, of the first consideration. . . .

In *The Financier* this poetry is almost absent, and that fact is largely to blame for the book's lack of charm. By the time we see him in *The Titan* Frank Cowperwood has taken on heroic proportions and the romance of great adventure is in him, but in *The Financier* he is still little more than an extra-pertinacious money-grubber, and not unrelated to the average stock broker or corner grocer. True enough, Dreiser says specifically that he is more, that the thing he craves is not money but power—power to force lesser men to execute his commands, power to surround himself with beautiful and splendid things, power to amuse himself with women, power to defy and nullify the laws made for the timorous and unimaginative. But the intent of the author never really gets into his picture. His Cowperwood in this first stage is hard, commonplace, unimaginative. In *The Titan* he flowers out as a blend of revolutionist and voluptuary, a highly civilized Lorenzo the Magnificent, an immoralist who would not hesitate two minutes about seducing a saint, but would turn sick at the thought of harming a child. But in *The Financier* he is still in the larval state, and a repellent sordidness hangs about him.

Moreover, the story of his rise is burdened by two defects which still further corrupt its effect. One lies in the fact that Dreiser is quite unable to get the feel, so to speak, of Philadelphia, just as he is unable to get the feel of New York in *The 'Genius.'* The other is that the style of the writing in the book reduces the dreiserian manner to absurdity, and almost to impossibility. The incredibly lazy, involved and unintelligent description of the trial of Cowperwood I have already mentioned. We get, in this lumbering chronicle, not a cohesive and luminous picture, but a dull, photographic representation of the whole tedious process, beginning with an account of the political obligations of the judge and district attorney, proceeding to a consideration of the habits of mind of each of the twelve jurymen, and ending with a summary of the majority and minority opinions of the court of appeals, and a discussion of the motives, ideals, traditions, prejudices, sympathies and chicaneries behind them, each and severally. When Cowperwood goes into the market, his operations are set forth in their last detail; we are told how many shares he buys, how much he pays for them, what the commission is, what his profit comes to. When he comes into chance contact with a politician, we hear all about that politician, including his family affairs. When he builds and furnishes a house, the chief rooms in it are inventoried with such care that not a chair or a rug or a picture on the wall is overlooked. The endless piling up of such non-essentials cripples and incommodes the story; its drama is too copiously swathed in words to achieve a sting; the Dreiser manner devours and defeats itself.

But none the less the book has compensatory merits. Its character sketches, for all the cloud of words, are lucid and vigorous. Out of that enormous complex of crooked politics and crookeder finance, Cowperwood himself stands out in the round, comprehensible and alive. And all the others, in their lesser measures, are done almost as well—Cowperwood's pale wife, whimpering in her empty house; Aileen Butler, his mistress; his doddering and eternally amazed old father; his old-fashioned, stupid, sentimental mother; Stener, the City Treasurer, a dish-rag in the face of danger; old Edward Malia Butler, that barbarian in a boiled shirt, with his Homeric hatred and his broken heart. Particularly old Butler. The years pass and he must be killed and put away, but not many readers of the book, I take it, will soon forget him. Dreiser is at his best, indeed, when he deals with old men. In their tragic helplessness they stand as symbols of that unfathomable cosmic cruelty which he sees as the motive power of life itself. More, even, than his women, he makes them poignant, vivid, memorable. The picture of old Gerhardt is full of a subtle brightness, though he is always in the background, as cautious and penny-wise as an ancient crow, trotting to his Lutheran church, pathetically ill-used by the world he never understands. Butler is another such, different in externals, but at bottom the same dismayed, questioning, pathetic old man. . . .

In *The Titan* there is a tightening of the screws, a clarifying of the action, an infinite improvement in the manner. The book, in truth, has the air of a new and clearer thinking out of *The Financier*, as *Jennie Gerhardt* is a new thinking out of *Sister Carrie*. With almost the same materials, the thing is given a new harmony and unity, a new plausibility, a new passion and purpose. In *The Financier* the artistic voluptuary is almost completely overshadowed by the dollar-chaser; in *The Titan* we begin to see clearly that grand battle between artist and man of money, idealist and materialist, spirit and flesh, which is the informing theme of the whole trilogy. The conflict that makes the drama, once chiefly external, now becomes more and more internal; it is played out within the soul of the man himself. The result is a character sketch of the highest colour and brilliance, a superb portrait of a complex and extremely fascinating man. Of all the personages in the Dreiser books, the Cowperwood of *The Titan* is perhaps the most radiantly real. He is accounted for in every detail, and yet, in the end, he is not accounted for at all; there hangs about him, to the last, that baffling mysteriousness which hangs about those we know most intimately. There is in him a complete and indubitable masculinity, as the eternal feminine is in Jennie. His struggle with the inexorable forces that urge him on as with whips, and lure him with false lights, and bring him to disillusion and dismay, is as typical as hers is, and as tragic. In his ultimate disaster, so plainly foreshadowed at the close, there is the clearest of all projections of the ideas that lie at the bottom of all Dreiser's work. Cowperwood, above any of them, is his protagonist.

The story, in its plan, is as transparent as in its burden. It has an austere simplicity in the telling that fits the directness of the thing told. Dreiser, as if to clear decks, throws over all the immemorial baggage of the novelist, making short shrift of "heart interest," conventional "sympathy," and even what ordinarily passes for romance. In *Sister Carrie,* as I have pointed out, there is still a sweet dish for the sentimentalists; if they don't like the history of Carrie as a work of art they may still wallow in it as a sad, sad love story. Carrie is appealing, melting; she moves, like Marguerite Gautier, in an atmosphere of romantic depression. And Jennie Gerhardt, in this aspect, is merely Carrie done over—a Carrie more carefully and objectively drawn, perhaps, but still conceivably to be mistaken for a "sympathetic" heroine in a bestseller. A lady eating chocolates might jump from *Laddie* to *Jennie Gerhardt* without knowing that she was jumping ten thousand miles. The tear jugs are there to cry into. Even in *The Financier* there is still a hint of familiar things. The first Mrs. Cowperwood is sorely put upon; old Butler has the markings of an irate father; Cowperwood himself suffers the orthodox injustice and languishes in a cell. But no one, I venture, will ever fall into any such mistake in identity in approaching *The Titan.* Not a single appeal to facile sentiment is in it. It proceeds from beginning to end in a forthright, uncompromising, confident manner. It is an almost purely objective account, as devoid of cheap heroics as a death certificate, of a strong man's contest with incontestable powers without and no less incontestable powers within. There is nothing of the conventional outlaw about him; he does not wear a red sash and bellow for liberty; fate wrings from him no melodramatic defiances. In the midst of the battle he views it with a sort of ironical detachment, as if lifted above himself by the sheer aesthetic spectacle. Even in disaster he asks for no quarter, no generosity, no compassion. Up or down, he keeps his zest for the game that is being played, and is sufficient unto himself.

Such a man as this Cowperwood of the Chicago days, described romantically, would be indistinguishable from the wicked earls and seven-foot guardsmen of Ouida, Robert W. Chambers and The Duchess. But described realistically and cold-bloodedly, with all that wealth of minute and apparently inconsequential detail which Dreiser piles up so amazingly, he becomes a figure astonishingly vivid, lifelike and engrossing. He fits into no a priori theory of conduct or scheme of rewards and punishments; he proves nothing and teaches nothing; the forces which move him are never obvious and frequently unintelligible. But in the end he seems genuinely a man—a man of the sort we see about us in the real world—not a patent and automatic fellow, reacting docilely and according to a formula, but a bundle of complexities and contradictions, a creature oscillating between the light and the shadow—at bottom, for all his typical representation of a race and a civilization, a unique and inexplicable personality. More, he is a man of the first class, an Achilles of his world; and here the achievement of Dreiser is most striking, for he succeeds where all fore-runners failed. It is easy enough to explain how John Smith courted his wife, and even how William Brown fought and died for his country, but it is inordinately difficult to give plausibility to the motives, feelings and processes of mind of a man whose salient character is that they transcend all ordinary experience. Too often, even when made by the highest creative and interpretative talent, the effort has resolved itself into a begging of the question. Shakespeare made Hamlet comprehensible to the groundlings by diluting that half of him which was Shakespeare with a half which was a college sophomore. In the same way he saved Lear by making him, in large part, a tedious and obscene old donkey—the blood brother of any average ancient of any average English taproom. Tackling Caesar, he was rescued by Brutus' knife. George Bernard Shaw, facing the same difficulty, resolved it by drawing a composite portrait of two or three London actor-managers and half a dozen English politicians. But Dreiser makes no such compromise. He bangs into the difficulties of his problem head on, and if he does not solve it absolutely, he at least makes an extraordinarily close approach to a solution. In *The Financier* a certain incredulity still hangs about Cowperwood; in *The Titan* he suddenly comes unquestionably real. If you want to get the true measure of this feat, put it beside the failure of Frank Norris with Curtis Jadwin in *The Pit*. . . .

The 'Genius,' which interrupted the "trilogy of desire," marks the nadir of Dreiser's accomplishment, as *The Titan* marks its apogee. The plan of it, of course, is simple enough, and it is one that Dreiser, at his best, might have carried out with undoubted success. What he is trying to show, in brief, is the battle that goes on in the soul of every man of active mind between the desire for self-expression and the desire for safety, for public respect, for emotional equanimity. It is, in a sense, the story of Cowperwood told over again, but with an important difference, for Eugene Witla is a much less self-reliant and powerful fellow than Cowperwood, and so he is unable to muster up the vast resolution of spirits that he needs to attain happiness. *The Titan* is the history of a strong man. *The 'Genius,'* is the history of a man essentially weak. Eugene Witla can never quite choose his route in life. He goes on sacrificing ease to aspiration and aspiration to ease to the end of the chapter. He vacillates abominably and forever between two irreconcilable desires. Even when, at the close, he sinks into a whining sort of resignation, the proud courage of Cowperwood is not in him; he is always a bit despicable in his pathos.

As I say, a story of simple outlines, and well adapted to the dreiserian pen. But it is spoiled and made a mock of by a donkeyish solemnity of attack which leaves it, on the one hand, diffuse, spineless and shapeless, and on the other hand, a compendium of platitudes. It is as if Dreiser, suddenly discovering himself a sage, put off the high passion of the artist and took to pounding a pulpit. It is almost as if he deliberately essayed upon a burlesque of himself. The book is an endless emission of the obvious, with touches of the scandalous to light up its killing monotony. It runs to 736 pages of small type; its reading is an unbearable weariness to the flesh; in the midst of it one has forgotten the beginning and is unconcerned about the end. Mingled with all the folderol, of course, there is stuff of nobler quality. Certain chapters stick in the memory; whole episodes lift themselves to the fervid luminosity of *Jennie Gerhardt*; there are character sketches that deserve all praise; one often pulls up with a reminder that the thing is the work of a proficient craftsman. But in the main it lumbers and jolts, wabbles and bores. A sort of ponderous imbecility gets into it. Both in its elaborate devices to shake up the pious and its imposing demonstrations of what every one knows, it somehow suggests the advanced thinking of Greenwich Village. I suspect, indeed, that the *vin rouge* was in Dreiser's arteries as he concocted it. He was at the intellectual menopause, and looking back somewhat wistfully and attitudinizingly toward the goatish days that were no more.

But let it go! A novelist capable of *Jennie Gerhardt* has rights, privileges, prerogatives. He may, if he will, go on a spiritual drunk now and then, and empty the stale bilges of his soul. Thackeray, having finished *Vanity Fair* and *Pendennis*, bathed himself in the sheep's milk of *The Newcomes*, and after *The Virginians* he did *The*

Adventures of Philip. Zola, with *Germinal, La Débâcle* and *La Terre* behind him, recreated himself horribly with *Fécondité.* Tolstoi, after *Anna Karenina,* wrote *What Is Art?* Ibsen, after *Et Dukkehjem* and *Gengangere,* wrote *Vildanden.* The good God himself, after all the magnificence of Kings and Chronicles, turned Dr. Frank Crane and so botched his Writ with Proverbs. . . . A weakness that we must allow for. Whenever Dreiser, abandoning his fundamental scepticism, yields to the irrepressible human (and perhaps also divine) itch to label, to moralize, to teach, he becomes a bit absurd. Observe *The 'Genius,'* and parts of *A Hoosier Holiday* and of *A Traveler at Forty,* and of *Plays of the Natural and the Supernatural.* But in this very absurdity, it seems to me, there is a subtle proof that his fundamental scepticism is sound. . . .

I mention the *Plays of the Natural and the Supernatural.* They are ingenious and sometimes extremely effective, but their significance is not great. The two that are "of the natural" are *The Girl in the Coffin* and *Old Ragpicker,* the first a laborious evocation of the gruesome, too long by half, and the other an experiment in photographic realism, with a pair of policemen as its protagonists. All five plays "of the supernatural" follow a single plan. In the foreground, as it were, we see a sordid drama played out on the human plane, and in the background (or in the empyrean above, as you choose) we see the operation of the god-like imbecilities which sway and flay us all. The technical trick is well managed. It would be easy for such four-dimensional pieces to fall into burlesque, but in at least two cases, to wit, in *The Blue Sphere* and *In the Dark,* they go off with an air. Superficially, these plays "of the supernatural" seem to show an abandonment to the wheezy, black bombazine mysticism which crops up toward the end of The *'Genius.'* But that mysticism, at bottom, is no more than the dreiserian scepticism made visible. "For myself," says Dreiser somewhere, "I do not know what truth is, what beauty is, what love is, what hope is." And in another place: "I admit a vast compulsion which has nothing to do with the individual desires or tastes or impulses." The jokers behind the arras pull the strings. It is pretty, but what is it all about? . . . The criticism which deals only with externals sees *Sister Carrie* as no more than a deft adventure into realism. Dreiser is praised, when he is praised at all, for making Carrie so clear, for understanding her so well. But the truth is, of course, that his achievement consists precisely in making patent the impenetrable mystery of her, and of the tangled complex of striving and aspiration of which she is so helplessly a part. It is in this sense that *Sister Carrie* is a profound work. It is not a book of glib explanations, of ready formulae; it is, above all else, a book of wonder. . . .

Of *A Traveler at Forty* I have spoken briefly. It is heavy with the obvious; the most interesting thing in it is the fact that Dreiser had never seen St. Peter's or Piccadilly Circus until he was too old for either reverence or romance. *A Hoosier Holiday* is far more illuminating, despite its platitudinizing. Slow in tempo, discursive, reflective, intimate, the book covers a vast territory, and lingers in pleasant fields. One finds in it an almost complete confession of faith, artistic, religious, even political. And not infrequently that confession takes the form of ingenuous confidences—about the fortunes of the house of Dreiser, the dispersed Dreiser clan, the old neighbours in Indiana, new friends made along the way. In *A Traveler at Forty* Dreiser is surely frank enough in his vivisections; he seldom forgets a vanity or a wart. In *A Hoosier Holiday* he goes even further; he speculates heavily about all his *dramatis personae,* prodding into the motives behind their acts, wondering what they would do in this or that situation, forcing them painfully into laboratory jars. They become, in the end, not unlike characters in a novel; one misses only the neatness of a plot. Strangely enough, the one personage of the chronicle who remains dim throughout is the artist,

Franklin Booth, Dreiser's host and companion on the long motor ride from New York to Indiana, and the maker of the book's excellent pictures. One gets a brilliant etching of Booth's father, and scarcely less vivid portraits of Speed, the chauffeur; of various persons encountered on the way, and of friends and relatives dredged up out of the abyss of the past. But of Booth one learns little save that he is a Christian Scientist and a fine figure of a man. There must have been much talk during those two weeks of careening along the high-road, and Booth must have borne some part in it, but what he said is very meagrely reported, and so he is still somewhat vague at the end—a personality sensed but scarcely apprehended.

However, it is Dreiser himself who is the chief character of the story, and who stands out from it most brilliantly. One sees in the man all the special marks of the novelist: his capacity for photographic and relentless observation, his insatiable curiosity, his keen zest in life as a spectacle, his comprehension of and sympathy for the poor striving of humble folks, his endless mulling of insoluble problems, his recurrent Philistinism, his impatience of restraints, his fascinated suspicion of messiahs, his passion for physical beauty, his relish for the gaudy drama of big cities; his incurable Americanism. The panorama that he enrols runs the whole scale of the colours; it is a series of extraordinarily vivid pictures. The sombre gloom of the Pennsylvania hills, with Wilkes-Barre lying among them like a gem; the procession of little country towns, sleepy and a bit hoggish; the flash of Buffalo, Cleveland, Indianapolis; the gargantuan coal-pockets and ore-docks along the Erie shore; the tinsel summer resorts; the lush Indiana farmlands, with their stodgy, bovine people—all of these things are sketched in simply, and yet almost magnificently. I know, indeed, of no book which better describes the American hinterland. Here we have no idle spying by a stranger, but a full-length representation by one who knows the thing he describes intimately, and is himself a part of it. Almost every mile of the road travelled has been Dreiser's own road in life. He knew those unkempt Indiana towns in boyhood; he wandered in the Indiana woods; he came to Toledo, Cleveland, Buffalo as a young man; all the roots of his existence are out there. And so he does his chronicle *con amore,* with many a sentimental dredging up of old memories, old hopes and old dreams.

Save for passages in *The Titan, A Hoosier Holiday* marks the high tide of Dreiser's writing —that is, as sheer writing. His old faults are in it, and plentifully. There are empty, brackish phrases enough, God knows—"high noon" among them. But for all that, there is an undeniable glow in it; it shows, in more than one place, an approach to style; the mere wholesaler of words has become, in some sense a connoisseur, even a voluptuary. The picture of Wilkes-Barre girt in by her hills is simply done, and yet there is imagination in it, and touches of brilliance. The sombre beauty of the Pennsylvania mountains is vividly transferred to the page. The towns by the wayside are differentiated, swiftly drawn, made to live. There are excellent sketches of people—a courtly hotelkeeper in some God-forsaken hamlet, his self-respect triumphing over his wallow; a group of babbling Civil War veterans, endlessly mouthing incomprehensible jests; the half-grown beaux and belles of the summer resorts, enchanted and yet a bit staggered by the awakening of sex; Booth *père* and his sinister politics; broken and forgotten men in the Indiana towns; policemen, waitresses, farmers, country characters; Dreiser's own people—the boys and girls of his youth; his brother Paul, the Indiana Schneckenburger and Francis Scott Key; his sisters and brothers; his beaten, hopeless, pious father; his brave and noble mother. The book is dedicated to this mother, now long dead, and in a way it is a memorial to her, a monument to affection. Life bore upon her cruelly; she knew poverty at its lowest ebb and despair at its bitterest; and yet there was in her a touch of fineness that never yielded, a gallant spirit that faced and fought things through. One thinks, somehow, of the mother of Gounod. . . . Her son has not forgotten her. His book is her epitaph. He enters into her presence with love and with reverence and with something not far from awe. . . .

As for the rest of the Dreiser compositions, I leave them to your curiosity.

§ 6

Dr. William Lyon Phelps, the Lampson professor of English language and literature at Yale, opens his chapter on Mark Twain in his *Essays on Modern Novelists* with a humorous account of the critical imbecility which pursued Mark in his own country down to his last years. The favourite national critics of that era (and it extended to 1895, at the least) were wholly blind to the fact that he was a great artist. They admitted him, somewhat grudgingly, a certain low dexterity as a clown, but that he was an imaginative writer of the first rank, or even of the fifth rank, was something that, in their insanest moments, never so much as occurred to them. Phelps cites, in particular, an ass named Professor Richardson, whose *American Literature,* it appears, "is still a standard work" and "a deservedly high authority"—apparently in colleges. In the 1892 edition of this *magnum opus,* Mark is dismissed with less than four lines, and ranked below Irving, Holmes and Lowell—nay, actually below Artemus Ward, Josh Billings and Petroleum V Nasby! The thing is fabulous, fantastic, *unglaublich*—but nevertheless true. Lacking the "higher artistic or moral purpose of the greater humourists" (*exempli gratia,* Rabelais, Molière, Aristophanes!!), Mark is dismissed by this Professor Balderdash as a hollow buffoon. . . . But stay! Do not laugh yet! Phelps himself, indignant at the stupidity, now proceeds to credit Mark with a moral purpose! . . . Turn to *The Mysterious Stranger,* or *What is Man?* . . .

College professors, alas, never learn anything. The identical gentleman who achieved this discovery about old Mark in 1910, now seeks to dispose of Dreiser in the exact manner of Richardson. That is to say, he essays to finish him by putting him into Coventry, by loftily passing over him. "Do not speak of him," said Kingsley of Heine; "he was a wicked man!" Search the latest volume of the Phelps revelation, *The Advance of the English Novel*, and you will find that Dreiser is not once mentioned in it. The late O. Henry is hailed as a genius who will have "abiding fame"; Henry Sydnor Harrison is hymned as "more than a clever novelist," nay, "a valuable ally of the angels" (the right-thinker complex! art as a form of snuffling!), and an obscure Pagliaccio named Charles D. Stewart is brought forward as "the American novelist most worthy to fill the particular vacancy caused by the death of Mark Twain"—but Dreiser is not even listed in the index. And where Phelps leads with his baton of birch most of the other drovers of rah-rah boys follow. I turn, for example, to *An Introduction to American Literature*, by Henry S. Pancoast, A.M., L.H.D., dated 1912. There are kind words for Richard Harding Davis, for Amélie Rives, and even for Will N. Harben, but not a syllable for Dreiser. Again, there is a *A History of American Literature*, by Reuben Post Halleck, A.M., LL.D., dated 1911. Lew Wallace, Marietta Holley, Owen Wister and Augusta Evans Wilson have their hearings, but not Dreiser. Yet again, there is *A History of American Literature Since 1870*, by Prof. Fred Lewis Pattee,[8] instructor in "the English language and literature" somewhere in Pennsylvania. Pattee has praises for Marion Crawford, Margaret Deland and F. Hopkinson Smith, and polite bows for Richard Harding Davis and Robert W. Chambers, but from end to end of his fat tome I am unable to find the slightest mention of Dreiser.

So much for one group of heroes of the new Dunciad. That it includes most of the acknowledged heavyweights of the craft—the Babbitts, Mores, Brownells and so on—goes without saying; as Van

Wyck Brooks has pointed out,[9] these magnificoes are austerely above any consideration of the literature that is in being. The other group, more courageous and more honest, proceeds by direct attack; Dreiser is to be disposed of by a moral *attentat.* Its leaders are two more professors, Stuart P. Sherman and H. W. Boynton, and in its ranks march the lady critics of the newspapers, with much shrill, falsetto clamour. Sherman is the only one of them who shows any intelligible reasoning. Boynton, as always, is a mere parroter of conventional phrases, and the objections of the ladies fade imperceptibly into a pious indignation which is indistinguishable from that of the professional suppressors of vice.

What, then, is Sherman's complaint? In brief, that Dreiser is a liar when he calls himself a realist; that he is actually a naturalist, and hence accursed. That "he has evaded the enterprise of representing human conduct, and confined himself to a representation of animal behaviour." That he "imposes his own naturalistic philosophy" upon his characters, making them do what they ought not to do, and think what they ought not to think. That "he has just two things to tell us about Frank Cowperwood: that he has a rapacious appetite for money, and a rapacious appetite for women." That this alleged "theory of animal behaviour" is not only incorrect but downright immoral, and that "when one-half the world attempts to assert it, the other half rises in battle."[10]

Only a glance is needed to show the vacuity of all this *brutum fulmen.* Dreiser, in point of fact, is scarcely more the realist or the naturalist, in any true sense, than H. G. Wells or the later George Moore, nor has he ever announced himself in either the one character or the other—if there be, in fact, any difference between them that any one save a pigeonholding pedagogue can discern. He is really something quite different, and, in his moments, something far more stately. His aim is not merely to record, but to translate and understand; the thing he exposes is not the empty event and act, but the endless mystery out of which it springs; his pictures have a passionate compassion in them that it is hard to separate from poetry. If this sense of the universal and inexplicable tragedy, if this vision of life as a seeking without a finding, if this adept summoning up of moving images, is mistaken by college professors for the empty, meticulous nastiness of Zola in "Pot-Bouille"—in Nietzsche's phrase, for "the delight to stink"—then surely the folly of college professors, as vast as it seems, has been underestimated. What is the fact? The fact is that Dreiser's attitude of mind, his manner of reaction to the phenomena he represents, the whole of his alleged "naturalistic philosophy," stems directly, not from Zola, Flaubert, Augier and the younger Dumas, but from the Greeks. In the midst of democratic cocksureness and Christian sentimentalism, of doctrinaire shallowness and professorial smugness, he stands for a point of view which at least has something honest and courageous about it; here, at all events, he is a realist. Let him put a motto to his books, and it might be:

> *Ἰὼ γενεαὶ βροτῶν,*
> *Ὡς ὑμᾶς ἴσα χαὶ τὸ μηδὲν*
> *Ζώσας ἐναριθμῶ.*

If you protest against that as too harsh for Christians and college professors, right-thinkers and forward-lookers, then you protest against "Oedipus Rex."[11]

As for the animal behaviour prattle of the learned head-master, it reveals, on the one hand, only the academic fondness for seizing upon high-sounding but empty phrases and using them to alarm the populace, and on the other hand, only the academic incapacity for observing facts correctly and reporting them honestly. The truth is, of course, that the behaviour of such men as Cowperwood and Witla and of such women as Carrie and Jennie, as Dreiser describes it, is no more merely animal than the behaviour of such acknowledged and undoubted human beings as Woodrow Wilson and Jane Addams. The whole point of the story of Witla, to take the example which seems to concern the horrified watchmen most, is this: that his life is a bitter conflict between the animal in him and the aspiring soul, between the flesh and the spirit, between what is weak in him and what is strong, between what is base and what is noble. Moreover, the good, in the end, gets its hooks into the bad: as we part from Witla he is actually bathed in the tears of remorse, and resolved to be a correct and godfearing man. And what have we in *The Financier* and *The Titan?* A conflict, in the ego of Cowperwood, between aspiration and ambition, between the passion for beauty and the passion for power. Is either passion animal? To ask the question is to answer it.

I single out Dr. Sherman, not because his pompous syllogisms have any plausibility in fact or logic, but simply because he may well stand as archetype of the booming, indignant corrupter of criteria, the moralist turned critic. A glance at his paean to Arnold Bennett[12] at once reveals the true gravamen of his objection to Dreiser. What offends him is not actually Dreiser's shortcoming as an artist, but Dreiser's shortcoming as a Christian and an American. In Bennett's volumes of pseudo-philosophy—e.g., *The Plain Man and His Wife* and *The Feast of St. Friend*—he finds the intellectual victuals that are to his taste. Here we have a sweet commingling of virtuous conformity and complacent optimism, of sonorous platitude and easy certainty—here, in brief, we have the philosophy of the English middle classes—and here, by the same token, we have the sort of guff that the half-educated of our own country can understand. It is the calm, superior numskullery that was Victorian; it is by Samuel Smiles out of Hannah More. The offence of Dreiser is that he has disdained this revelation and gone back to the Greeks. Lo, he reads poetry into "the appetite for women"—he rejects the Pauline doctrine that all love is below the diaphragm! He thinks of Ulysses, not as a mere heretic and criminal, but as a great artist. He sees the life of man, not as a simple theorem in Calvinism, but as a vast adventure, an enchantment, a mystery. It is no wonder that respectable school-teachers are against him. . . .

The comstockian attack upon *The 'Genius'* seems to have sprung out of the same muddled sense of Dreiser's essential hostility to all that is safe and regular—of the danger in him to that mellowed Methodism which has become the national ethic. The book, in a way, was a direct challenge, for though it came to an end upon a note which even a Methodist might hear as sweet, there were undoubted provocations in detail. Dreiser, in fact, allowed his scorn to make off with his taste—and *es ist nichts fürchterlicher als Einbildungskraft ohne Geschmack*. The Comstocks arose to the bait a bit slowly, but none the less surely. Going through the volume with the terrible industry of a Sunday-school boy dredging up pearls of smut from the Old Testament, they achieved a list of no less than 89 alleged floutings of the code—75 described as lewd and 14 as profane. An inspection of these specifications affords mirth of a rare and lofty variety; nothing could more cruelly expose the inner chambers of the moral mind. When young Witla, fastening his best girl's skate, is so overcome by the carnality of youth that he hugs her, it is set down as lewd. On page 51, having become an art student, he is fired by "a great, warm-tinted nude of Bouguereau"—lewd again. On page 70 he begins to draw from the figure, and his instructor cautions him that the female breast is round, not square—more lewdness. On page 151 he kisses a girl on mouth and neck and she cautions him: "Be careful! Mamma may come in"—still more. On page 161, having got rid of mamma, she yields "herself to him gladly, joyously" and he is greatly shocked when she argues that an artist (she is by way of being a singer) had better not marry—lewdness doubly damned. On page 245 he and his bride, being ignorant, neglect the principles laid down by Dr. Sylvanus Stall in his great works on sex hygiene—lewdness most horrible! But there is no need to proceed further. Every kiss, hug and tickle of the chin in the chronicle is laboriously snouted out, empanelled, exhibited. Every hint that Witla is no vestal, that he indulges his unchristian fleshliness, that he burns in the manner of I Corinthians, VII, 9, is uncovered to the moral inquisition.

On the side of profanity there is a less ardent pursuit of evidences, chiefly, I daresay, because their unearthing is less stimulating. (Beside, there is no law prohibiting profanity in books: the whole inquiry here is but so much *lagniappe.*) On page 408, in describing a character called Daniel C. Summerfield, Dreiser says that the fellow is "very much given to swearing, more as a matter of habit than of foul intention," and then goes on to explain somewhat lamely that "no picture of him would be complete without the interpolation of his various expressions." They turn out to be *God damn* and *Jesus Christ*—three of the latter and five or six of the former. All go down; the pure in heart must be shielded from the knowledge of them. (But what of the immoral French? They call the English *Goddams.*) Also, three plain *damns,* eight *hells,* one *my God,* five *by Gods,* one *go to the devil,* one *God Almighty* and one plain *God.* Altogether, 31 specimens are listed. *The 'Genius'* runs to 350,000 words. The profanity thus works out to somewhat less than one word in 10,000. . . . Alas, the comstockian proboscis, feeling for such offendings, is not as alert as when uncovering more savoury delicacies. On page 191 find an overlooked *by God.* On page 372 there are *Oh God, God curse her,* and *God strike her dead.* On page 373 there are *Ah God, Oh God* and three other invocations of God. On page 617 there is *God help me.* On page 720 there is *as God is my judge.* On page 723 there is *I'm no damned good.* . . . But I begin to blush.

When the Comstock Society began proceedings against *The 'Genius,'* a group of English novelists, including Arnold Bennett, H. G. Wells, W. L. George and Hugh Walpole, cabled an indignant caveat. This bestirred the Author's League of America to activity, and its executive committee issued a minute denouncing the business. Later on a protest of American *literati* was circulated, and more than 400 signed, including such highly respectable authors as Winston Churchill, Percy MacKaye, Booth Tarkington and James Lane Allen, and such critics as Lawrence Gilman, Clayton Hamilton and James Huneker, and the editors of such journals as the *Century*, the *Atlantic Monthly* and the *New Republic.* Among my literary lumber is all the correspondence relating to this protest, not forgetting the letters of those who refused to sign, and some day I hope to publish it, that posterity may not lose the joy of an extremely diverting episode. The case attracted wide attention and was the theme of an extraordinarily violent discussion, but the resultant benefits to Dreiser were more than counterbalanced, I daresay, by the withdrawal of *The 'Genius'* itself.[13]

§ 7

Dreiser, like Mark Twain and Emerson before him, has been far more hospitably greeted in his first stage, now drawing to a close, in England than in his own country. The cause of this, I daresay, lies partly in the fact that *Sister Carrie* was in general circulation over there during the seven years that it remained suppressed on this side. It was during these years that such men as Arnold Bennett, Theodore Watts-Dunton, Frank Harris and H. G. Wells, and such critical journals as the *Spectator,* the *Saturday Review* and the *Athenaeum* became aware of him, and so laid the foundations of a sound appreciation of his subsequent work. Since the beginning of the war, certain English newspapers have echoed the alarmed American discovery that he is a literary agent of the Wilhelmstrasse, but it is to the honour of the English that this imbecility has got no countenance from reputable authority and has not injured his position.

At home, as I have shown, he is less fortunate. When criticism is not merely an absurd effort to chase him out of court because his ideas are not orthodox, as the Victorians tried to chase out Darwin and Swinburne, and their predecessors pursued Shelley and Byron, it is too often designed to identify him with some branch or other of "radical" poppycock, and so credit him with purposes he has never imagined. Thus Chautauqua pulls and Greenwich Village pushes. In the middle ground there proceeds the pedantic effort to dispose of him by labelling him. One faction maintains that he is a realist; another calls him a naturalist; a third argues that he is really a disguised romanticist. This debate is all sound and fury, signifying nothing, but out of it has come a valuation by Lawrence Gilman[14] which perhaps strikes very close to the truth. He is, says Mr. Gilman, "a sentimental mystic who employs the mimetic gestures of the realist." This judgment is apt in particular and sound in general. No such thing as a pure method is possible in the novel. Plain realism, as in Gorky's *Nachtasyl* and the war stories of Ambrose Bierce, simply wearies us by its vacuity; plain romance, if we ever get beyond our nonage, makes us laugh. It is their artistic combination, as in life itself, that fetches us—the subtle projection of the concrete muddle that is living against the ideal orderliness that we reach out for—the eternal war of experience and aspiration—the contrast between the world as it is and the world as it might be or ought to be. Dreiser describes the thing that he sees, laboriously and relentlessly, but he never forgets the dream that is behind it. "He gives you," continues Mr. Gilman, "a sense of actuality; but he gives you more than that: out of the vast welter and surge, the plethoric irrelevancies, . . . emerges a sense of the infinite sadness and mystery of human life." . . .[15]

"To see truly," said Renan, "is to see dimly." Dimness or mystery, call it what you will: it is in all these overgrown and formless, but profoundly moving books. Just what do they mean? Just what is Dreiser driving at? That such questions should be asked is only a proof of the straits to which pedagogy has brought criticism. The answer is simple: he is driving at nothing, he is merely trying to represent what he sees and feels. His moving impulse is no flabby yearning to teach, to expound, to make simple; it is that "obscure inner necessity" of which Conrad tells us, the irresistible creative passion of a genuine artist, standing spell-bound before the impenetrable enigma that is life, enamoured by the strange beauty that plays over its sordidness, challenged to a wondering and half-terrified sort of representation of what passes understanding. And *jenseits von Gut und Böse*. "For myself," says Dreiser, "I do not know what truth is, what beauty is, what love is, what hope is. I do not believe any one absolutely and I do not doubt any one absolutely. I think people are both evil and well-intentioned." The hatching of the Dreiser bugaboo is here; it is the flat rejection of the rubber-stamp formulae that outrages petty minds; not being "good," he must be "evil"—as William Blake said of Milton, a true poet is always "of the devil's party." But in that very groping toward a light but dimly seen there is a measure, it seems to me, of Dreiser's rank and consideration as an artist. "Now comes the public," says Hermann Bahr, "and demands that we explain what the poet is trying to say. The answer is this: If we knew exactly he would not be a poet. . . ."

→ CHAPTER THREE ←

JAMES HUNEKER

§ 1

EDGAR ALLAN POE, I AM FOND OF BELIEVING, EARNED AS A CRITIC a good deal of the excess of praise that he gets as a romancer and a poet, and another over-estimated American dithyrambist, Sidney Lanier, wrote the best textbook of prosody in English;[1] but in general the critical writing done in the United States has been of a low order, and most American writers of any genuine distinction, like most American painters and musicians, have had to wait for understanding until it appeared abroad. The case of Emerson is typical. At thirty, he was known in New England as a heretical young clergyman and no more, and his fame threatened to halt at the tea-tables of the Boston Brahmins. It remained for Landor and Carlyle, in a strange land, to discern his higher potentialities, and to encourage him to his real life-work. Mark Twain, as I have hitherto shown, suffered from the same lack of critical perception at home. He was quickly recognized as a funny fellow, true enough, but his actual stature was not even faintly apprehended, and even after *Huckleberry Finn* he was still bracketed with such laborious farceurs as Artemus Ward. It was Sir Walter Besant, an Englishman, who first ventured to put him on his right shelf, along with Swift,

Cervantes and Molière. As for Poe and Whitman, the native recognition of their genius was so greatly conditioned by a characteristic horror of their immorality that it would be absurd to say that their own country understood them. Both were better and more quickly apprehended in France, and it was in France, not in America, that each founded a school. What they had to teach we have since got back at second hand—the tale of mystery, which was Poe's contribution, through Gaboriau and Boisgobey; and *vers libre,* which was Whitman's, through the French *imagistes.*

The cause of this profound and almost unbroken lack of critical insight and enterprise, this puerile Philistinism and distrust of ideas among us, is partly to be found, it seems to me, in the fact that the typical American critic is quite without any adequate cultural equipment for the office he presumes to fill. Dr. John Dewey, in some late remarks upon the American universities, has perhaps shown the cause thereof. The trouble with our educational method, he argues, is that it falls between the two stools of English humanism and German relentlessness—that it produces neither a man who intelligently feels nor a man who thoroughly knows. Criticism, in America, is a function of this half-educated and conceited class; it is not a popular art, but an esoteric one; even in its crassest journalistic manifestations it presumes to a certain academic remoteness from the concerns and carnalities of everyday. In every aspect it shows the defects of its practitioners. The American critic of beautiful letters, in his common incarnation, is no more than a talented sophomore, or, at best, a somewhat absurd professor. He suffers from a palpable lack of solid preparation; he has no background of moving and illuminating experience behind him; his soul has not sufficiently adventured among masterpieces, nor among men. Imagine a Taine or a Sainte-Beuve or a Macaulay—man of the world, veteran of philosophies, "lord of life"—and you imagine his complete antithesis. Even on the side of mere professional knowledge, the primary material of his craft, he always appears incompletely outfitted. The grand sweep and direction of the literary currents elude him; he is eternally on the surface, chasing bits of driftwood. The literature he knows is the fossil literature taught in colleges—worse, in high schools. It must be dead before he is aware of it. And in particular he appears ignorant of what is going forward in other lands. An exotic idea, to penetrate his consciousness, must first become stale, and even then he is apt to purge it of all its remaining validity and significance before adopting it.

This has been true since the earliest days. Emerson himself, though a man of unusual discernment and a diligent drinker from German spigots, nevertheless remained a *dilettante* in both aesthetics and metaphysics to the end of his days, and the incompleteness of his equipment never showed more plainly than in his criticism of books. Lowell, if anything, was even worse; his aesthetic theory, first and last, was nebulous and superficial, and all that remains of his pleasant essays today is their somewhat smoky pleasantness. He was a Charles Dudley Warner in nobler trappings, but still, at bottom, a Charles Dudley Warner. As for Poe, though he was by nature a far more original and penetrating critic than either Emerson or Lowell, he was enormously ignorant of good books, and moreover, he could never quite throw off a congenital vulgarity of taste, so painfully visible in the strutting of his style. The man, for all his grand dreams, had a shoddy soul; he belonged authentically to the era of cuspidors, "females" and Sons of Temperance. His occasional affectation of scholarship has deceived no one. It was no more than Yankee bluster; he constantly referred to books that he had never read. Beside, the typical American critic of those days was not Poe, but his arch-enemy, Rufus Wilmot Griswold, that almost fabulous ass—a Baptist preacher turned taster of the beautiful. Imagine a Baptist valuing Balzac, or Molière, or Shakespeare, or Goethe—or Rabelais!

Coming down to our own time, one finds the same endless amateurishness, so characteristic of everything American, from politics to cookery—the same astounding lack of training and vocation. Consider the solemn ponderosities of the pious old maids, male and female, who write book reviews for the newspapers. Here we have a heavy pretension to culture, a campus cocksureness, a laborious righteousness—but of sound aesthetic understanding, of alertness and hospitality to ideas, not a trace. The normal American book reviewer, indeed, is an elderly virgin, a superstitious bluestocking, an apostle of Vassar *Kultur;* and her customary attitude of mind is one of fascinated horror. (The Hamilton Wright Mabie complex! The "white list" of novels!) William Dean Howells, despite a certain jauntiness and even kittenishness of manner, was spiritually of that company. For all his phosphorescent heresies, he was what the uplifters call a right-thinker at heart, and soaked in the national tradition. He was easiest intrigued, not by force and originality, but by a sickly, *Ladies' Home Journal* sort of piquancy; it was this that made him see a genius in the Philadelphia Zola, W. B. Trites, and that led him to hymn an abusive business letter by Frank A. Munsey, author of *The Boy Broker* and *Afloat in a Great City,* as a significant human document. Moreover Howells ran true to type in another way, for he long reigned as the leading Anglo-Saxon authority on the Russian novelists without knowing, so far as I can make out, more than ten words of Russian. In the same manner, we have had enthusiasts for D'Annunzio and Mathilde Serao who knew no Italian, and celebrants of Maeterlinck and Verhaeren whose French was of the finishing school, and Ibsen authorities without a single word of Dano-Norwegian—I met one once who failed to recognize *Et Dukkehje* as the original title of *A Doll's House,*—and performers upon Hauptmann who could no more read *Die Weber* than they could decipher a tablet of Tiglath-Pileser III.

Here and there, of course, a more competent critic of beautiful letters flings out his banner—for example, John Macy, Ludwig Lewisohn, André Tridon, Francis Hackett, Van Wyck Brooks, Burton Rascoe, E. A. Boyd, Llewellyn Jones, Otto Heller, J. E. Spingarn, Lawrence Gilman, the late J. Percival Pollard. Well-informed, intelligent, wide-eyed men—but only four of them even Americans, and not one of them with a wide audience, or any appreciable influence upon the main stream of American criticism. Pollard's best work is buried in the perfumed pages of *Town Topics;* his book on the Munich wits and dramatists[2] is almost unknown. Heller and Lewisohn make their way slowly; a patriotic wariness, I daresay, mixes itself up with their acceptance. Gilman disperses his talents; he is quite as much musician as critic of the arts. As for Macy, I recently found his *The Spirit of American Literature,*[3] by long odds the soundest, wisest book on its subject, selling for fifty cents on a Fifth Avenue remainder counter.

How many remain? A few competent reviewers who are primarily something else—Harvey, Aikin, Untermeyer and company. A few youngsters on the newspapers, struggling against the business office. And then a leap to the Victorians, the crêpe-clad pundits, the bombastic word-mongers of the campus school—H. W. Boynton, W. C. Brownell, Paul Elmer More, William Lyon Phelps, Frederick Taber Cooper *et al.* Here, undoubtedly, we have learning of a sort. More, it appears, once taught Sanskrit to the adolescent suffragettes of Bryn Mawr—an enterprise as stimulating (and as intelligible) as that of setting off fire-works in a blind asylum. Phelps sits in a chair at Yale. Boynton is a master of arts in English literature, whatever that may mean. Brownell is both L.H.D. and Litt.D., thus surpassing Samuel Johnson by one point, and Hazlitt, Coleridge and Malone by two. But the learning of these august *umbilicarii,* for all its pretensions, is precisely the sterile, foppish sort one looks for in second-rate college professors. The appearance is there, but not the substance. One ingests a horse-doctor's dose of words, but fails to acquire any illumination. Read More on Nietzsche[4] if you want to find out just how stupid criticism can be, and yet show the outward forms of sense. Read Phelps' *The Advance of the English Novel*[5] if you would see a fine art treated as a moral matter, and great works tested by the criteria of a small-town Sunday-school, and all sorts of childish sentimentality whooped up. And plough through Brownell's "Standards,"[6] if you have the patience, and then try to reduce its sonorous platitudes to straightforward and defensible propositions.

§ 2

Now for the exception. He is, of course, James Gibbons Huneker, the solitary Iokanaan in this tragic aesthetic wilderness, the only critic among us whose vision sweeps the whole field of beauty, and whose reports of what he sees there show any genuine gusto. That gusto of his, I fancy, is two-thirds of his story. It is unquenchable, contagious, inflammatory; he is the only performer in the commissioned troupe who knows how to arouse his audience to anything approaching enthusiasm. The rest, even including Howells, are pedants lecturing to the pure in heart, but Huneker makes a joyous story of it; his exposition, transcending the merely expository, takes on the quality of an adventure hospitably shared. One feels, reading him, that he is charmed by the men and women he writes about, and that their ideas, even when he rejects them, give him an agreeable stimulation. And to the charm that he thus finds and exhibits in others, he adds the very positive charm of his own personality. He seems a man who has found the world fascinating, if perhaps not perfect; a friendly and good-humoured fellow; no frigid scholiast, but something of an epicure; in brief, the reverse of the customary maker of books about books. Compare his two essays on Ibsen, in *Egoists* and *Iconoclasts,* to the general body of American writing upon the great Norwegian. The difference is that between a portrait and a Bertillon photograph, Richard Strauss and Czerny, a wedding and an autopsy. Huneker displays Ibsen, not as a petty mystifier of the women's clubs, but as a literary artist of large skill and exalted passion, and withal a quite human and understandable man. These essays were written at the height of the symbolism madness; in their own way, they even show some reflection of it; but taking them in their entirety, how clearly they stand above the ignorant obscurantism of the prevailing criticism of the time—how immeasurably superior they are, for example, to that favourite hymn-book of the Ibsenites, *The Ibsen Secret* by Jennette Lee! For the causes of this difference one need not seek far. They are to be found in the difference between the bombastic half-knowledge of a school teacher and the discreet and complete knowledge of a man of culture. Huneker is that man of culture. He has reported more of interest and value than any other American critic, living or dead, but the essence of his criticism does not lie so much in what he specifically reports as in the civilized point of view from which he reports it. He is a true cosmopolitan, not only in the actual range of his adventurings, but also and more especially in his attitude of mind. His world is not America, nor Europe, nor Christendom, but the whole universe of beauty. As Jules Simon said of Taine: *"Aucun écrivain de nos jours n'a . . . découvert plus d'horizons variés et immenses."*

Need anything else be said in praise of a critic? And does an extravagance or an error here and there lie validly against the saying of it? I think not. I could be a professor if I would and show you slips enough—certain ponderous nothings in the Ibsen essays, already mentioned; a too easy bemusement at the hands of Shaw; a vacillating over Wagner; a habit of yielding to the hocus-pocus of the mystics, particularly Maeterlinck. On the side of painting, I am told, there are even worse aberrations; I know too little about painting to judge for myself. But the list, made complete, would still not be over-long, and few of its items would be important. Huneker, like the rest of us, has sinned his sins, but his judgments, in the overwhelming main, hold water. He has resisted the lure of all the wild movements of the generation; the tornadoes of doctrine have never knocked him over. Nine times out of ten, in estimating a new man in music or letters, he has come curiously close to the truth at the first attempt. And he has always announced it in good time; his solo has always preceded the chorus. He was, I believe, the first American (not forgetting William Morton Payne and Hjalmar Hjorth Boyesen, the pioneers) to write about Ibsen with any understanding of the artist behind the prophet's mask; he was the first to see the rising star of Nietzsche (this was back in 1888); he was beating a drum for Shaw the critic before ever Shaw the dramatist and mob philosopher was born (*circa* 1886–1890); he was writing about Hauptmann and Maeterlinck before they had got well set on their legs in their own countries; his estimate of Sudermann, bearing date of 1905, may stand with scarcely the change of a word today; he did a lot of valiant pioneering for Strindberg, Hervieu, Stirner and Gorki, and later on helped in the pioneering for Conrad; he was in the van of the MacDowell enthusiasts; he fought for the ideas of such painters as Davies, Lawson, Luks, Sloan and Prendergest (Americans all, by the way: an answer to the hollow charge of exotic obsession) at a time when even Manet, Monet and Degas were laughed at; he was among the first to give a hand to Frank Norris, Theodore Dreiser, Stephen Crane and H. B. Fuller. In sum, he gave some semblance of reality in the United States, after other men had tried and failed, to that great but ill-starred revolt against Victorian pedantry, formalism and sentimentality which began in the early 90's. It would be difficult, indeed, to overestimate the practical value to all the arts in America of his intellectual alertness, his catholic hospitality to ideas, his artistic courage, and above all, his powers of persuasion. It was not alone that he saw clearly what was sound and significant;

it was that he managed, by the sheer charm of his writings, to make a few others see and understand it. If the United States is in any sort of contact today, however remotely, with what is aesthetically going on in the more civilized countries—if the Puritan tradition, for all its firm entrenchment, has eager and resourceful enemies besetting it—if the pall of Harvard quasiculture, by the Oxford manner out of Calvinism, has been lifted ever so little—there is surely no man who can claim a larger share of credit for preparing the way. . . .

§ 3

Huneker comes out of Philadelphia, that depressing intellectual slum, and his first writing was for the Philadelphia *Evening Bulletin.* He is purely Irish in blood, and is of very respectable ancestry, his maternal grandfather and godfather having been James Gibbons, the Irish poet and patriot, and president of the Fenian Brotherhood in America. Once, in a review of *The Pathos of Distance,* I ventured the guess that there was a German strain in him somewhere, and based it upon the beery melancholy visible in parts of that book. Who but a German sheds tears over the empty bottles of day before yesterday, the Adelaide Neilson of 1877? Who but a German goes into woollen undershirts at 45, and makes his will, and begins to call his wife "Mamma"? The green-sickness of youth is endemic from pole to pole, as much so as measles; but what race save the wicked one is floored by a blue distemper in middle age, with sentimental burblings *a cappella,* hallucinations of lost loves, and an unquenchable lacrymorrhea? . . . I made out a good case, but I was wrong, and the penalty came swiftly and doubly, for on the one hand the Boston *Transcript* sounded an alarm against both Huneker and me as German spies, and on the other hand Huneker himself proclaimed that, even spiritually, he was less German than Magyar, less "Hun" than Hun. "I am," he said, "a Celto-Magyar: Pilsner at Donneybrook Fair. Even the German beer and cuisine are not in it with the Austro-Hungarian." Here, I suspect, he meant to say Czech instead of Magyar, for isn't Pilsen in Bohemia? Moreover, turn to the chapter on Prague in *New Cosmopolis,* and you will find out in what highland his heart really is. In this book, indeed, is a vast hymn to all things Czechic—the Pilsen *Urquell,* the muffins stuffed with poppy-seed jam, the spiced chicken liver *en casserole,* the pretty Bohemian girls, the rose and golden glory of Hradschin Hill. . . . One thinks of other strange infatuations: the Polish Conrad's for England, the Scotch Mackay's for Germany, the Low German Brahms' for Italy. Huneker, I daresay, is the first Celto-Czech—or Celto-Magyar, as you choose. (Maybe the name suggests something. It is not to be debased to *Hoon*-eker, remember, but kept at *Hun*-eker, rhyming initially with *nun* and *gun.*) An unearthly marriage of elements, by all the gods! but there are pretty children of it. . . .

Philadelphia humanely disgorged Huneker in 1878. His father designed him for the law, and he studied the institutes at the Philadelphia Law Academy, but like Schumann, he was spoiled for briefs by the stronger pull of music and the *cacoëthes scribendi.* (Grandpa John Huneker had been a composer of church music, and organist at St. Mary's.) In the year mentioned he set out for Paris to see Liszt; his aim was to make himself a piano virtuoso. His name does not appear on his own exhaustive list of Liszt pupils, but he managed to quaff of the Pierian spring at second-hand, for he had lessons from Theodore Ritter (*né* Bennet), a genuine pupil of the old walrus, and he was also taught by the venerable Georges Mathias, a pupil of Chopin. These days laid the foundations for two subsequent books, the *Chopin: the Man and His Music* of 1900, and the *Franz Liszt* of 1911. More, they prepared the excavations for all of the others, for Huneker began sending home letters to the Philadelphia *Bulletin* on the pictures that he saw, the books that he read and the music that he heard in Paris, and out of them gradually grew a body of doctrine that was to be developed into full-length criticism on his return to the United States. He stayed in Paris until the middle 80's, and then settled in New York.

All the while his piano studies continued, and in New York he became a pupil of Rafael Joseffy. He even became a teacher himself and was for ten years on the staff of the National Conservatory, and showed himself at all the annual meetings of the Music Teachers' Association. But bit by bit criticism elbowed out music-making, as music-making had elbowed out criticism with Schumann and Berlioz. In 1886 or thereabout he joined the *Musical Courier;* then he went, in succession, to the old *Recorder,* to the *Morning Advertiser,* to the *Sun,* to the *Times,* and finally to the Philadelphia *Press* and the New York *World.* Various weeklies and monthlies have also enlisted him: *Mlle. New York,* the *Atlantic Monthly,* the *Smart Set,* the *North American Review* and *Scribner's.* He has even stooped to *Puck,* vainly trying to make an American *Simplicissimus* of that dull offspring of synagogue and barbershop. He has been, in brief, an extremely busy and not too fastidious journalist, writing first about one of the arts, and then about another, and then about all seven together. But music has been the steadiest of all his loves; his first three books dealt almost wholly with it; of his complete canon more than half have to do with it.

§ 4

His first book, *Mezzotints in Modern Music,* published in 1899, revealed his predilections clearly, and what is more, his critical insight and sagacity. One reads it today without the slightest feeling that it is an old story; some of the chapters, obviously reworkings of articles for the papers, must go back to the middle 90's, and yet the judgments they proclaim scarcely call for the change of a word. The single noticeable weakness is a too easy acquiescence in the empty showiness of Saint-Saëns, a tendency to bow to the celebrated French parlour magician too often. Here, I daresay, is an echo of old Paris days, for Camille was a hero on the Seine in 1880, and there was even talk of pitting him against Wagner. The estimates of other men are judiciously arrived at and persuasively stated. Tschaikowsky is correctly put down as a highly talented but essentially shallow fellow—a blubberer in the regalia of a philosopher. Brahms, then still under attack by Henry T. Finck, of the *Evening Post* (the press-agent of Massenet: ye gods, what Harvard can do, even to a Würtemberger!) is subjected to a long, an intelligent and an extremely friendly analysis; no better has got into English since, despite too much stress on the piano music. And Richard Strauss, yet a nine days' wonder, is described clearly and accurately, and his true stature indicated. The rest of the book is less noteworthy; Huneker says the proper things about Chopin, Liszt and Wagner, and adds a chapter on piano methods, the plain fruit of his late pedagogy. But the three chapters I have mentioned are enough; they fell, in their time, into a desert of stupidity; they set a standard in musical criticism in America that only Huneker himself has ever exceeded.

The most popular of his music books, of course, is the *Chopin* (1900). Next to *Iconoclasts,* it is the best seller of them all. More, it has been done into German, French and Italian, and is chiefly responsible for Huneker's celebrity abroad as the only critic of music that America has ever produced. Superficially, it seems to be a monument of pedantry, a meticulous piling up of learning, but a study of it shows that it is very much more than that. Compare it to Sir George Grove's staggering tome on the Beethoven symphonies if you want to understand the difference between mere scholastic diligence and authentic criticism. The one is simply a top-heavy mass of disorderly facts and worshipping enthusiasm; the other is an analysis that searches out every nook and corner of the subject, and brings it into coherence and intelligibility. The Chopin rhapsodist is always held in check by the sound musician; there is a snouting into dark places as well as a touching up of high lights. I myself am surely no disciple of the Polish tuberose—his sweetness, in fact, gags me, and I turn even to Moszkowski for relief—but I have read and re-read this volume with endless interest, and I find it more bethumbed than any other Huneker book in my library, saving only *Iconoclasts* and *Old Fogy*. Here, indeed, Huneker is on his own ground. One often feels, in his discussions of orchestral music, that he only thinks orchestrally, like Schumann, with an effort—that all music, in his mind, gets itself translated into terms of piano music. In dealing with Chopin no such transvaluation of values is necessary; the raw materials are ready for his uses without preparation; he is wholly at home among the black keys and white.

His *Liszt* is a far less noteworthy book. It is, in truth, scarcely a book at all, but merely a collection of notes for a book, some of them considerably elaborated, but others set down in the altogether. One reads it because it is about Liszt, the most fantastic figure that ever came out of Hungary, half devil and half clown; not because there is any conflagration of ideas in it. The chapter that reveals most of Huneker is the appendix on latter-day piano virtuosi, with its estimates of such men as de Pachmann, Rosenthal, Paderewski and Hofmann. Much better stuff is to be found in *Overtones, The Pathos of Distance* and *Ivory, Apes and Peacocks*—brilliant, if not always profound studies of Strauss, Wagner, Schoenberg, Moussorgsky, and even Verdi. But if I had my choice of the whole shelf, it would rest, barring the *Chopin*, on *Old Fogy*—the *scherzo* of the Hunekeran symphony, the critic taking a holiday, the Devil's Mass in the tonal sanctuary. In it Huneker is at his very choicest, making high-jinks with his Davidsbund of one, rattling the skeletons in all the musical closets of the world. Here, throwing off his critic's black gown, his lays about him right and left, knocking the reigning idols off their perches; resurrecting the old, old dead and trying to pump the breath into them; lambasting on one page and lauding on the next; lampooning his fellow critics and burlesquing their rubber stamp fustian; extolling Dussek and damning Wagner; swearing mighty oaths by Mozart, and after him, Strauss—not Richard, but Johann! The Old Fogy, of course, is the thinnest of disguises, a mere veil of gossamer for "Editor" Huneker. That Huneker in false whiskers is inimitable, incomparable, almost indescribable. On the one hand, he is a prodigy of learning, a veritable warehouse of musical information, true, half-true and apocryphal; on the other hand, he is a jester who delights in reducing all learning to absurdity. Reading him somehow suggests hearing a Bach mass re-scored for two fifes, a tambourine in B, a wind machine, two tenor harps, a contrabass oboe, two banjos, eight tubas and the usual clergy and strings. The substance is there; every note is struck exactly in the middle—but what outlandish tone colours, what strange, unearthly sounds! It is not Bach, however, who first comes to mind when Huneker is at his tricks, but Papa Haydn—the Haydn of the Surprise symphony and the Farewell. There is the same gargantuan gaiety, the same magnificent irreverence. Haydn did more for the symphony than any other man, but he also got more fun out of it than any other man.

Old Fogy, of course, is not to be taken seriously: it is frankly a piece of fooling. But all the same a serious idea runs through the book from end to end, and that is the idea that music is getting too subjective to be comfortable. The makers of symphonies tend to forget beauty altogether; their one effort is to put all their own petty trials and tribulations, their empty theories and speculations into cacophony. Even so far back as Beethoven's day that autobiographical habit had begun. "Beethoven," says Old Fogy, is "dramatic, powerful, a maker of storms, a subduer of tempests; but his speech is the speech of a self-centred egotist. He is the father of all the modern melomaniacs, who, looking into their own souls, write what they see therein—misery, corruption, slighting selfishness and ugliness." Old Ludwig's groans, of course, we can stand. He was not only a great musician, but also a great man. It is just as interesting to hear him sigh and complain as it would be to hear the private prayers of Julius Caesar. But what of Tschaikowsky, with his childish Slavic whining? What of Liszt, with his cheap playacting, his incurable lasciviousness, his plebeian warts? What of Wagner, with his delight in imbecile fables, his popinjay vanity, his soul of a *Schnorrer?* What of Richard Strauss, with his warmed-over Nietzscheism, his flair for the merely horrible? Old Fogy sweeps them all into his ragbag. If art is to be defined as beauty seen through a temperament, then give us more beauty and cleaner temperaments! Back to the old gods, Mozart and Bach, with a polite bow to Brahms and a sentimental tear for Chopin! Beethoven tried to tell his troubles in his music; Mozart was content to ravish the angels of their harps. And as for Johann Sebastian, "there was more real musical feeling, uplifting and sincerity in the old Thomaskirche in Leipzig . . . than in all your modern symphony and oratorio machine-made concerts put together."

All this is argued, to be sure, in extravagant terms. Wagner is a mere ghoul and impostor: "The Flying Dutchman" is no more than a parody on Weber, and "Parsifal" is "an outrage against religion, morals and music." Daddy Liszt is "the inventor of the Liszt pupil, a bad piano player, a venerable man with a purple nose—a Cyrano de Cognac nose." Tschaikowsky is the Slav gone crazy on vodka. He transformed Hamlet into "a yelling man" and Romeo and Juliet into "two monstrous Cossacks, who gibber and squeak at each other while reading some obscene volume." "His Manfred is a libel on Byron, who was a libel on God." And even Schumann is a vanishing star, a literary man turned composer, a pathological case. But, as I have said, a serious idea runs through all this concerto for slapstick and seltzer siphon, and to me, at least, that idea has a plentiful reasonableness. We are getting too much melodrama, too much vivisection, too much rebellion—and too little music. Turn from Tschaikowsky's Pathétique or from any of his wailing tone-poems to Schubert's C major, or to Mozart's Jupiter, or to Beethoven's *kleine Sinfonie in F dur:* it is like coming out of a *Kaffeeklatsch* into the open air, almost like escaping from a lunatic asylum. The one unmistakable emotion that much of this modern music from the steppes and morgues and *Biertische* engenders is a longing for form, clarity, coherence, a self-respecting tune. The snorts and moans of the pothouse Werthers are as irritating, in the long run, as the bawling of a child, the squeak of a pig under a gate. One yearns unspeakably for a composer who gives out his pair of honest themes, and then develops them with both ears open, and then recapitulates them unashamed, and then hangs a brisk coda to them, and then shuts up.

§ 5

So much for *Old Fogy* and the musical books. They constitute, not only the best body of work that Huneker himself has done, but the best body of musical criticism that any American has done. Musical criticism, in our great Calvinist republic, confines itself almost entirely to transient reviewing, and even when it gets between covers, it keeps its trivial quality. Consider, for example, the published work of Henry Edward Krehbiel, for long the *doyen* of the New York critics. I pick up his latest book, *A Second Book of Operas,*[7] open it at random, and find this:

> *On January 31, 1893, the Philadelphia singers, aided by the New York Symphony Society, gave a performance of the opera, under the auspices of the Young Men's Hebrew Association, for the benefit of its charities, at the Carnegie Music Hall, New York. Mr. Walter Damrosch was to have conducted, but was detained in Washington by the funeral of Mr. Blaine, and Mr. Hinrichs took his place.*

O Doctor *admirabilis, acutus et illuminatissimus!* Needless to say the universities have not overlooked this geyser of buttermilk: he is an honourary A.M. of Yale. His most respectable volume, that on negro folksong, impresses one principally by its incompleteness. It may be praised as a sketch, but surely not as a book. The trouble with Krehbiel, of course, is that he mistakes a newspaper morgue for Parnassus. He has all of the third-rate German's capacity for unearthing facts, but he doesn't know how either to think or to write, and so his criticism is mere pretence and pishposh. W. J. Henderson, of the *Sun,* doesn't carry that handicap. He is as full of learning as Krehbiel, as his books on singing and on the early Italian opera show, but he also wields a slippery and intriguing pen, and he could be hugely entertaining if he would. Instead, he devotes himself to manufacturing primers for the newly intellectual. I can find little of the charm of his *Sun* articles in his books. Lawrence Gilman? A sound musician but one who of late years has often neglected music for the other arts. Philip H. Goepp? His three volumes on the symphonic repertoire leave twice as much to be said as they say. Carl Van Vechten? A very promising novice, but not yet at full growth. Philip Hale? His gigantic annotations scarcely belong to criticism at all; they are musical talmudism. Beside, they are buried in the program books of the Boston Symphony Orchestra, and might as well be inscribed on the temple walls of Baalbec. As for Upton and other such fellows, they are merely musical chautauquans, and their tedious commentaries have little more value than the literary criticisms in the religious weeklies. One of them, a Harvard *maestro,* has published a book on the orchestra in which, on separate pages, the reader is solemnly presented with pictures of first and second violins!

It seems to me that Huneker stands on a higher level than any of these industrious gentlemen, and that his writings on music are of much more value, despite his divided allegiance among the *beaux arts.* Whatever may be said against him, it must at least be admitted that he knows Chopin, and that he has written the best volumes upon the tuberculous Pole in English. Vladimir de Pachmann, that king of all Chopin players, once bore characteristic testimony to the fact—I think it was in London. The program was heavy with the études and ballades, and Huneker sat in the front row of fanatics. After a storm of applause de Pachmann rose from the piano stool, levelled a bony claw at Huneker, and pronounced his dictum: "*He* knows more than *all* of you." Joseffy seems to have had the same opinion, for he sought the aid of his old pupil in preparing his new edition of Chopin, the first volume of which is all he lived to see in print. . . . And, beyond all the others, Huneker disdains writing for the kindergarten. There is no stooping in his discourse; he frankly addresses himself to an audience that has gone through the forms, and so he avoids the tediousness of the A B C expositors. He is the only American musical critic, save Van Vechten, who thus assumes invariably that a musical audience exists, and the only one who constantly measures up to its probable interests, supposing it to be there. Such a book as *Old Fogy*, for all its buffoonery, is conceivable only as the work of a sound musician. Its background is one of the utmost sophistication; in the midst of its wildest extravagances there is always a profound knowledge of music on tap, and a profound love of it to boot. Here, perhaps, more than anywhere else, Huneker's delight in the things he deals with is obvious. It is not a seminary that he keeps, but a sort of club of tone enthusiasts, and membership in it is infinitely charming.

§ 6

This capacity for making the thing described seem important and delightful, this quality of infectious gusto, this father-talent of all the talents that a critic needs, sets off his literary criticism no less than his discourse on music and musicians. Such a book as *Iconoclasts* or *Egoists* is full of useful information, but it is even more full of agreeable adventure. The style is the book, as it is the man. It is arch, staccato, ironical, witty, galloping, playful, polyglot, allusive—sometimes, alas, so allusive as to reduce the Drama Leaguer and women's clubber to wonderment and ire. In writing of plays or of books, as in writing of cities, tone-poems or philosophies, Huneker always assumes that the elements are already well-grounded, that he is dealing with the initiated, that a pause to explain would be an affront. Sad work for the Philistines—but a joy to the elect! All this polyphonic allusiveness, this intricate fuguing of ideas, is not to be confused, remember, with the hollow showiness of the academic soothsayer. It is as natural to the man, as much a part of him as the clanging Latin of Johnson, or, to leap from art to art Huneker-wise, the damnable cross-rhythms of Brahms. He could no more write without his stock company of heretic sages than he could write without his ration of malt. And, on examination, all of them turned out to be real. They are far up dark alleys, but they are there! . . . And one finds them, at last, to be as pleasant company as the multilingual puns of Nietzsche or Debussy's chords of the second.

As for the origin of that style, it seems to have a complex ancestry. Huneker's first love was Poe, and even today he still casts affectionate glances in that direction, but there is surely nothing of Poe's elephantine labouring in his skipping, *pizzicato* sentences. Then came Carlyle—the Carlyle of "Sartor Resartus"—a god long forgotten. Huneker's mother was a woman of taste; on reading his first scribblings, she gave him Cardinal Newman, and bade him consider the Queen's English. Newman achieved a useful purging; the style that remained was ready for Flaubert. From the author of *L'Education Sentimentale,* I daresay, came the deciding influence, with Nietzsche's staggering brilliance offering suggestions later on. Thus Huneker, as stylist, owes nearly all to France, for Nietzsche, too, learned how to write there, and to the end of his days he always wrote more like a Frenchman than a German. His greatest service to his own country, indeed, was not as anarch, but as teacher of writing.

He taught the Germans that their language had a snap in it as well as sighs and gargles—that it was possible to write German and yet not wander in a wood. There are whole pages of Nietzsche that suggest such things, say, as the essay on Maurice Barrès in *Egoists,* with its bold tropes, its rapid gait, its sharp *sforzandos.* And you will find old Friedrich at his tricks from end to end of *Old Fogy.*

Of the actual contents of such books as *Egoists* and *Iconoclasts* it is unnecessary to say anything. One no longer reads them for their matter, but for their manner. Every flapper now knows all that is worth knowing about Ibsen, Strindberg, Maeterlinck and Shaw, and a great deal that is not worth knowing. We have disentangled Hauptmann from Sudermann, and, thanks to Dr. Lewisohn, may read all his plays in English. Even Henry Becque has got into the vulgate and is familiar to the Drama League. As for Anatole France, his "Revolt of the Angels" is on the shelves of the Carnegie Libraries, and the Comstocks have let it pass. New gods whoop and rage in Valhalla: Verhaeren, Artzibashef, Przybyszewski. Huneker, alas, seems to drop behind the procession. He writes nothing about these second-hand third-raters. He has come to Wedekind, Schnitzler, Schoenberg, Korngold and Moussorgsky, and he has discharged a few rounds of shrapnel at the Gallo-Asiatic petticoat philosopher, Henri Bergson, but here he has stopped, as he has stopped at Matisse, Picasso, Epstein and Augustus John in painting. As he says himself, "one must get off somewhere." . . .

Particularly if one grows weary of criticism—and in Huneker, of late, I detect more than one sign of weariness. Youth is behind him, and with it some of its zest for exploration and combat. "The pathos of distance" is a phrase that haunts him as poignantly as it haunted Nietzsche, its maker. Not so long ago I tried to induce him to write some new Old Fogy sketches, nominating Puccini, Strawinsky, Schoenberg, Korngold, Elgar. He protested that the mood was gone from him forever, that he could not turn the clock back twenty years. His late work in *Puck,* the *Times* and the *Sun,* shows an unaccustomed acquiescence in current valuations. He praises such one-day masterpieces as McFee's "Casuals of the Sea"; he is polite to the gaudy heroines of the opera-house; he gags a bit at Wright's "Modern Painting"; he actually makes a gingery curtsy to Frank Jewett Mather, a Princeton professor. . . . The pressure in the gauges can't keep up to 250 pounds forever. Man must tire of fighting after awhile, and seek his ease in his inn. . . .

Perhaps the post-bellum transvaluation of all values will bring Huneker to his feet again, and with something of the old glow and gusto in him. And if the new men do not stir up, then assuredly the wrecks of the ancient cities will: the Paris of his youth; Munich, Dresden, Vienna, Brussels, London; above all, Prague. Go to "New Cosmopolis" and you will find where his heart lies, or, if not his heart, then at all events his oesophagus and pylorus. . . . Here, indeed, the thread of his meditations is a thread of nutriment. However diverted by the fragrance of the Dutch woods, the church bells of Belgium, the music of Stuttgart, the bad pictures of Dublin, the plays of Paris, the musty romance of old Wien, he always comes back anon to such ease as a man may find in his inn. "The stomach of Vienna," he says, "first interested me, not its soul." And so, after a dutiful genuflexion to St. Stephen's ("Old Steffel," as the Viennese call it), he proceeds to investigate the paprika-chicken, the *Gulyas,* the *Risi-bisi,* the *Apfelstrudel,* the *Kaiserschmarrn* and the native and authentic *Wienerschnitzel.* And from food to drink—specifically, to the haunts of Pilsner, to "certain semi-sacred houses where the ritual of beer-drinking is observed," to the shrines at which beer maniacs meet, to "a little old house near a Greek church" where "the best-kept Pilsner in Vienna may be found."

The best-kept Pilsner in Vienna! The phrase enchants like an entrance of the horns. The best caviare in Russia, the worst actor on Broadway, the most virtuous angel in Heaven! Such superlatives are transcendental. And yet,—so rare is perfection in this world!—the news swiftly follows, unexpected, disconcerting, that the best Pilsner in Vienna is far short of the ideal. For some undetermined reason—the influence of the American tourist? the decay of the Austrian national character?—the Vienna *Bierwirte* freeze and paralyze it with too much ice, so that it chills the nerves it should caress, and fills the heart below with heaviness and repining. Avoid Vienna, says Huneker, if you are one who understands and venerates the great Bohemian brew! And if, deluded, you find yourself there, take the first *D-zug* for Prague, that lovely city, for in it you will find the Pilsen *Urquell,* and in the Pilsen *Urquell* you will find the best Pilsner in Christendom—its colour a phosphorescent, translucent, golden yellow, its foam like whipped cream, its temperature exactly and invariably right. Not even at Pilsen itself (which the Bohemians call Plezen) is the emperor of malt liquors more stupendously grateful to the palate. Write it down before you forget: the Pilsen *Urquell,* Prague, Bohemia, 120 miles S. S. E. of Dresden, on the river Moldau (which the natives call the Vitava). Ask for Fräulein Ottilie. Mention the name of Herr Huneker, the American *Schriftsteller.*

Of all the eminent and noble cities between the Alleghenies and the Balkans, Prague seems to be Huneker's favourite. He calls it poetic, precious, delectable, original, dramatic—a long string of adjectives, each argued for with eloquence that is unmistakably sincere. He stands fascinated before the towers and pinnacles of the Hradschin, "a miracle of tender rose and marble white with golden spots of sunshine that would have made Claude Monet envious." He pays his devotions to the Chapel of St. Wenceslaus, "crammed with the bones of buried kings," or, at any rate, to the shrine of St. John Nepomucane, "composed of nearly two tons of silver." He is charmed by the beauty of the stout, black-haired, red-cheeked Bohemian girls, and hopes that enough of them will emigrate to the United States to improve the fading pulchritude of our own houris. But most of all, he has praises for the Bohemian cuisine, with its incomparable apple tarts, and its dumplings of cream cheese, and for the magnificent, the overpowering, the ineffable Pilsner of

Prague. This Pilsner motive runs through the book from cover to cover. In the midst of Dutch tulip-beds, Dublin cobblestones, Madrid sunlight and Atlantic City leg-shows, one hears it insistently, deep down in the orchestra. The cellos weave it into the polyphony, sometimes clearly, sometimes in scarcely recognizable augmentation. It is heard again in the wood-wind; the bassoons grunt it thirstily; it slides around in the violas; it rises to a stately choral in the brass. And chiefly it is in minor. Chiefly it is sounded by one who longs for the Pilsen *Urquell* in a far land, and among a barbarous and teetotaling people, and in an atmosphere as hostile to the recreations of the palate as it is to the recreations of the intellect.

As I say, this Huneker is a foreigner and hence accursed. There is something about him as exotic as a samovar, as essentially un-American as a bashi-bazouk, a nose-ring or a fugue. He is filled to the throttle with strange and unnational heresies. He ranks Beethoven miles above the native gods, and not only Beethoven, but also Bach and Brahms, and not only Bach and Brahms, but also Berlioz, Bizet, Bruch and Bülow and perhaps even Balakirew, Bellini, Balfe, Borodin and Boïeldieu. He regards Budapest as a more civilized city than his native Philadelphia, Stendhal as a greater literary artist than Washington Irving, "Künstler Leben" as better music than "There is Sunlight in My Soul." Irish? I still doubt it, despite the *Stammbaum.* Who ever heard of an Irish epicure, an Irish *flâneur,* or, for that matter, an Irish contrapuntist? The arts of the voluptuous category are unknown west of Cherbourg; one leaves them behind with the French pilot. Even the Czech-Irish hypothesis (or is it Magyar-Irish?) has a smell of the lamp. Perhaps it should be Irish-Czech. . . .

§ 7

There remain the books of stories, *Visionaries* and *Melomaniacs.* It is not surprising to hear that both are better liked in France and Germany than in England and the United States. (*Visionaries* has even appeared in Bohemian.) Both are made up of what the Germans call *Kultur-Novellen*—that is, stories dealing, not with the emotions common to all men, but with the clash of ideas among the civilized and godless minority. In some of them, e.g., "Rebels of the Moon," what one finds is really not a story at all, but a static discussion, half aesthetic and half lunatic. In others, e.g., "Isolde's Mother," the whole action revolves around an assumption incomprehensible to the general. One can scarcely imagine most of these tales in the magazines. They would puzzle and outrage the readers of Gouverneur Morris and Gertrude Atherton, and the readers of Howells and Mrs. Wharton no less. Their point of view is essentially the aesthetic one; the overwhelming importance of beauty is never in any doubt. And the beauty thus vivisected and fashioned into new designs is never the simple Wordsworthian article, of fleecy clouds and primroses all compact; on the contrary, it is the highly artificial beauty of pigments and tone-colours, of Cézanne landscapes and the second act of *Tristan und Isolde,* of Dunsanyan dragons and Paracelsian mysteries. Here, indeed, Huneker riots in the aesthetic occultism that he loves. Music slides over into diabolism; the Pobloff symphony rends the firmament of Heaven; the ghost of Chopin drives Mychowski to drink; a single drumbeat finishes the estimable consort of the composer of the Tympani symphony. In *The Eighth Deadly Sin* we have a paean to perfume—the only one, so far as I know, in English. In *The Hall of the Missing Footsteps* we behold the reaction of hasheesh upon Chopin's ballade in F major. . . . Strangely-flavoured, unearthly, perhaps unhealthy stuff. I doubt that it will ever be studied for its style in our new Schools of Literature; a devilish cunning if often there, but it leaves a smack of the pharmacopoeia. However, as George Gissing used to say, "the artist should be free from everything like moral prepossession." This lets in the Antichrist. . . .

Huneker himself seems to esteem these fantastic tales above all his other work. Story-writing, indeed, was his first love, and his Opus 1, a bad imitation of Poe, by name "The Comet," was done in Philadelphia so long ago as July 4, 1876. (Temperature, 105 degrees Fahrenheit.) One rather marvels that he has never attempted a novel. It would have been as bad, perhaps, as "Love Among the Artists," but certainly no bore. He might have given George Moore useful help with "Evelyn Innes" and "Sister Teresa": they are about music, but not by a musician. As for me, I see no great talent for fiction *qua* fiction in these two volumes of exotic tales. They are interesting simply because Huneker the story teller so often yields place to Huneker the playboy of the arts. Such things as "Antichrist" and "The Woman Who Loved Chopin" are no more, at bottom, than second-rate anecdotes; it is the filling, the sauce, the embroidery that counts. But what filling! What sauce! What embroidery! . . . One never sees more of Huneker. . . .

§ 8

He must stand or fall, however, as critic. It is what he has written about other men, not what he has concocted himself, that makes a figure of him, and gives him his unique place in the sterile literature of the republic's second century. He stands for a *Weltanschauung* that is not only un-national, but anti-national; he is the chief of all the curbers and correctors of the American Philistine; in praising the arts he has also criticized a civilization. In the large sense, of course, he has had but small influence. After twenty years of earnest labour, he finds himself almost as alone as a Methodist in Bavaria. The body of native criticism remains as I have described it; an endless piling up of platitudes, an homeric mass of false assumptions and jejune conclusions, an insane madness to reduce beauty to terms of a petty and pornographic morality. One might throw a thousand bricks in any American city without striking a single man who could give an intelligible account of either Hauptmann or Cézanne, or of the reasons for holding Schumann to have been a better composer than Mendelssohn. The boys in our colleges are still taught that Whittier was a great poet and Fennimore Cooper a great novelist. Nine-tenths of our people—perhaps ninety-nine hundredths of our native-born—have yet to see their first good picture, or to hear their first symphony. Our Chamberses and Richard Harding Davises are national figures; our Norrises and Dreisers are scarcely tolerated. Of the two undoubted world figures that we have contributed to letters, one was allowed to die like a stray cat up an alley and the other was mistaken for a cheap buffoon. Criticism, as the average American "intellectual" understands it, is what a Frenchman, a German or a Russian would call donkeyism. In all the arts we still cling to the ideals of the dissenting pulpit, the public cemetery, the electric sign, the bordello parlour.

But for all that, I hang to a somewhat battered optimism, and one of the chief causes of that optimism is the fact that Huneker, after all these years, yet remains unhanged. A picturesque and rakish fellow, a believer in joy and beauty, a disdainer of petty bombast and moralizing, a sworn friend of all honest purpose and earnest striving, he has given his life to a work that must needs bear fruit hereafter. While the college pedagogues of the Brander Matthews type still worshipped the dead bones of Scribe and Sardou, Robertson and Bulwer-Lytton, he preached the new and revolutionary gospel of Ibsen. In the golden age of Rosa Bonheur's "The Horse Fair," he was expounding the principles of the post-impressionists. In the midst of the Sousa marches he whooped for Richard Strauss. Before the rev. professors had come to Schopenhauer, or even to Spencer, he was hauling ashore the devil-fish, Nietzsche. No stranger poisons have ever passed through the customs than those he has brought in his baggage. No man among us has ever urged more ardently, or with sounder knowledge or greater persuasiveness, that catholicity of taste and sympathy which stands in such direct opposition to the booming certainty and snarling narrowness of Little Bethel.

If he bears a simple label, indeed, it is that of anti-Philistine. And the Philistine he attacks is not so much the vacant and harmless fellow who belongs to the Odd Fellows and recreates himself with *Life* and *Leslie's Weekly* in the barber shop, as that more belligerent and pretentious donkey who presumes to do battle for "honest" thought and a "sound" ethic—the "forward looking" man, the university ignoramus, the conservator of orthodoxy, the rattler of ancient phrases—what Nietzsche called "the Philistine of culture." It is against this fat milch cow of wisdom that Huneker has brandished a spear since first there was a Huneker. He is a sworn foe to "the traps that snare the attention from poor or mediocre workmanship—the traps of sentimentalism, of false feeling, of cheap pathos, of the cheap moral." He is on the trail of those pious mountebanks who "clutter the marketplaces with their booths, mischievous half-art and tubs of tripe and soft soap." Superficially, as I say, he seems to have made little progress in this benign *pogrom*. But under the surface, concealed from a first glance, he has undoubtedly left a mark—faint, perhaps, but still a mark. To be a civilized man in America is measurably less difficult, despite the war, than it used to be, say, in 1890. One may at least speak of "Die Walküre" without being laughed at as a half-wit, and read Stirner without being confused with Castro and Raisuli, and argue that Huxley got the better of Gladstone without being challenged at the polls. I know of no man who pushed in that direction harder than James Huneker.

CHAPTER FOUR

PURITANISM AS A LITERARY FORCE

§ 1

"CALVINISM," SAYS DR. LEON KELLNER, IN HIS EXCELLENT LITTLE history of American literature,[1] "is the natural theology of the disinherited; it never flourished, therefore, anywhere as it did in the barren hills of Scotland and in the wilds of North America." The learned doctor is here speaking of theology in what may be called its narrow technical sense—that is, as a theory of God. Under Calvinism, in the New World as well as in the Old, it became no more than a luxuriant demonology; even God himself was transformed into a superior sort of devil, ever wary and wholly merciless. That primitive demonology still survives in the barbaric doctrines of the Methodists and Baptists, particularly in the South; but it has been ameliorated, even there, by a growing sense of the divine grace, and so the old God of Plymouth Rock, as practically conceived, is now scarcely worse than the average jail warden or Italian padrone. On the ethical side, however, Calvinism is dying a much harder death, and we are still a long way from the enlightenment. Save where Continental influences have measurably corrupted the Puritan idea—e.g., in such cities as New York, San Francisco and New Orleans,—the prevailing American view of the world and its mysteries is still a moral one, and no other human concern gets half the attention that is endlessly lavished upon the problem of conduct, particularly of the other fellow. It needed no official announcement to define the function and office of the republic as that of an international expert in morals, and the mentor and exemplar of the more backward nations. Within, as well as without, the eternal rapping of knuckles and proclaiming of new austerities goes on. The American, save in moments of conscious and swiftly lamented deviltry, casts up all ponderable values, including even the values of beauty, in terms of right and wrong. He is beyond all things else, a judge and a policeman; he believes firmly that there is a mysterious power in law; he supports and embellishes its operation with a fanatical vigilance.

Naturally enough, this moral obsession has given a strong colour to American literature. In truth, it has coloured it so brilliantly that American literature is set off sharply from all other literatures. In none other will you find so wholesale and ecstatic a sacrifice of aesthetic ideas, of all the fine gusto of passion and beauty, to notions of what is meet, proper and nice. From the books of grisly sermons that were the first American contribution to letters down to that amazing literature of "inspiration" which now flowers so prodigiously, with two literary ex-Presidents among its chief virtuosi, one observes no relaxation of the moral pressure. In the history of every other literature there have been periods of what might be called moral innocence—periods in which a naif *joie de vivre* has broken through all concepts of duty and responsibility, and the wonder and glory of the universe have been hymned with unashamed zest. The age of Shakespeare comes to mind at once: the violence of the Puritan reaction offers a measure of the pendulum's wild swing. But in America no such general rising of the blood has ever been seen. The literature of the nation, even the literature of the enlightened minority, has been under harsh Puritan restraints from the beginning, and despite a few stealthy efforts at revolt—usually quite without artistic value or even common honesty, as in the case of the cheap fiction magazines and that of smutty plays on Broadway, and always very short-lived—it shows not the slightest sign of emancipating itself today. The American, try as he will, can never imagine any work of the imagination as wholly devoid of moral content. It must either tend toward the promotion of virtue, or be suspect and abominable.

If any doubt of this is in your mind, turn to the critical articles in the newspapers and literary weeklies; you will encounter enough proofs in a month's explorations to convince you forever. A novel or a play is judged among us, not by its dignity of conception, its artistic honesty, its perfection of workmanship, but almost entirely by its orthodoxy of doctrine, its platitudinousness, its usefulness as a moral tract. A digest of the reviews of such a book as David Graham Phillips' *Susan Lenox* or of such a play as Ibsen's "Hedda Gabler" would make astounding reading for a Continental European. Not only the childish incompetents who write for the daily press, but also most of our critics of experience and reputation, seem quite unable to estimate a piece of writing as a piece of writing, a work of art as a work of art; they almost inevitably drag in irrelevant gabble as to whether this or that personage in it is respectable, or this or that situation in accordance with the national notions of what is edifying and nice. Fully nine-tenths of the reviews of Dreiser's *The Titan,* without question the best American novel of its year, were devoted chiefly to indignant denunciations of the morals of Frank Cowperwood, its central character. That the man was superbly imagined and magnificently depicted, that he stood out from the book in all the flashing vigour of life, that his creation was an artistic achievement of a very high and difficult order—these facts seem to have made no impression upon the reviewers whatever. They were Puritans writing for Puritans, and all they could see in Cowperwood was an anti-Puritan, and in his creator another. It will remain for Europeans, I daresay, to discover the true stature of *The Titan,* as it remained for Europeans to discover the true stature of *Sister Carrie.*

Just how deeply this corrective knife has cut you may find plainly displayed in Dr. Kellner's little book. He sees the throttling influence of an ever alert and bellicose Puritanism, not only in our grand literature, but also in our petit literature, our minor poetry, even in our humour. The Puritan's utter lack of aesthetic sense, his distrust of all romantic emotion, his unmatchable intolerance of opposition, his unbreakable belief in his own bleak and narrow views, his savage cruelty of attack, his lust for relentless and barbarous persecution—these things have put an almost unbearable burden upon the exchange of ideas in the United States, and particularly upon that form of it which involves playing with them for the mere game's sake. On the one hand, the writer who would deal seriously and honestly with the larger problems of life, particularly in the rigidly-partitioned ethical field, is restrained by laws that would have kept a Balzac or a Zola in prison from year's end to year's end; and on the other hand the writer who would proceed against the reigning superstitions by mockery has been silenced by taboos that are quite as stringent, and by an indifference that is even worse. For all our professed delight in and capacity for jocosity, we have produced so far but one genuine wit—Ambrose Bierce—and, save to a small circle, he remains unknown today. Our great humourists, including even Mark Twain, have had to take protective colouration, whether willingly or unwillingly, from the prevailing ethical foliage, and so one finds them levelling their darts, not at the stupidities of the Puritan majority, but at the evidences of lessening stupidity in the anti-Puritan minority. In other words, they have done battle, not against, but *for* Philistinism—and Philistinism is no more than another name for Puritanism. Both wage a ceaseless warfare upon beauty in its every form, from painting to religious ritual, and from the drama to the dance—the first because it holds beauty to be a mean and stupid thing, and the second because it holds beauty to be distracting and corrupting.

Mark Twain, without question, was a great artist; there was in him something of that prodigality of imagination, that aloof engrossment in the human comedy, that penetrating cynicism, which one associates with the great artists of the Renaissance. But his nationality hung around his neck like a millstone; he could never throw off his native Philistinism. One ploughs through *The Innocents Abroad* and through parts of *A Tramp Abroad* with incredulous amazement. Is such coarse and ignorant clowning to be accepted as humour, as great humour, as the best humour that the most humorous of peoples has produced? Is it really the mark of a smart fellow to lift a peasant's cackle over "Lohengrin"? Is Titian's chromo of Moses in the bullrushes seriously to be regarded as the noblest picture in Europe? Is there nothing in Latin Christianity, after all, save petty grafting, monastic scandals and the worship of the knuckles and shin-bones of dubious saints? May not a civilized man, disbelieving in it, still find himself profoundly moved by its dazzling history, the lingering remnants of its old magnificence, the charm of its gorgeous and melancholy loveliness? In the presence of all beauty of man's creation—in brief, of what we roughly call art, whatever its form—the voice of Mark Twain was the voice of the Philistine. A literary artist of very high rank himself, with instinctive gifts that lifted him, in *Huckleberry Finn* to kinship with Cervantes and Aristophanes, he was yet so far the victim of his nationality that he seems to have had no capacity for distinguishing between the good and the bad in the work of other men of his own craft. The literary criticism that one occasionally finds in his writings is chiefly trivial and ignorant; his private inclination appears to have been toward such romantic sentimentality as entrances school-boys; the thing that interested him in Shakespeare was not the man's colossal genius, but the absurd theory that Bacon wrote his plays. Had he been born in France (the country of his chief abomination!) instead of in a Puritan village of the American hinterland, I venture that he would have conquered the world. But try as he would, being what he was, he could not get rid of the Puritan smugness and cock-sureness, the Puritan distrust of new ideas, the Puritan incapacity for seeing beauty as a thing in itself, and the full peer of the true and the good.

It is, indeed, precisely in the works of such men as Mark Twain that one finds the best proofs of the Puritan influence in American letters, for it is there that it is least expected and hence most significant. Our native critics, unanimously Puritans themselves, are anaesthetic to the flavour, but to Dr. Kellner, with his half-European, half-Oriental culture, it is always distinctly perceptible. He senses it, not only in the harsh Calvinistic fables of Hawthorne and the pious gurglings of Longfellow, but also in the poetry of Bryant, the tea-party niceness of Howells, the "maiden-like reserve" of James Lane Allen, and even in the work of Joel Chandler Harris. What! A Southern Puritan? Well, why not? What could be more erroneous than the common assumption that Puritanism is exclusively a Northern, a New England, madness? The truth is that it is as thoroughly national as the kindred belief in the devil, and runs almost unobstructed from Portland to Portland and from the Lakes to the Gulf. It is in the South, indeed, and not in the North, that it takes on its most bellicose and extravagant forms. Between the upper tier of New England and the Potomac river there was not a single prohibition state—but thereafter, alas, they came in huge blocks! And behind that infinitely prosperous Puritanism there is a long and unbroken tradition. Berkeley, the last of the Cavaliers, was kicked out of power in Virginia so long ago as 1650. Lord Baltimore, the Proprietor of Maryland, was brought to terms by the Puritans of the Severn in 1657. The Scotch Covenanter, the most uncompromising and unenlightened of all Puritans, flourished in the Carolinas from the start, and in 1698, or thereabout, he was reinforced from New England. In 1757 a band of Puritans invaded what is now Georgia—and Georgia has been a Puritan barbarism ever since. Even while the early (and half-mythical) Cavaliers were still in nominal control of all these Southern plantations, they clung to the sea-coast. The population that moved down the chain of the Appalachians during the latter part of the eighteenth century, and then swept over them into the Mississippi valley, was composed almost entirely of Puritans—chiefly intransigeants from New England (where Unitarianism was getting on its legs), kirk-crazy Scotch, and that plupious and beauty-hating folk, the Scotch-Irish. "In the South today," said John Fiske a generation ago, "there is more Puritanism surviving than in New England." In that whole region, an area three times as large as France or Germany, there is not a single orchestra capable of playing Beethoven's C minor symphony, or a single painting worth looking at, or a single public building or monument of any genuine distinction, or a single factory devoted to the making of beautiful things, or a single poet, novelist, historian, musician, painter or sculptor whose reputation extends beyond his own country. Between the Mason and Dixon line and the mouth of the Mississippi there is but one opera-house, and that one was built by a Frenchman, and is now, I believe, closed. The only domestic art this huge and opulent empire knows is in the hands of Mexican greasers; its only native music it owes to the despised negro; its only genuine poet was permitted to die up an alley like a stray dog.

§ 2

In studying the anatomy and physiology of American Puritanism, and its effects upon the national literature, one quickly discerns two main streams of influence. On the one hand, there is the influence of the original Puritans—whether of New England or of the South—, who came to the New World with a ready-made philosophy of the utmost clarity, positiveness and inclusiveness of scope, and who attained to such a position of political and intellectual leadership that they were able to force it almost unchanged upon the whole population, and to endow it with such vitality that it successfully resisted alien opposition later on. And on the other hand, one sees a complex of social and economic conditions which worked in countless irresistible ways against the rise of that dionysian spirit, that joyful acquiescence in life, that philosophy of the *Ja-sager*, which offers to Puritanism, today as in times past, its chief and perhaps only effective antagonism. In other words, the American of the days since the Revolution has had Puritanism diligently pressed upon him from without, and at the same time he has led, in the main, a life that has engendered a chronic hospitality to it, or at all events to its salient principles, within.

Dr. Kellner accurately describes the process whereby the aesthetic spirit, and its concomitant spirit of joy, were squeezed out of the original New Englanders, so that no trace of it showed in their literature, or even in their lives, for a century and a half after the first settlements. "Absorption in God," he says, "seems incompatible with the presentation (i.e., aesthetically) of mankind. The God of the Puritans was in this respect a jealous God who brooked no sort of creative rivalry. The inspired moments of the loftiest souls were filled with the thought of God and His designs; spiritual life was wholly dominated by solicitude regarding salvation, the hereafter, grace; how could such petty concerns as personal experience of a lyric nature, the transports or the pangs of love, find utterance? What did a lyric occurrence like the first call of the cuckoo, elsewhere so welcome, or the first sight of the snowdrop, signify compared with the last Sunday's sermon and the new interpretation of the old riddle of evil in the world? And apart from the fact that everything of a personal nature must have appeared so trivial, all the sources of secular lyric poetry were offensive and impious to Puritan theology. . . . One thing is an established fact: up to the close of the eighteenth century America had no belletristic literature."

This Puritan bedevilment by the idea of personal sin, this reign of the God-crazy, gave way in later years, as we shall see, to other and somewhat milder forms of pious enthusiam. At the time of the Revolution, indeed, the importation of French political ideas was accompanied by an importation of French theological ideas, and such men as Franklin and Jefferson dallied with what, in those days at least, was regarded as downright atheism. Even in New England this influence made itself felt; there was a gradual letting down of Calvinism to the softness of Unitarianism, and that change was presently to flower in the vague temporizing of Transcendentalism. But as Puritanism, in the strict sense, declined in virulence and took deceptive new forms, there was a compensating growth of its brother, Philistinism, and by the first quarter of the nineteenth century, the distrust of beauty, and of the joy that is its object, was as firmly established throughout the land as it had ever been in New England. The original Puritans had at least been men of a certain education, and even of a certain austere culture. They were inordinately hostile to beauty in all its forms, but one somehow suspects that much of their hostility was due to a sense of their weakness before it, a realization of its disarming psychical pull. But the American of the new republic was of a different kidney. He was not so much hostile to beauty as devoid of any consciousness of it; he stood as unmoved before its phenomena as a savage before a table of logarithms. What he had set up on this continent, in brief, was a commonwealth of peasants and small traders, a paradise of the third-rate, and its national philosophy, almost wholly unchecked by the more sophisticated and civilized ideas of an aristocracy, was precisely the philosophy that one finds among peasants and small traders at all times and everywhere. The difference between the United States and any other nation did not lie in any essential difference between American peasants and other peasants, but simply in the fact that here, alone, the voice of the peasant was the single voice of the nation—that here, alone, the only way to eminence and public influence was the way of acquiescence in the opinions and prejudices of the untutored and Philistine mob. Jackson was the *Stammvater* of the new statesmen and philosophers; he carried the mob's distrust of good taste even into the field of conduct; he was the first to put the rewards of conformity above the dictates of common decency; he founded a whole hierarchy of Philistine messiahs, the roaring of which still belabours the ear.

Once established, this culture of the intellectually disinherited tended to defend and perpetuate itself. On the one hand, there was no appearance of a challenge from within, for the exigent problems of existence in a country that was yet but half settled and organized left its people with no energy for questioning what at least satisfied their gross needs, and so met the pragmatic test. And on the other hand, there was no critical pressure from without, for the English culture which alone reached over the sea was itself entering upon its Victorian decline, and the influence of the native aristocracy—the degenerating *Junkers* of the great estates and the boorish magnates of the city *bourgeoisie*—was quite without any cultural direction at all. The chief concern of the American people, even above the bread-and-butter question, was politics. They were incessantly hag-ridden by political difficulties, both internal and external, of an inordinate complexity, and these occupied all the leisure they could steal from the sordid work of everyday. More, their new and troubled political ideas tended to absorb all the rancorous certainty of their fading religious ideas, so that devotion to a theory or a candidate became translated into devotion to a revelation, and the game of politics turned itself into a holy war. The custom of connecting purely political doctrines with pietistic concepts of an inflammable nature, then firmly set up by skilful persuaders of the mob, has never quite died out in the United States. There has not been a presidential contest since Jackson's day without its Armageddons, its marching of Christian soldiers, its crosses of gold, its crowns of thorns. The most successful American politicians, beginning with the anti-slavery agitators, have been those most adept at twisting the ancient gauds and shibboleths of Puritanism to partisan uses. Every campaign that we have seen for eighty years has been, on each side, a pursuit of bugaboos, a denunciation of heresies, a snouting up of immoralities.

But it was during the long contest against slavery, beginning with the appearance of William Lloyd Garrison's *Liberator* in 1831 and ending at Appomattox, that this gigantic supernaturalization of politics reached its most astounding heights. In those days, indeed, politics and religion coalesced in a manner not seen in the world since the Middle Ages, and the combined pull of the two was so powerful that none could quite resist it. All men of any ability and ambition turned to political activity for self-expression. It engaged the press to the exclusion of everything else; it conquered the pulpit; it even laid its hand upon industry and trade. Drawing the best imaginative talent into its service—Jefferson and Lincoln may well stand as examples—it left the cultivation of belles lettres, and of all the other arts no less, to women and admittedly second-rate men. And when, breaking through this taboo, some chance first-rate man gave himself over to purely aesthetic expression, his reward was not only neglect, but even a sort of ignominy, as if such enterprises were not fitting for males with hair on their chests. I need not point to Poe and Whitman, both disdained as dreamers and wasters, and both proceeded against with the utmost rigours of outraged Philistinism.

In brief, the literature of that whole period, as Algernon Tassin shows in "The Magazine in America,"[2] was almost completely disassociated from life as men were then living it. Save one counts in such crude politico-puritan tracts as *Uncle Tom's Cabin,* it is difficult to find a single contemporaneous work that interprets the culture of the time, or even accurately represents it. Later on, it found historians and anatomists, and in one work, at least, to wit, *Huckleberry Finn,* it was studied and projected with the highest art, but no such impulse to make imaginative use of it showed itself contemporaneously, and there was not even the crude sentimentalization of here and now that one finds in the popular novels of today. Fenimore Cooper filled his romances, not with the people about him, but with the Indians beyond the sky-line, and made them half-fabulous to boot. Irving told fairy tales about the forgotten Knickerbockers; Hawthorne turned backward to the Puritans of Plymouth Rock; Longfellow to the Acadians and the prehistoric Indians; Emerson took flight from earth altogether; even Poe sought refuge in a land of fantasy. It was only the frank second-raters—e.g., Whittier and Lowell—who ventured to turn to the life around them, and the banality of the result is a sufficient indication of the crudeness of the current taste, and the mean position assigned to the art of letters. This was pre-eminently the era of the moral tale, the Sunday-school book. Literature was conceived, not as a thing in itself, but merely as a hand-maiden to politics or religion. The great celebrity of Emerson in New England was not the celebrity of a literary artist, but that of a theologian and metaphysician; he was esteemed in much the same way that Jonathan Edwards had been esteemed. Even down to our own time, indeed, his vague and empty philosophizing has been put above his undeniable capacity for graceful utterance, and it remained for Dr. Kellner to consider him purely as a literary artist, and to give him due praise for his skill.

The Civil War brought that era of sterility to an end. As I shall show later on, the shock of it completely reorganized the American scheme of things, and even made certain important changes in the national Puritanism, or, at all events, in its machinery. Whitman, whose career straddled, so to speak, the four years of the war, was the leader—and for a long while, the only trooper—of a double revolt. On the one hand he offered a courageous challenge to the intolerable prudishness and dirty-mindedness of Puritanism, and on the other hand he boldly sought the themes and even the modes of expression of his poetry in the arduous, contentious and highly melodramatic life that lay all about him. Whitman, however, was clearly before his time. His countrymen could see him only as immoralist; save for a pitiful few of them, they were dead to any understanding of his stature as artist, and even unaware that such a category of men existed. He was put down as an invader of the public decencies, a disturber of the public peace; even his eloquent war poems, surely the best of all his work, were insufficient to get him a hearing; the sentimental rubbish of *The Blue and the Gray* and the ecstatic supernaturalism of *The Battle Hymn of the Republic* were far more to the public taste. Where Whitman failed, indeed, all subsequent explorers of the same field have failed with him, and the great war has left no more mark upon American letters than if it had never been fought. Nothing remotely approaching the bulk and beam of Tolstoi's *War and Peace,* or, to descend to a smaller scale, Zola's *The Attack on the Mill,* has come out of it. Its appeal to the national imagination was undoubtedly of the most profound character; it coloured politics for fifty years, and is today a dominating influence in the thought of whole sections of the American people. But in all that stirring up there was no upheaval of artistic consciousness, for the plain reason that there was no artistic consciousness there to heave up, and all we have in the way of Civil War literature is a few conventional melodramas, a few half-forgotten short stories by Ambrose Bierce and Stephen Crane, and a half dozen idiotic popular songs in the manner of Randall's "Maryland, My Maryland."

In the seventies and eighties, with the appearance of such men as Henry James, William Dean Howells, Mark Twain and Bret Harte, a better day seemed to be dawning. Here, after a full century of infantile romanticizing, were four writers who at least deserved respectful consideration as literary artists, and what is more, three of them turned from the conventionalized themes of the past to the teeming and colourful life that lay under their noses. But this promise of better things was soon found to be no more than a promise. Mark Twain, after *The Gilded Age,* slipped back into romanticism tempered by Philistinism, and was presently in the era before the Civil War, and finally in the Middle Ages, and even beyond. Harte, a brilliant technician, had displayed his whole stock when he had displayed his technique: his stories were not even superficially true to the life they presumed to depict; one searched them in vain for an interpretation of it; they were simply idle tales. As for Howells and James, both quickly showed that timorousness and reticence which are the distinguishing marks of the Puritan, even in his most intellectual incarnations. The American scene that they depicted with such meticulous care was chiefly peopled with marionettes. They shrunk, characteristically, from those larger, harsher clashes of will and purpose which one finds in all truly first-rate literature. In particular, they shrunk from any interpretation of life which grounded itself upon an acknowledgment of its inexorable and inexplicable tragedy. In the vast combat of instincts and aspirations about them they saw only a feeble jousting of comedians, unserious and insignificant. Of the great questions that have agitated the minds of men in Howells' time one gets no more than a faint and far-away echo in his novels. His investigations, one may say, are carried on *in vacuo;* his discoveries are not expressed in terms of passion, but in terms of giggles.

In the followers of Howells and James one finds little save an empty imitation of their emptiness, a somewhat puerile parodying of their highly artful but essentially personal technique. To wade through the books of such characteristic American fictioneers as Frances Hodgson Burnett, Mary E. Wilkins Freeman, F. Hopkinson Smith, Alice Brown, James Lane Allen, Winston Churchill, Ellen

Glasgow, Gertrude Atherton and Sarah Orne Jewett is to undergo an experience that is almost terrible. The flow of words is completely purged of ideas; in place of them one finds no more than a romantic restatement of all the old platitudes and formulae. To call such an emission of graceful poppycock a literature, of course, is to mouth an absurdity, and yet, if the college professors who write treatises on letters are to be believed, it is the best we have to show. Turn, for example, to *A History of American Literature Since 1870,* by Prof. Fred Lewis Pattee, one of the latest and undoubtedly one of the least unintelligent of these books. In it the gifted pedagogue gives extended notice to no less than six of the nine writers I have mentioned, and upon all of them his verdicts are flattering. He bestows high praises, direct and indirect, upon Mrs. Freeman's "grim and austere" manner, her "repression," her entire lack of poetical illumination. He compares Miss Jewett to both Howells and Hawthorne, not to mention Mrs. Gaskell—and Addison! He grows enthusiastic over a hollow piece of fine writing by Miss Brown. And he forgets altogether to mention Dreiser, or Sinclair, or Medill Patterson, or Harry Leon Wilson, or George Ade! . . .

So much for the best. The worst is beyond description. France has her Brieux and her Henry Bordeaux; Germany has her Mühlbach, her stars of the *Gartenlaube;* England contributes Caine, Corelli, Oppenheim and company. But it is in our country alone that banality in letters takes on the proportions of a national movement; it is only here that a work of the imagination is habitually judged by its sheer emptiness of ideas, its fundamental platitudinousness, its correspondence with the imbecility of mob thinking; it is only here that "glad" books run up sales of hundreds of thousands. Richard Harding Davis, with his ideals of a floorwalker; Gene Stratton-Porter, with her snuffling sentimentality; Robert W. Chambers, with his "society" romances for shop-girls; Irvin Cobb, with his laboured, *Ayers' Almanac* jocosity; the authors of the *Saturday Evening Post* school, with their heroic drummers and stockbrokers, their ecstatic celebration of the stupid, the sordid, the ignoble—these, after all, are our typical *literati.* The Puritan fear of ideas is the master of them all. Some of them, in truth, most of them, have undeniable talent; in a more favourable environment not a few of them might be doing sound work. But they see how small the ring is, and they make their tricks small to fit it. Not many of them ever venture a leg outside. The lash of the ringmaster is swift, and it stings damnably. . . .

I say not many; I surely do not mean none at all. As a matter of fact, there have been intermittent rebellions against the prevailing pecksniffery and sentimentality ever since the days of Irving and Hawthorne. Poe led one of them—as critic more than as creative artist. His scathing attacks upon the Gerald Stanley Lees, the Hamilton Wright Mabies and the George E. Woodberrys of his time keep a liveliness and appositeness that the years have not staled; his criticism deserves to be better remembered. Poe sensed the Philistine pull of a Puritan civilization as none had before him, and combated it with his whole artillery of rhetoric. Another rebel, of course, was Whitman; how he came to grief is too well known to need recalling. What is less familiar is the fact that both the *Atlantic Monthly* and the *Century* (first called *Scribner's*) were set up by men in revolt against the reign of mush, as *Putnam's* and the *Dial* had been before them. The salutatory of the *Dial,* dated 1840, stated the case against the national mugginess clearly. The aim of the magazine, it said, was to oppose "that rigour of our conventions of religion and education which is turning us to stone" and to give expression to "new views and the dreams of youth." Alas, for these brave *révoltés! Putnam's* succumbed to the circumambient rigours and duly turned to stone, and is now no more. The *Atlantic,* once so heretical, has become as respectable as the New York *Evening Post.* As for the *Dial,* it was until lately the very pope of orthodoxy and jealously guarded the college professors who read it from the pollution of ideas. Only the *Century* has kept the faith unbrokenly. It is, indeed, the one first-class American magazine that has always welcomed newcomers, and that maintains an intelligent contact with the literature that is in being, and that consistently tries to make the best terms possible with the dominant Philistinism. It cannot go the whole way without running into danger; let it be said to the credit of its editors that they have more than once braved that danger.

The tale might be lengthened. Mark Twain, in his day, felt the stirrings of revolt, and not all his Philistinism was sufficient to hold him altogether in check. If you want to find out about the struggle that went on within him, read the biography by Albert Bigelow Paine, or, better still, *The Mysterious Stranger* and *What is Man?* Alive, he had his position to consider; dead, he now speaks out. In the preface to *What is Man?* dated 1905, there is a curious confession of his incapacity for defying the taboos which surrounded him. The studies for the book, he says, were begun "twenty-five or twenty-seven years ago"—the period of *A Tramp Abroad* and *The Prince and the Pauper.* It was actually written "seven years ago"—that is, just after *Following the Equator* and *Personal Recollections of Joan of Arc.* And why did it lie so long in manuscript, and finally go out stealthily, under a private imprint?[3] Simply because, as Mark frankly confesses, he "dreaded *(and could not bear)* the disapproval of the people around" him. He knew how hard his fight for recognition had been; he knew what direful penalties outraged orthodoxy could inflict; he had in him the somewhat pathetic discretion of a respectable family man. But, dead, he is safely beyond reprisal, and so, after a prudent interval, the faithful Paine begins printing books in which, writing knowingly behind six feet of earth, he could set down his true ideas without fear. Some day, perhaps, we shall have his microbe story, and maybe even his picture of the court of Elizabeth.

A sneer in Prof. Pattee's history, before mentioned, recalls the fact that Hamlin Garland was also a rebel in his day and bawled for the Truth with a capital T. That was in 1893. Two years later the guardians of the national rectitude fell afoul of "Rose of Dutchers' Coolly" and Garland began to think it over; today he devotes himself to the safer enterprise of chasing spooks; his name is conspicuously absent from the Dreiser Protest. Nine years before his brief offending John Hay had set off a discreet bomb in "The Bread-Winners"—anonymously because "my standing would be seriously compromised" by an avowal. Six years later Frank Norris shook up the Phelpses and Mores of the time with *McTeague*. Since then there have been assaults timorous and assaults head-long—by Bierce, by Dreiser, by Phillips, by Fuller—by Mary MacLanes and by Upton Sinclairs—by ploughboy poets from the Middle West and by jitney geniuses in Greenwich Village—assaults gradually tapering off to a mere sophomoric brashness and deviltry. And all of them like snow-ballings of Verdun. All of them petered out and ineffectual. The normal, the typical American book of today is as fully a remouthing of old husks as the normal book of Griswold's day. The whole atmosphere of our literature, in William James' phrase, is "mawkish and dishwatery." Books are still judged among us, not by their form and organization as works of art, their accuracy and vividness as representations of life, their validity and perspicacity as interpretations of it, but by their conformity to the national prejudices, their accordance with set standards of niceness and propriety. The thing irrevocably demanded is a "sane" book; the ideal is a "clean," an "inspiring," a "glad" book.

§ 3

All this may be called the Puritan impulse from within. It is, indeed, but a single manifestation of one of the deepest prejudices of a religious and half-cultured people—the prejudice against beauty as a form of debauchery and corruption—the distrust of all ideas that do not fit readily into certain accepted axioms—the belief in the eternal validity of moral concepts—in brief, the whole mental sluggishness of the lower orders of men. But in addition to this internal resistance, there has been laid upon American letters the heavy hand of a Puritan authority from without, and no examination of the history and present condition of our literature could be of any value which did not take it constantly into account, and work out the means of its influence and operation. That authority, as I shall show, transcends both in power and in alertness the natural reactions of the national mind, and is incomparably more potent in combating ideas. It is supported by a body of law that is unmatched in any other country of Christendom, and it is exercised with a fanatical harshness and vigilance that make escape from its operations well nigh impossible. Some of its effects, both direct and indirect, I shall describe later, but before doing so it may be well to trace its genesis and development.

At bottom, of course, it rests upon the inherent Puritanism of the people; it could not survive a year if they were opposed to the principle visible in it. That deep-seated and uncorrupted Puritanism, that conviction of the pervasiveness of sin, of the supreme importance of moral correctness, of the need of savage and inquisitorial laws, has been a dominating force in American life since the very beginning. There has never been any question before the nation, whether political or economic, religious or military, diplomatic or sociological, which did not resolve itself, soon or late, into a purely moral question. Nor has there ever been any surcease of the spiritual eagerness which lay at the bottom of the original Puritan's moral obsession: the American has been, from the very start, a man genuinely interested in the eternal mysteries, and fearful of missing their correct solution. The frank theocracy of the New England colonies had scarcely succumbed to the libertarianism of a godless Crown before there came the Great

Awakening of 1734, with its orgies of homiletics and its restoration of talmudism to the first place among polite sciences. The Revolution, of course, brought a set-back: the colonists faced so urgent a need of unity in politics that they declared a sort of *Treuga Dei* in religion, and that truce, armed though it was, left its imprint upon the First Amendment to the Constitution. But immediately the young Republic emerged from the stresses of adolescence, a missionary army took to the field again, and before long the Asbury revival was paling that of Whitefield, Wesley and Jonathan Edwards, not only in its hortatory violence but also in the length of its lists of slain.

Thereafter, down to the outbreak of the Civil War, the country was rocked again and again by furious attacks upon the devil. On the one hand, this great campaign took a purely theological form, with a hundred new and fantastic creeds as its fruits; on the other hand, it crystallized into the hysterical temperance movement of the 30's and 40's, which penetrated to the very floor of Congress and put "dry" laws upon the statute-books of ten States; and on the third hand, as it were, it established a prudery in speech and thought from which we are yet but half delivered. Such ancient and innocent words as "bitch" and "bastard" disappeared from the American language; Bartlett tells us, indeed, in his "Dictionary of Americanisms,"[4] that even "bull" was softened to "male cow." This was the Golden Age of euphemism, as it was of euphuism; the worst inventions of the English mid-Victorians were adopted and improved. The word "woman" became a term of opprobrium, verging close upon downright libel; legs became the inimitable "limbs"; the stomach began to run from the "bosom" to the pelvic arch; pantaloons faded into "unmentionables"; the newspapers spun their parts of speech into such gossamer webs as "a statutory offence," "a house of questionable repute" and "an interesting condition." And meanwhile the Good Templars and Sons of Temperance swarmed in the land like a plague of celestial locusts.

There was not a hamlet without its uniformed phalanx, its affecting exhibit of reformed drunkards. The Kentucky Legislature succumbed to a travelling recruiting officer, and two-thirds of the members signed the pledge. The National House of Representatives took recess after recess to hear eminent excoriators of the Rum Demon, and more than a dozen of its members forsook their duties to carry the new gospel to the bucolic heathen—the vanguard, one may note in passing, of the innumerable Chautauquan caravan of later years.

Beneath all this bubbling on the surface, of course, ran the deep and swift undercurrent of anti-slavery feeling—a tide of passion which historians now attempt to account for on economic grounds, but which showed no trace of economic origin while it lasted. Its true quality was moral, devout, ecstatic; it culminated, to change the figure, in a supreme discharge of moral electricity, almost fatal to the nation. The crack of that great spark emptied the jar; the American people forgot all about their pledges and pruderies during the four years of Civil War. The Good Templars, indeed, were never heard of again, and with them into memory went many other singular virtuosi of virtue—for example, the Millerites. But almost before the last smoke of battle cleared away, a renaissance of Puritan ardour began, and by the middle of the 70's it was in full flower. Its high points and flashing lighthouses halt the backward-looking eye; the Moody and Sankey uproar, the triumphal entry of the Salvation Army, the recrudescence of the temperance agitation and its culmination in prohibition, the rise of the Young Men's Christian Association and of the Sunday-school, the almost miraculous growth of the Christian Endeavour movement, the beginnings of the vice crusade, the renewed injection of moral conceptions and rages into party politics (the "crime" of 1873!), the furious preaching of baroque Utopias, the invention of muckraking, the mad, glad war of extermination upon the Mormons, the hysteria over the

Breckenridge-Pollard case and other like causes, the enormous multiplication of moral and religious associations, the spread of zoöphilia, the attack upon Mammon, the dawn of the uplift, and last but far from least, comstockery.

In comstockery, if I do not err, the new Puritanism gave a sign of its formal departure from the old, and moral endeavour suffered a general overhauling and tightening of the screws. The difference between the two forms is very well represented by the difference between the program of the half-forgotten Good Templars and the program set forth in the Webb Law of 1913, or by that between the somewhat diffident prudery of the 40's and the astoundingly ferocious and uncompromising vice-crusading of today. In brief, a difference between the *re*nunciation and *de*nunciation, asceticism and Mohammedanism, the hair shirt and the flaming sword. The distinguishing mark of the elder Puritanism, at least after it had attained to the stature of a national philosophy, was its appeal to the individual conscience, its exclusive concern with the elect, its strong flavour of self-accusing. Even the rage against slavery was, in large measure, an emotion of the mourners' bench. The thing that worried the more ecstatic Abolitionists was their sneaking sense of responsibility, the fear that they themselves were flouting the fire by letting slavery go on. The thirst to punish the concrete slave-owner, as an end in itself, did not appear until opposition had added exasperation to fervour. In most of the earlier harangues against his practice, indeed, you will find a perfect willingness to grant that slave-owner's good faith, and even to compensate him for his property. But the new Puritanism—or, perhaps more accurately, considering the shades of prefixes, the neo-Puritanism—is a frank harking back to the primitive spirit. The original Puritan of the bleak New England coast was not content to flay his own wayward carcass: full satisfaction did not sit upon him until he had jailed a Quaker. That is to say, the sinner who excited his highest zeal and passion was not so much himself as his neighbour; to borrow a term from psychopathology, he was less the masochist than the sadist. And it is that very peculiarity which sets off his descendant of today from the ameliorated Puritan of the era between the Revolution and the Civil War. The new Puritanism is not ascetic, but militant. Its aim is not to lift up saints but to knock down sinners. Its supreme manifestation is the vice crusade, an armed pursuit of helpless outcasts by the whole military and naval forces of the Republic. Its supreme hero is Comstock Himself, with his pious boast that the sinners he jailed during his astounding career, if gathered into one penitential party, would have filled a train of sixty-one coaches, allowing sixty to the coach.

So much for the general trend and tenor of the movement. At the bottom of it, it is plain, there lies that insistent presentation of the idea of sin, that enchantment by concepts of carnality, which has engaged a certain type of man, to the exclusion of all other notions, since the dawn of history. The remote ancestors of our Puritan-Philistines of today are to be met with in the Old Testament and the New, and their nearer grandfathers clamoured against the snares of the flesh in all the councils of the Early Church. Not only Western Christianity has had to reckon with them: they have brothers today among the Mohammedan Sufi and in obscure Buddhist sects, and they were the chief preachers of the Russian Raskol, or Reformation. "The Ironsides of Cromwell and the Puritans of New England," says Heard, in his book on the Russian church, "bear a strong resemblance to the Old Believers." But here, in the main, we have asceticism more than Puritanism, as it is now visible; here the sinner combated is chiefly the one within. How are we to account for the wholesale transvaluation of values that came after the Civil War, the transfer of ire from the Old Adam to the happy rascal across the street, the sinister rise of a new Inquisition in the midst of a growing luxury that even the Puritans themselves succumbed to? The answer is to be sought, it seems to me, in the direction of the Golden Calf—in the direction of the fat fields of our Midlands, the full nets of our lakes and coasts, the factory smoke of our cities—even in the direction of Wall Street, that devil's chasm. In brief, Puritanism has become bellicose and tyrannical by becoming rich. The will to power has been aroused to a high flame by an increase in the available draught and fuel, as militarism is engendered and nourished by the presence of men and materials. Wealth, discovering its power, has reached out its long arms to grab the distant and innumerable sinner; it has gone down into its deep pockets to pay for his costly pursuit and flaying; it has created the Puritan *entrepreneur,* the daring and imaginative organizer of Puritanism, the baron of moral endeavour, the invincible prophet of new austerities. And, by the same token, it has issued its letters of marque to the Puritan mercenary, the professional hound of heaven, the moral *Junker,* the Comstock, and out of his skill at his trade there has arisen the whole machinery, so complicated and so effective, of the new Holy Office.

Poverty is a soft pedal upon all branches of human activity, not excepting the spiritual, and even the original Puritans, for all their fire, felt its throttling caress. I think it is Bill Nye who has humorously pictured their arduous life: how they had to dig clams all winter that they would have strength enough to plant corn, and how they had to hoe corn all summer that they would have strength enough to dig clams. That low ebb of fortune worked against the full satisfaction of their zeal in two distinct ways. On the one hand, it kept them but ill-prepared for the cost of offensive enterprise: even their occasional missionarying raids upon the Indians took too much productive energy from their business with the corn and the clams. And on the other hand, it kept a certain restraining humility in their hearts, so that for every Quaker they hanged, they let a dozen go. Poverty, of course, is no discredit, but at all events, it is a subtle criticism. The man oppressed by material wants is not in the best of moods for the more ambitious forms of moral adventure. He not only lacks the means; he is also deficient in the self-assurance, the sense of superiority, the secure and lofty point of departure. If he is haunted by notions of the sinfulness of his neighbours, he is apt to see some of its worst manifestations within himself, and that disquieting discovery will tend to take his thoughts from the other fellow. It is by no arbitrary fiat, indeed, that the brothers of all the expiatory orders are vowed to poverty. History teaches us that wealth, whenever it has come to them by chance, has put an end to their soul-searching. The Puritans of the elder generations, with few exceptions, were poor. Nearly all Americans, down to the Civil War, were poor. And being poor, they subscribed to a *Sklavenmoral.* That is to say, they were spiritually humble. Their eyes were fixed, not upon the abyss below them, but upon the long and rocky road ahead of them. Their moral passion spent most of its force in self-accusing, self-denial and self-scourging. They began by howling their sins from the mourners' bench; they came to their end, many of them, in the supreme immolation of battle.

But out of the War came prosperity, and out of prosperity came a new morality, to wit, the *Herrenmoral.* Many great fortunes were made in the War itself; an uncountable number got started during the two decades following. What is more, this material prosperity was generally dispersed through all classes: it affected the common workman and the remote farmer quite as much as the actual merchant and manufacturer. Its first effect, as we all know, was a universal cockiness, a rise in pretensions, a comforting feeling that the Republic was a success, and with it, its every citizen. This change made itself quickly obvious, and even odious, in all the secular relations of life. The American became a sort of braggart playboy of the western world, enormously sure of himself and ludicrously contemptuous of all other men. And on the ghostly side there appeared the same accession of confidence, the same sure assumption of authority, though at first less self-evidently and offensively. The religion of the American thus began to lose its inward direction; it became less and less a scheme of personal salvation and more and more a scheme of pious derring-do. The revivals of the 70s had all the bounce and fervour of those of half a century before, but the mourners' bench began to lose its standing as their symbol, and in its place appeared the collection basket. Instead of accusing himself, the convert volunteered to track down and bring in the other fellow. His enthusiasm was not for repentance, but for what he began to call service. In brief, the national sense of energy and fitness gradually superimposed itself upon the national Puritanism, and from that marriage sprung a keen *Wille zur Macht,* a lusty will to power.[5] The American Puritan, by now, was not content with the rescue of his own soul; he felt an irresistible impulse to hand salvation on, to disperse and multiply it, to ram it down reluctant throats, to make it free, universal and compulsory. He had the men, he had the guns and he had the money too. All that was needed was organization. The rescue of the unsaved could be converted into a wholesale business, unsentimentally and economically conducted, and with all the usual aids to efficiency, from skilful sales management to seductive advertising, and from rigorous accounting to the diligent shutting off of competition.

Out of that new will to power came many enterprises more or less futile and harmless, with the "institutional" church at their head. Piety was cunningly disguised as basketball, billiards and squash; the sinner was lured to grace with Turkish baths, lectures on foreign travel, and free instructions in stenography, rhetoric and double-entry bookkeeping. Religion lost all its old contemplative and esoteric character, and became a frankly worldly enterprise, a thing of balance-sheets and ponderable profits, heavily capitalized and astutely manned. There was no longer any room for the spiritual type of leader, with his white choker and his interminable fourthlies. He was displaced by a brisk gentleman in a "business suit" who looked, talked and thought like a seller of Mexican mine stock. Scheme after scheme for the swift evangelization of the nation was launched, some of them of truly astonishing sweep and daring. They kept pace, step by step, with the mushroom growth of enterprise in the commercial field. The Y. M. C. A. swelled to the proportions of a Standard Oil Company, a United States Steel Corporation. Its hugh buildings began to rise in every city; it developed a swarm of specialists in new and fantastic moral and social sciences; it enlisted the same gargantuan talent which managed the railroads, the big banks and the larger national industries. And beside it rose the Young People's Society of Christian Endeavour, the Sunday-school associations and a score of other such grandiose organizations, each with its seductive baits for recruits and money. Even the enterprises that had come down from an elder and less expansive day were pumped up and put on a Wall Street basis: the American Bible Society, for example, began to give away Bibles by the million instead of by the thousand, and the venerable Tract Society took on the feverish ardour of a daily newspaper, even of a yellow journal. Down into our own day this trustification of pious endeavour has gone on. The Men and Religion Forward Movement proposed to convert the whole country by 12 o'clock noon of such and such a day; the Order of Gideons plans to make every traveller read the Bible (American Revised Version!) whether he will or not; in a score of cities there are committees of opulent devotees who take half-pages in the newspapers, and advertise the Decalogue and the Beatitudes as if they were commodities of trade.

Thus the national energy which created the Beef Trust and the Oil Trust achieved equal marvels in the field of religious organization and by exactly the same methods. One needs be no psychologist to perceive in all this a good deal less actual religious zeal than mere lust for staggering accomplishment, for empty bigness, for the unprecedented and the prodigious. Many of these great religious enterprises, indeed, soon lost all save the faintest flavour of devotion—for example, the Y. M. C. A., which is now no more than a sort of national club system, with its doors open to any one not palpably felonious. (I have drunk cocktails in Y. M. C. A. lamaseries, and helped fallen lamas to bed.) But while the war upon godlessness thus degenerated into a secular sport in one direction, it maintained all its pristine quality, and even took on a new ferocity in another direction. Here it was that the lamp of American Puritanism kept on burning; here, it was, indeed, that the lamp became converted into a huge bonfire, or rather a blast-furnace, with flames mounting to the very heavens, and sinners stacked like cordwood at the hand of an eager black gang. In brief, the new will to power, working in the true Puritan as in the mere religious sportsman, stimulated him to a campaign of repression and punishment perhaps unequalled in the history of the world, and developed an art of militant morality as complex in technique and as rich in professors as the elder art of iniquity.

If we take the passage of the Comstock Postal Act, on March 3, 1873, as a starting point, the legislative stakes of this new Puritan movement sweep upward in a grand curve to the passage of the Mann and Webb Acts, in 1910 and 1913, the first of which ratifies the Seventh Commandment with a salvo of artillery, and the second of which put the overwhelming power of the Federal Government behind the enforcement of the prohibition laws in the so-called "dry" States. The mind at once recalls the salient campaigns of this war of a generation: first the attack upon "vicious" literature, begun by Comstock and the New York Society for the Suppression of Vice, but quickly extending to every city in the land; then the long fight upon the open gambling house, culminating in its practical disappearance; then the recrudesence of prohibition, abandoned at the outbreak of the Civil War, and the attempt to enforce it in a rapidly growing list of States; then the successful onslaught upon the Louisiana lottery, and upon its swarm of rivals and successors; then the gradual stamping-out of horse-racing, until finally but two or three States permitted it, and the consequent attack upon the poolroom; then the rise of a theatre-censorship in most of the large cities, and of a moving picture censorship following it; then the revival of Sabbatarianism, with the Lord's Day Alliance, a Canadian invention, in the van; then the gradual tightening of the laws against sexual irregularity, with the unenforceable New York Adultery Act as a typical product; and lastly, the general ploughing up and emotional discussion of sexual matters, with compulsory instruction in "sex hygiene" as its mildest manifestation and the mediaeval fury of the vice crusade as its worst. Differing widely in their targets, these various Puritan enterprises had one character in common: they were all efforts to combat immorality with the weapons designed for crime. In each of them there was a visible effort to erect the individual's offence against himself into an offence against society. Beneath all of them there was the dubious principle—the very determining principle, indeed, of Puritanism—that it is competent for the community to limit and condition the private acts of its members, and with it the inevitable corollary that there are some members of the community who have a special talent for such legislation, and that their arbitrary fiats are, and of a right ought to be, binding upon all.

§ 4

This is the essential fact of the new Puritanism; its recognition of the moral expert, the professional sinhound, the virtuoso of virtue. Under the original Puritan theocracy, as in Scotland, for example, the chase and punishment of sinners was a purely ecclesiastical function, and during the slow disintegration of the theocracy the only change introduced was the extension of that function to lay helpers, and finally to the whole body of laymen. This change, however, did not materially corrupt the ecclesiastical quality of the enterprise: the leader in the so-called militant field still remained the same man who led in the spiritual field. But with the capitalization of Puritan effort there came a radical overhauling of method. The secular arm, as it were, conquered as it helped. That is to say, the special business of forcing sinners to be good was taken away from the preachers and put into the hands of laymen trained in its technique and mystery, and there it remains. The new Puritanism has created an army of gladiators who are not only distinct from the hierarchy, but who, in many instances, actually command and intimidate the hierarchy. This is conspicuously evident in the case of the Anti-Saloon League, an enormously effective fighting organization, with a large staff of highly accomplished experts in its service. These experts do not wait for ecclesiastical support, nor even ask for it; they force it. The clergyman who presumes to protest against their war upon the saloon, even upon the quite virtuous ground that it is not effective enough, runs a risk of condign and merciless punishment. So plainly is this understood, indeed, that in more than one State the clergy of the Puritan denominations openly take orders from these specialists in excoriation, and court their favour without shame. Here a single moral enterprise, heavily capitalized and carefully officered, has engulfed the entire Puritan movement, and a part has become more than the whole.[6]

In a dozen other directions this tendency to transform a religious business into a purely secular business, with lay backers and lay officers, is plainly visible. The increasing wealth of Puritanism has not only augmented its scope and its daring, but it has also had the effect of attracting clever men, of no particular spiritual enthusiasm, to its service. Moral endeavour, in brief, has become a recognized trade, or rather a profession, and there have appeared men who pretend to a special and enormous knowledge of it, and who show enough truth in their pretension to gain the unlimited support of Puritan capitalists. The vice crusade, to mention one example, has produced a large crop of such self-constituted experts, and some of them are in such demand that they are overwhelmed with engagements. The majority of these men have wholly lost the flavour of sacerdotalism. They are not pastors, but detectives, statisticians and mob orators, and not infrequently their secularity becomes distressingly evident. Their aim, as they say, is to do things. Assuming that "moral sentiment" is behind them, they override all criticism and opposition without argument, and proceed to the business of dispersing prostitutes, of browbeating and terrorizing weak officials, and of forcing legislation of their own invention through City Councils and State Legislatures. Their very cocksureness is their chief source of strength. They combat objection with such violence and with such a devastating cynicism that it quickly fades away. The more astute politicians, in the face of so ruthless a fire, commonly profess conversion and join the colours, just as their brethren went over to prohibition in the "dry" States, and the newspapers seldom hold out much longer. The result is that the "investigation" of the social evil becomes an orgy, and that the ensuing "report" of the inevitable "vice commission" is made up of two parts sensational fiction and three parts platitude. Of all the vice commissions that have sat of late in the United States, not one has done its work without the aid of these singularly confident experts, and not one has contributed an original and sagacious idea, nor even an idea of ordinary common sense, to the solution of the problem.

I need not go on piling up examples of this new form of Puritan activity, with its definite departure from a religious foundation and its elaborate development as an everyday business. The impulse behind it I have called a *Wille zur Macht,* a will to power. In terms more homely, it was described by John Fiske as "the disposition to domineer," and in his usual unerring way, he saw its dependence on the gratuitous assumption of infallibility. But even stronger than the Puritan's belief in his own inspiration is his yearning to make some one jump. In other words, he has an ineradicable liking for cruelty in him: he is a sportsman even before he is a moralist, and very often his blood-lust leads him into lamentable excesses. The various vice crusades afford innumerable cases in point. In one city, if the press dispatches are to be believed, the proscribed women of the Tenderloin were pursued with such ferocity that seven of them were driven to suicide. And in another city, after a campaign of repression so unfortunate in its effects that there were actually protests against it by clergymen elsewhere, a distinguished (and very friendly) connoisseur of such affairs referred to it ingenuously as more fun "than a fleet of aeroplanes." Such disorderly combats with evil, of course, produce no permanent good. It is a commonplace, indeed, that a city is usually in worse condition after it has been "cleaned up" than it was before, and I need not point to New York, Los Angeles and Des Moines for the evidence as to the social evil, and to any large city, East, West, North, South, for the evidence as to the saloon. But the Puritans who finance such enterprises get their thrills, not out of any possible obliteration of vice, but out of the galloping pursuit of the vicious. The new Puritan gives no more serious thought to the rights and feelings of his quarry than the gunner gives to the rights and feelings of his birds. From the beginning of the prohibition campaign, for example, the principle of compensation has been violently opposed, despite its obvious justice, and a complaisant judiciary has ratified the Puritan position. In England and on the Continent that principle is safeguarded by the fundamental laws, and during the early days of the anti-slavery agitation in this country it was accepted as incontrovertible, but if any American statesman were to propose today that it be applied to the license-holder whose lawful franchise has been taken away from him arbitrarily, or to the brewer or distiller whose costly plant has been rendered useless and valueless, he would see the days of his statesmanship brought to a quick and violent close.

But does all this argue a total lack of justice in the American character, or even a lack of common decency? I doubt that it would be well to go so far in accusation. What it does argue is a tendency to put moral considerations above all other considerations, and to define morality in the narrow Puritan sense. The American, in other words, thinks that the sinner has no rights that any one is bound to respect, and he is prone to mistake an unsupported charge of sinning, provided it be made violently enough, for actual proof and confession. What is more, he takes an intense joy in the mere chase: he has the true Puritan taste for an *auto da fé* in him. "I am ag'inst capital punishment," said Mr. Dooley, "but we won't get rid av it so long as the people enjie it so much." But though he is thus an eager spectator, and may even be lured into taking part in the pursuit, the average American is not disposed to initiate it, nor to pay for it. The larger Puritan enterprises of today are not popular in the sense of originating in the bleachers, but only in the sense of being applauded from the bleachers. The burdens of the fray, both of toil and of expense, are always upon a relatively small number of men. In a State rocked and racked by a war upon the saloon, it was recently shown, for example, that but five percent of the members of the Puritan denominations contributed to the war-chest. And yet the Anti-Saloon League of that State was so sure of support from below that it presumed to stand as the spokesman of the whole Christian community, and even ventured to launch excommunications upon contumacious Christians, both lay and clerical, who objected to its methods. Moreover, the great majority of the persons included in the contributing five percent gave no more than a few cents a year. The whole support of the League devolved upon a dozen men, all of them rich and all of them Puritans of purest ray serene. These men supported a costly organization for their private entertainment and stimulation. It was their means of recreation, their sporting club. They were willing to spend a lot of money to procure good sport for themselves—i.e., to procure the best crusading talent available—and they were so successful in that endeavour that they enchanted the populace too, and so shook the State.

Naturally enough, this organization of Puritanism upon a business and sporting basis has had a tendency to attract and create a type of "expert" crusader whose determination to give his employers a good show is uncontaminated by any consideration for the public welfare. The result has been a steady increase of scandals, a constant collapse of moral organizations, a frequent unveiling of whited sepulchres. Various observers have sought to direct the public attention to this significant corruption of the new Puritanism. The New York *Sun,* for example, in the course of a protest against the appointment of a vice commission for New York, has denounced the paid agents of private reform organizations as "notoriously corrupt, undependable and dishonest," and the Rev. Dr. W. S. Rainsford, supporting the charge, has borne testimony out of his own wide experience to their lawlessness, their absurd pretensions to special knowledge, their habit of manufacturing evidence, and their devious methods of shutting off criticism. But so far, at all events, no organized war upon them has been undertaken, and they seem to flourish more luxuriantly year after year. The individual whose common rights are invaded by such persons has little chance of getting justice, and less of getting redress. When he attempts to defend himself he finds that he is opposed, not only by a financial power that is ample for all purposes of the combat and that does not shrink at intimidating juries, prosecuting officers and judges, but also by a shrewdness which shapes the laws to its own uses, and takes full advantage of the miserable cowardice of legislatures. The moral gladiators, in brief, know the game. They come before a legislature with a bill ostensibly designed to cure some great and admitted evil, they procure its enactment by scarcely veiled insinuations that all who stand against it must be apologists for the evil itself, and then they proceed to extend its aims by bold inferences, and to dragoon the courts into ratifying those inferences, and to employ it as a means of persecution, terrorism and blackmail. The history of the Mann Act offers a shining example of this purpose. It was carried through Congress, over the veto of President Taft, who discerned its extravagance, on the plea that it was needed to put down the traffic in prostitutes; it is enforced today against men who are no more engaged in the traffic in prostitutes than you or I. Naturally enough, the effect of this extension of its purposes, against which its author has publicly protested, has been to make it a truly deadly weapon in the hands of professional Puritans and of denouncers of delinquency even less honest. "Blackmailers of both sexes have arisen," says Mr. Justice McKenna, "using the terrors of the construction now sanctioned by the [Supreme] Court as a help—indeed, the means—for their brigandage. The result is grave and should give us pause."[7]

But that is as far as objection has yet gone; the majority of the learned jurist's colleagues swallowed both the statute and its consequences.[8] There is, indeed, no sign as yet of any organized war upon the alliance between the blackmailing Puritan and the pseudo-Puritan blackmailer. It must wait until a sense of reason and justice shows itself in the American people, strong enough to overcome their prejudice in favour of the moralist on the one hand, and their delight in barbarous pursuits and punishments on the other. I see but faint promise of that change today.

§ 5

I have gone into the anatomy and physiology of militant Puritanism because, so far as I know, the inquiry has not been attempted before, and because a somewhat detailed acquaintance with the forces behind so grotesque a manifestation as comstockery, the particular business of the present essay, is necessary to an understanding of its workings, and of its prosperity, and of its influence upon the arts. Save one turn to England or to the British colonies, it is impossible to find a parallel for the astounding absolutism of Comstock and his imitators in any civilized country. No other nation has laws which oppress the arts so ignorantly and so abominably as ours do, nor has any other nation handed over the enforcement of the statutes which exist to agencies so openly pledged to reduce all aesthetic expression to the service of a stupid and unworkable scheme of rectitude. I have before me as I write a pamphlet in explanation of his aims and principles, prepared by Comstock himself and presented to me by his successor. Its very title is a sufficient statement of the Puritan position: "MORALS, Not Art or Literature."[9] The capitals are in the original. And within, as a sort of general text, the idea is amplified: "It is a question of peace, good order and morals, and not art, literature or science." Here we have a statement of principle that, at all events, is at least quite frank. There is not the slightest effort to beg the question; there is no hypocritical pretension to a desire to purify or safeguard the arts; they are dismissed at once as trivial and degrading. And jury after jury has acquiesced in this; it was old Anthony's boast, in his last days, that his percentage of convictions, in 40 years, had run to 98.5.[10]

Comstockery is thus grounded firmly upon that profound national suspicion of the arts, that truculent and almost unanimous Philistinism, which I have described. It would be absurd to dismiss it as an excrescence, and untypical of the American mind. But it is typical, too, in the manner in which it has gone beyond that mere partiality to the accumulation of a definite power, and made that power irresponsible and almost irresistible. It was Comstock himself, in fact, who invented the process whereby his followers in other fields of moral endeavour have forced laws into the statute books upon the pretence of putting down John Doe, an acknowledged malefactor, and then turned them savagely upon Richard Roe, a peaceable, well-meaning and hitherto law-abiding man. And it was Comstock who first capitalized moral endeavour like baseball or the soap business, and made himself the first of its kept professors, and erected about himself a rampart of legal and financial immunity which rid him of all fear of mistakes and their consequences, and so enabled him to pursue his jehad with all the advantages in his favour. He was, in brief, more than the greatest Puritan gladiator of his time; he was the Copernicus of a quite new art and science, and he devised a technique and handed down a professional ethic that no rival has been able to better.

The whole story is naïvely told in *Anthony Comstock, Fighter,*[11] a work which passed under the approving eye of the old war horse himself and is full of his characteristic pecksniffery.[12] His beginnings, it appears, were very modest. When he arrived in New York from the Connecticut hinterland, he was a penniless and uneducated clodhopper, just out of the Union army, and his first job was that of a porter in a wholesale dry-goods house. But he had in him several qualities of the traditional Yankee which almost always insure success, and it was not long before he began to make his way. One of these qualities was a talent for bold and ingratiating address; another was a vast appetite for thrusting himself into affairs, a yearning to run things—what the Puritan calls public spirit. The two constituted his fortune. The second brought him into intimate relations with the newly-organized Young Men's Christian Association, and led him to the discovery of a form of moral endeavour that was at once novel and fascinating—the unearthing and denunciation of "immoral" literature. The first, once he had attracted attention thereby, got him the favourable notice, and finally the unlimited support, of the late Morris K. Jesup, one of the earliest and perhaps the greatest of the moral *entrepreneurs* that I have described. Jesup was very rich, and very eager to bring the whole nation up to grace by *force majeure.* He was the banker of at least a dozen grandiose programs of purification in the seventies and eighties. In Comstock he found precisely the sort of field agent that he was looking for, and the two presently constituted the most formidable team of professional reformers that the country had ever seen.

The story of the passage of the Act of Congress of March 3, 1873,[13] under cover of which the Comstock Society still carries on its campaigns of snouting and suppression, is a classical tale of Puritan impudence and chicanery. Comstock, with Jesup and other rich men backing him financially and politically,[14] managed the business. First, a number of spectacular raids were made on the publishers of such pornographic books as *The Memoirs of Fanny Hill* and *Only a Boy.* Then the newspapers were filled with inflammatory matter about the wide dispersal of such stuff, and its demoralizing effects upon the youth of the republic. Then a committee of self-advertising clergymen and "Christian millionaires" was organized to launch a definite "movement." And then a direct attack was made upon Congress, and, to the tune of fiery moral indignation, the bill prepared by Comstock himself was forced through both houses. All opposition, if only the opposition of inquiry, was overborne in the usual manner. That is to say, every Congressman who presumed to ask what it was all about, or to point out obvious defects in the bill, was disposed of by the insinuation, or even the direct charge, that he was a covert defender of obscene books, and, by inference, of the carnal recreations described in them. We have grown familiar of late with this process: it was displayed at full length in the passage of the Mann Act, and again when the Webb Act and the Prohibition Amendment were before Congress. In 1873 its effectiveness was helped out by its novelty, and so the Comstock bill was rushed through both houses in the closing days of a busy session, and President Grant accommodatingly signed it.

Once it was upon the books, Comstock made further use of the prevailing uproar to have himself appointed a special agent of the Postoffice Department to enforce it, and with characteristic cunning refused to take any salary. Had his job carried a salary, it would have excited the acquisitiveness of other virtuosi; as it was, he was secure. As for the necessary sinews of war, he knew well that he could get them from Jesup. Within a few weeks, indeed, the latter had perfected a special organization for the enforcement of the new statute, and it still flourishes as the New York Society for the Suppression of Vice; or, as it is better known, the Comstock Society. The new Federal Act, dealing only with the mails, left certain loopholes; they were plugged up by fastening drastic amendments upon the New York Code of Criminal Procedure—amendments forced through the legislature precisely as the Federal Act had been forced through Congress.[15] With these laws in his hands Comstock was ready for his career. It was his part of the arrangement to supply the thrills of the chase; it was Jesup's part to find the money. The partnership kept up until the death of Jesup, in 1908, and after that Comstock readily found new backers. Even his own death, in 1915, did not materially alter a scheme of things which offered such admirable opportunities for the exercise of the Puritan love of spectacular and relentless pursuit, the Puritan delusion of moral grandeur and infallibility, the Puritan will to power.

Ostensibly, as I have said, the new laws were designed to put down the traffic in frankly pornographic books and pictures—a traffic which, of course, found no defenders—but Comstock had so drawn them that their actual sweep was vastly wider, and once he was firmly in the saddle his enterprises scarcely knew limits. Having disposed of "The Confessions of Maria Monk" and "Night Life in Paris," he turned to Rabelais and the Decameron, and having driven these ancients under the book-counters, he pounced upon Zola, Balzac and Daudet, and having disposed of these too, he began a *pogrom* which, in other hands, eventually brought down such astounding victims as Thomas Hardy's "Jude the Obscure" and Harold Frederic's "The Damnation of Theron Ware." All through the eighties and nineties this ecstatic campaign continued, always increasing in violence and effectiveness. Comstock became a national celebrity; his doings were as copiously reported by the newspapers as those of P. T. Barnum or John L. Sullivan. Imitators sprang up in all the larger cities: there was hardly a public library in the land that did not begin feverishly expurgating its shelves; the publication of fiction, and particularly of foreign fiction, took on the character of an extra hazardous enterprise. Not, of course, that the reign of terror was not challenged, and Comstock himself denounced. So early as 1876 a national organization demanding a reasonable amendment of the postal laws got on its legs; in the late eighties "Citizen" George Francis Train defied the whirlwind by printing the Old Testament as a serial; many indignant victims, acquitted by some chance in the courts, brought suit against Comstock for damages. Moreover, an occasional judge, standing out boldly against the usual intimidation, denounced him from the bench; one of them, Judge Jenkins, accused him specifically of "fraud and lying" and other "dishonest practices."[16] But the spirit of American Puritanism was on his side. His very extravagances at once stimulated and satisfied the national yearning for a hot chase, a good show—and in the complaints of his victims, that the art of letters was being degraded, that the country was made ridiculous, the newspaper-reading populace could see no more than an affectation. The reform organization of 1876 lasted but five years; and then disbanded without having accomplished anything; Train was put on trial for "debauching the young" with an "obscene" serial;[17] juries refused to bring in punitive verdicts against the master showman.

In carrying on this way of extermination upon all ideas that violated their private notions of virtue and decorum, Comstock and his followers were very greatly aided by the vagueness of the law. It prohibited the use of the mails for transporting all matter of an "obscene, lewd, lascivious . . . or filthy" character, but conveniently failed to define these adjectives. As a result, of course, it was possible to bring an accusation against practically *any* publication that aroused the comstockian blood-lust, however innocently, and to subject the persons responsible for it to costly, embarrassing and often dangerous persecution. No man, said Dr. Johnson, would care to go on trial for his life once a week, even if possessed of absolute proofs of his innocence. By the same token, no man wants to be arraigned in a criminal court, and displayed in the sensational newspapers, as a purveyor of indecency, however strong his assurance of innocence. Comstock made use of this fact in an adroit and characteristically unconscionable manner. He held the menace of prosecution over all who presumed to dispute his tyranny, and when he could not prevail by a mere threat, he did not hesitate to begin proceedings, and to carry them forward with the aid of florid proclamations to the newspapers and ill concealed intimidations of judges and juries.

The last-named business succeeded as it always does in this country, where the judiciary is quite as sensitive to the suspicion of sinfulness as the legislative arm. A glance at the decisions handed down during the forty years of Comstock's chief activity shows a truly amazing willingness to accommodate him in his pious enterprises. On the one hand, there was gradually built up a court-made definition of obscenity which eventually embraced almost every conceivable violation of Puritan prudery, and on the other hand the victim's means of defence were steadily restricted and conditioned, until in the end he had scarcely any at all. This is the state of the law today. It is held in the leading cases that anything is obscene which may excite "impure thoughts" in "the minds . . . of persons that are susceptible to impure thoughts,"[18] or which "tends to deprave the minds" of any who, because they are "young and inexperienced," are "open to such influences"[19]—in brief, that anything is obscene that is not fit to be handed to a child just learning to read, or that may imaginably stimulate the lubricity of the most foul-minded. It is held further that words that are perfectly innocent in themselves—"words, abstractly considered, [that] may be free from vulgarism"—may yet be assumed, by a friendly jury, to be likely to "arouse a libidinous passion . . . in the mind of a modest woman." (I quote exactly! The court failed to define "modest woman.")[20] Yet further, it is held that any book is obscene "which is unbecoming, immodest. . . ."[21] Obviously, this last decision throws open the door to endless imbecilities, for its definition merely begs the question, and so makes a reasonable solution ten times harder. It is in such mazes that the Comstocks safely lurk. Almost any printed allusion to sex may be argued against as unbecoming in a moral republic, and once it is unbecoming it is also obscene.

In meeting such attacks the defendant must do his fighting without weapons. He cannot allege in his defence that the offending work was put forth for a legitimate, necessary and decent purpose;[22] he cannot allege that a passage complained of is from a standard work, itself in general circulation;[23] he cannot offer evidence that the person to whom a book or picture was sold or exhibited was not actually depraved by it, or likely to be depraved by it;[24] he cannot rest his defence on its lack of such effect upon the jurymen themselves;[25] he cannot plead that the alleged obscenity, in point of fact, is couched in decent and unobjectionable language;[26] he cannot plead that the same or a similar work has gone unchallenged elsewhere;[27] he cannot argue that the circulation of works of the same class has set up a presumption of toleration, and a tacit limitation of the definition of obscenity.[28] The general character of a book is not a defence of a particular passage, however unimportant; if there is the slightest descent to what is "unbecoming," the whole may be ruthlessly condemned.[29] Nor is it an admissible defence to argue that the book was not generally circulated, and that the copy in evidence was obtained by an *agent provocateur,* and by false representations.[30] Finally, all the decisions deny the defendant the right to introduce any testimony, whether expert or otherwise, that a book is of artistic value and not pornographic, and that its effect upon normal persons is not pernicious. Upon this point the jury is the sole judge, and it cannot be helped to its decision by taking other opinions, or by hearing evidence as to what is the general opinion.

Occasionally, as I have said, a judge has revolted against this intolerable state of the court- and Comstock-made law, and directed a jury to disregard these astounding decisions.[31] In a recent New York case Judge Samuel Seabury actually ruled that "it is no part of the duty of courts to exercise a censorship over literary productions."[32] But in general the judiciary has been curiously complaisant, and more than once a Puritan on the bench has delighted the Comstocks by prosecuting their case for them.[33] With such decisions in their hands and such aid from the other side of the bar, it is no wonder that they enter upon their campaigns with impudence and assurance. All the odds are in their favour from the start. They have statutes deliberately designed to make the defence onerous; they are familiar by long experience with all the tricks and surprises of the game; they are sheltered behind organizations, incorporated without capital and liberally chartered by trembling legislatures, which make reprisals impossible in case of failure; above all, they have perfected the business of playing upon the cowardice and vanity of judges and prosecuting officers. The newspapers, with very few exceptions, give them ready aid. Theoretically, perhaps, many newspaper editors are opposed to comstockery, and sometimes they denounce it with great eloquence, but when a good show is offered they are always in favour of the showman[34]—and the Comstocks are showmen of undoubted skill. They know how to make a victim jump and writhe in the ring; they have a talent for finding victims who are prominent enough to arrest attention; they shrewdly capitalize the fact that the pursuer appears more heroic than the prey, and the further fact that the newspaper reader is impatient of artistic pretensions and glad to see an artist made ridiculous. And behind them there is always the steady pressure of Puritan prejudice—the Puritan feeling that "immorality" is the blackest of crimes, and that its practitioner has no rights. It was by making use of these elements that Comstock achieved his prodigies, and it is by making use of them that his heirs and assigns keep up the sport today. Their livelihood depends upon the money they can raise among the righteous, and the amount they can raise depends upon the quality of the entertainment they offer. Hence their adept search for shining marks. Hence, for example, the spectacular raid upon the Art Students' League, on August 2, 1906. Hence the artful turning to their own use of the vogue of such sensational dramatists as Eugène Brieux and George Bernard Shaw, and of such isolated plays as "Trilby" and "Sapho." Hence the barring from the mails of the inflammatory report of the Chicago Vice Commission—a strange, strange case of dog eating dog.

But here we have humour. There is, however, no humour in the case of a serious author who sees his work damaged and perhaps ruined by a malicious and unintelligent attack, and himself held up to public obloquy as one with the vendors of pamphlets of flagellation and filthy "marriage guides." He finds opposing him a flat denial of his decent purpose as an artist, and a stupid and ill-natured logic that baffles sober answer.[35] He finds on his side only the half-hearted support of a publisher whose interest in a single book is limited to his profits from it, and who desires above all things to evade a nuisance and an expense. Not a few publishers, knowing the constant possibility of sudden and arbitrary attack, insert a clause in their contracts whereby an author must secure them against damage from any "immoral" matter in his book. They read and approve the manuscript, they print the book and sell it—but if it is unlucky enough to attract the comstockian lightning, the author has the whole burden to bear,[36] and if they seek safety and economy by yielding, as often happens, he must consent to the mutilation or even the suppression of his work. The result is that a writer in such a situation, is practically beaten before he can offer a defence. The professional book-baiters have laws to their liking, and courts pliant to their exactions; they fill the newspapers with inflammatory charges before the accused gets his day in court; they have the aid of prosecuting officers who fear the political damage of their enmity, and of the enmity of their wealthy and influential backers; above all, they have the command of far more money than any author can hope to muster. Finally, they derive an advantage from two of the most widespread of human weaknesses, the first being envy and the second being fear. When an author is attacked, a good many of his rivals see only a personal benefit in his difficulties, and not a menace to the whole order, and a good many others are afraid to go to his aid because of the danger of bringing down the moralists' rage upon themselves. Both of these weaknesses revealed themselves very amusingly in the Dreiser case, and I hope to detail their operations at some length later on, when I describe that *cause célèbre* in a separate work.

Now add to the unfairness and malignancy of the attack its no less disconcerting arbitrariness and fortuitousness, and the path of the American author is seen to be strewn with formidable entanglements indeed. With the law what it is, he is quite unable to decide a priori what is permitted by the national delicacy and what is not, nor can he get any light from the recorded campaigns of the moralists.

They seem to strike blindly, unintelligently, without any coherent theory or plan. "Trilby" is assaulted by the united comstockery of a dozen cities, and "The Yoke" somehow escapes. "Hagar Revelly" is made the subject of a double prosecution in the State and Federal courts, and "Love's Pilgrimage" and "One Man" go unmolested. The publisher of Przybyszewski's "Homo Sapiens" is forced to withdraw it; the publisher of Artzibashef's "Sanine" follows it with "The Breaking Point." The serious work of a Forel is brought into court as pornography, and the books of Havelock Ellis are barred from the mails; the innumerable volumes on "sex hygiene" by tawdry clergymen and smutty old maids are circulated by the million and without challenge. Frank Harris is deprived of a publisher for his "Oscar Wilde: His Life and Confession" by threats of immediate prosecution; the newspapers meanwhile dedicate thousands of columns to the filthy amusements of Harry Thaw. George Moore's "Memoirs of My Dead Life" are bowdlerized, James Lane Allen's "A Summer in Arcady" is barred from libraries, and a book by D. H. Lawrence is forbidden publication altogether; at the same time half a dozen cheap magazines devoted to sensational sex stories attain to hundreds of thousands of circulation. A serious book by David Graham Phillips, published serially in a popular monthly, is raided the moment it appears between covers; a trashy piece of nastiness by Elinor Glyn goes unmolested. Worse, books are sold for months and even years without protest, and then suddenly attacked; Dreiser's "The 'Genius,'" Kreymborg's "Edna" and Forel's "The Sexual Question" are examples. Still worse, what is held to be unobjectionable in one State is forbidden in another as *contra bonos mores*.[37] Altogether, there is madness, and no method in it. The livelihoods and good names of hard-striving and decent men are at the mercy of the whims of a horde of fanatics and mountebanks, and they have no way of securing themselves against attack, and no redress for their loss when it comes.

§ 6

So beset, it is no wonder that the typical American maker of books becomes a timorous and ineffective fellow, whose work tends inevitably toward a feeble superficiality. Sucking in the Puritan spirit with the very air he breathes, and perhaps burdened inwardly with an inheritance of the actual Puritan stupidity, he is further kept upon the straight path of chemical purity by the very real perils that I have just rehearsed. The result is a literature full of the mawkishness that the late Henry James so often roared against—a literature almost wholly detached from life as men are living it in the world—in George Moore's phrase, a literature still at nurse. It is on the side of sex that the appointed virtuosi of virtue exercise their chief repressions, for it is sex that especially fascinates the lubricious Puritan mind; but the conventual reticence that thus becomes the enforced fashion in one field extends itself to all others. Our fiction, in general, is marked by an artificiality as marked as that of Eighteenth Century poetry or the later Georgian drama. The romance in it runs to set forms and stale situations; the revelation, by such a book as *The Titan*, that there may be a glamour as entrancing in the way of a conqueror of men as in the way of a youth with a maid, remains isolated and exotic. We have no first-rate political or religious novel; we have no first-rate war story; despite all our national engrossment in commercial enterprise, we have few second-rate tales of business. Romance, in American fiction, still means only a somewhat childish amorousness and sentimentality—the love affairs of Paul and Virginia, or the pale adulteries of their elders. And on the side of realism there is an almost equal vacuity and lack of veracity. The action of all the novels of the Howells school goes on within four walls of painted canvas; they begin to shock once they describe an attack of asthma or a steak burning below stairs; they never penetrate beneath the flow of social concealments and urbanities to the passions that actually move men and women to their acts, and the great forces that circumscribe and condition personality. So obvious a piece of reporting as Upton Sinclair's *The Jungle* or Robert Herrick's *Together* makes a sensation; the appearance of a *Jennie Gerhardt* or a *Hagar Revelly* brings forth a growl of astonishment and rage.

In all this dread of free inquiry, this childish skittishness in both writers and public, this dearth of courage and even of curiosity, the influence of comstockery is undoubtedly to be detected. It constitutes a sinister and ever-present menace to all men of ideas; it affrights the publisher and paralyzes the author; no one on the outside can imagine its burden as a practical concern. I am, in moments borrowed from more palatable business, the editor of an American magazine, and I thus know at first hand what the burden is. That magazine is anything but a popular one, in the current sense. It sells at a relatively high price; it contains no pictures or other baits for the childish; it is frankly addressed to a sophisticated minority. I may thus assume reasonably, I believe, that its readers are not sex-curious and itching adolescents, just as my colleague of the *Atlantic Monthly* may assume reasonably that his readers are not Italian immigrants. Nevertheless, as a practical editor, I find that the Comstocks, near and far, are oftener in my mind's eye than my actual patrons. The thing I always have to decide about a manuscript offered for publication, before ever I give any thought to its artistic merit and suitability, is the question whether its publication will be permitted—not even whether it is intrinsically good or evil, moral or immoral, but whether some roving Methodist preacher, self-commissioned to keep watch on letters, will read indecency into it. Not a week passes that I do not decline some sound and honest piece of work for no other reason. I have a long list of such things by American authors, well-devised, well-imagined, well-executed, respectable as human documents and as works of art—but never to be printed in mine or any other

American magazine. It includes four or five short stories of the very first rank, and the best one-act play yet done, to my knowledge, by an American. All of these pieces would go into type at once on the Continent; no sane man would think of objecting to them; they are no more obscene, to a normal adult, than his own bare legs. But they simply cannot be printed in the United States, with the law what it is and the courts what they are.

I know many other editors. All of them are in the same boat. Some of them try to get around the difficulty by pecksniffery more or less open—for example, by fastening a moral purpose upon works of art, and hawking them as uplifting.[38] Others, facing the intolerable fact, yield to it with resignation. And if they didn't? Well, if one of them didn't, any professional moralist could go before a police magistrate, get a warrant upon a simple affidavit, raid the office of the offending editor, seize all the magazines in sight, and keep them impounded until after the disposition of the case. Editors cannot afford to take this risk. Magazines are perishable goods. Even if, after a trial has been had, they are returned, they are worthless save as waste paper. And what may be done with copies found in the actual office of publication may be done too with copies found on news-stands, and not only in one city, but in two, six, a dozen, a hundred. All the costs and burdens of the contest are on the defendant. Let him be acquitted with honour, and invited to dinner by the judge, he has yet lost his property, and the Comstock hiding behind the warrant cannot be made to pay. In this concealment, indeed, lurk many sinister things—not forgetting personal enmity and business rivalry. The actual complainant is seldom uncovered; Comstockery, taking on a semi-judicial character, throws its chartered immunity around the whole process. A hypothetical outrage? By no means. It has been perpetrated, in one American city or another, upon fully half of the magazines of general circulation published today. Its possibility sticks in the consciousness of every editor and publisher like a recurrent glycosuria.[39]

But though the effects of comstockery are thus abominably insane and irritating, the fact is not to be forgotten that, after all, the thing is no more than an effect itself. The fundamental causes of all the grotesque (and often half-fabulous) phenomena flowing out of it are to be sought in the habits of mind of the American people. They are, as I have shown, besotted by moral concepts, a moral engrossment, a delusion of moral infallibility. In their view of the arts they are still unable to shake off the naïve suspicion of the Fathers.[40] A work of the imagination can justify itself, in their sight, only if it show a moral purpose, and that purpose must be obvious and unmistakable. Even in their slow progress toward a revolt against the ancestral Philistinism, they cling to this ethical bemusement: a new gallery of pictures is welcomed as "improving," to hear Beethoven "makes one better." Any questioning of the moral ideas that prevail—the principal business, it must be plain, of the novelist, the serious dramatist, the professed inquirer into human motives and acts—is received with the utmost hostility. To attempt such an enterprise is to disturb the peace—and the disturber of the peace, in the national view, quickly passes over into the downright criminal.

These symptoms, it seems to me, are only partly racial, despite the persistent survival of that third-rate English strain which shows itself so ingenuously in the colonial spirit, the sense of inferiority, the frank craving for praise from home. The race, in truth, grows mongrel, and the protest against that mongrelism only serves to drive in the fact. But a mongrel race is necessarily a race still in the stage of reaching out for culture; it has not yet formulated defensible standards; it must needs rest heavily upon the superstitions that go with inferiority. The Reformation brought Scotland among the civilized nations, but it took Scotland a century and a half to live down the Reformation.[41] Dogmatism, conformity, Philistinism, the fear of rebels, the crusading spirit; these are the marks of an upstart people, uncertain of their rank in the world and even of their direction.[42] A cultured European, reading a typical American critical journal, must needs conceive the United States, says H. G. Wells, as "a vain, garrulous and prosperous female of uncertain age and still more uncertain temper, with unfounded pretensions to intellectuality and an ideal of refinement of the most negative description . . . the Aunt Errant of Christendom."[43] There is always that blushful shyness, that timorous uncertainty, broken by sudden rages, sudden enunciations of impeccable doctrine, sudden runnings amuck. Formalism is the hall-mark of the national culture, and sins against the one are sins against the other. The American is school-mastered out of gusto, out of joy, out of innocence. He can never fathom William Blake's notion that "the lust of the goat is also to the glory of God." He must be correct, or, in his own phrase, he must bust.

Via trita est tutissima. The new generation, urged to curiosity and rebellion by its mounting sap, is rigorously restrained, regimented, policed. The ideal is vacuity, guilelessness, imbecility. "We are looking at this particular book," said Comstock's successor of *The 'Genius,'* "from the standpoint of its harmful effect on female readers of immature mind."[44] To be curious is to be lewd; to know is to yield to fornication. Here we have the mediaeval doctrine still on its legs: a chance word may arouse "a libidinous passion" in the mind of a "modest" woman. Not only youth must be safeguarded, but also the "female," the untrustworthy one, the temptress. "Modest," is a euphemism; it takes laws to keep her "pure." The "locks of chastity" rust in the Cluny Museum; in place of them we have comstockery. . . .

But, as I have said in hymning Huneker, there is yet the munyonic consolation. Time is a great legalizer, even in the field of morals. We have yet no delivery, but we have at least the beginnings of a revolt, or, at all events, of a protest. We have already reached, in Howells, our Hannah More; in Clemens, our Swift; in Henry James, our Horace Walpole; in Woodberry, Robinson *et al.*, our

Cowpers, Southeys and Crabbes; perhaps we might even make a composite and call it our Johnson. We are sweating through our Eighteenth Century, our era of sentiment, our spiritual measles. Maybe a new day is not quite so far off as it seems to be, and with it we may get our Hardy, our Conrad, our Swinburne, our Thoma, our Moore, our Meredith and our Synge.

Damn! A Book of Calumny

CHAPTER ONE

PATER PATRIÆ

IF GEORGE WASHINGTON WERE ALIVE TODAY, WHAT A SHINING mark he would be for the whole camorra of uplifters, forward-lookers and professional patriots! He was the Rockefeller of his time, the richest man in the United States, a promoter of stock companies, a land-grabber, an exploiter of mines and timber. He was a bitter opponent of foreign alliances, and denounced their evils in harsh, specific terms. He had a liking for all fortright and pugnacious men, and a contempt for lawyers, schoolmasters, and all other such obscurantists. He was not pious. He drank whisky whenever he felt chilly, and kept a jug of it handy. He knew far more profanity than Scripture, and used and enjoyed it more. He had no belief in the infallible wisdom of the common people, but regarded them as inflammatory dolts, and tried to save the republic from them. He advocated no sure cure for all the sorrows of the world, and doubted that such a panacea existed. He took no interest in the private morals of his neighbors.

Inhabiting These States today, George would be ineligible for any office of honor or profit. The Senate would never dare confirm him; the President would not think of nominating him. He would be on trial in all the yellow journals for belonging to the Invisible Government, the Hell Hounds of Plutocracy, the Money Power, the

Interests. The Sherman Act would have him in its toils; he would be under indictment by every grand jury south of the Potomac; the triumphant prohibitionists of his native state would be denouncing him (he had a still at Mount Vernon) as a debaucher of youth, a recruiting officer for insane asylums, a poisoner of the home. The suffragettes would be on his trail, with sentinels posted all along the Accotink road. The initiators and referendors would be bawling for his blood. The young college men of the *Nation* and the *New Republic* would be lecturing him weekly. He would be used to scare children in Kansas and Arkansas. The chautauquas would shiver whenever his name was mentioned. . . .

And what a chance there would be for that ambitious young district attorney who thought to shadow him on his peregrinations—and grab him under the Mann Act!

CHAPTER TWO

THE REWARD OF THE ARTIST

A MAN LABORS AND FUMES FOR A WHOLE YEAR TO WRITE A symphony in G minor. He puts enormous diligence into it, and much talent, and maybe no little downright genius. It draws his blood and wrings his soul. He dies in it that he may live again. . . . Nevertheless, its final value, in the open market of the world, is a great deal less than that of a fur overcoat, half a Rolls-Royce automobile, or a handful of authentic hair from the whiskers of Henry Wadsworth Longfellow.

CHAPTER THREE

The Heroic Considered

For humility and poverty, in themselves, the world has little liking and less respect. In the folklore of all races, despite the sentimentalization of abasement for dramatic effect, it is always power and grandeur that count in the end. The whole point of the story of Cinderella, the most widely and constantly charming of all stories, is that the Fairy Prince lifts Cinderella above her cruel sisters and stepmother, and so enables her to lord it over them. The same idea underlies practically all other folk stories: the essence of each of them is to be found in the ultimate triumph and exaltation of its protagonist. And of the real men and women of history, the most venerated and envied are those whose early humiliations were but preludes to terminal glories; for example, Lincoln, Whittington, Franklin, Columbus, Demosthenes, Frederick the Great, Catherine, Mary of Magdala, Moses. Even the Man of Sorrows, cradled in a manger and done to death between two thieves, is seen, as we part from Him at last, in a situation of stupendous magnificence, with infinite power in His hands. Even the Beatitudes, in the midst of their eloquent counselling of renunciation, give it unimaginable splendor as its reward. The meek shall inherit—what? The whole earth! And the poor in spirit? They shall sit upon the right hand of God! . . .

→ CHAPTER FOUR ←

The Burden of Humor

What is the origin of the prejudice against humor? Why is it so dangerous, if you would keep the public confidence, to make the public laugh? Is it because humor and sound sense are essentially antagonistic? Has humanity found by experience that the man who sees the fun of life is unfitted to deal sanely with its problems? I think not. No man had more of the comic spirit in him than William Shakespeare, and yet his serious reflections, by the sheer force of their sublime obviousness, have pushed their way into the race's arsenal of immortal platitudes. So, too, with Aesop, and with Balzac, and with Dickens, to come down the scale. All of these men were fundamentally humorists, and yet all of them achieved what the race has come to accept as a penetrating sagacity. Contrariwise, many a haloed pundit has had his occasional guffaw. Lincoln, had there been no Civil War, might have survived in history chiefly as the father of the American smutty story—the only original art form that America has yet contributed to literature. Huxley, had he not been the greatest intellectual duellist of his age, might have been its greatest satirist. Bismarck, pursuing the gruesome trade of politics, concealed the devastating wit of a Molière; his surviving epigrams are truly stupendous. And

Beethoven, after soaring to the heights of tragedy in the first movement of the Fifth Symphony, turned to the sardonic bull-fiddling of the *scherzo*.

No, there is not the slightest disharmony between sense and nonsense, humor and respectability, despite the skittish tendency to assume that there is. But, why, then, that widespread error? What actual fact of life lies behind it, giving it a specious appearance of reasonableness? None other, I am convinced, than the fact that the average man is far too stupid to make a joke. He may *see* a joke and *love* a joke, particularly when it floors and flabbergasts some person he dislikes, but the only way he can himself take part in the priming and pointing of a new one is by acting as its target. In brief, his personal contact with humor tends to fill him with an accumulated sense of disadvantage, of pricked complacency, of sudden and crushing defeat; and so, by an easy psychological process, he is led into the idea that the thing itself is incompatible with true dignity of character and intellect. Hence his deep suspicion of jokers, however adept their thrusts. "What a damned fool!"—this same half-pitying tribute he pays to wit and butt alike. He cannot separate the virtuoso of comedy from his general concept of comedy itself, and that concept is inextricably mingled with memories of foul ambuscades and mortifying hurts. And so it is not often that he is willing to admit any wisdom in a humorist, or to condone frivolity in a sage.

CHAPTER FIVE

THE SAVING GRACE

LET US NOT BURN THE UNIVERSITIES—YET. AFTER ALL, THE DAMAGE they do might be worse. . . . Suppose Oxford had snared and disemboweled Shakespeare! Suppose Harvard had set its stamp upon Mark Twain!

→ CHAPTER SIX ←

MORAL INDIGNATION

THE LOUD, PREPOSTEROUS MORAL CRUSADES THAT SO ENDLESSLY rock the republic—against the rum demon, against Sunday baseball, against Sunday moving-pictures, against dancing, against fornication, against the cigarette, against all things sinful and charming—these astounding Methodist jehads offer fat clinical material to the student of mobocracy. In the long run, nearly all of them must succeed, for the mob is eternally virtuous, and the only thing necessary to get it in favor of some new and super-oppressive law is to convince it that that law will be distasteful to the minority that it envies and hates. The poor numskull who is so horribly harrowed by Puritan pulpit-thumpers that he can't go to a ball game on Sunday afternoon without dreaming of hell and the devil all Sunday night is naturally envious of the fellow who can, and being envious of him, he hates him and is eager to destroy his offensive happiness. The farmer who works eighteen hours a day and never gets a day off is envious of his farmhand who goes to the crossroads and barrels up on Saturday afternoon; hence the virulence of prohibition among the peasantry. The hard-working householder who, on some bitter evening, glances over the *Saturday Evening Post* for a square and honest look at his wife is envious of those gaudy drummers who go gallivanting about the country with scarlet girls; hence the Mann act. If these deviltries were equally open to all men, and all men were equally capable of appreciating them, their unpopularity would tend to wither.

I often think, indeed, that the prohibitionist tub-thumpers make a tactical mistake in dwelling too much upon the evils and horrors of alcohol, and not enough upon its delights. A few enlarged photographs of first-class barrooms, showing the rows of well-fed, well-dressed *bibuli* happily moored to the brass rails, their noses in fragrant mint and hops and their hands reaching out for free rations of olives, pretzels, cloves, pumpernickle, Bismarck herring, anchovies, *schwartenmagen,* wieners, Smithfield ham, and dill pickles—such a gallery of contentment would probably do far more execution among the dismal *shudra* than all the current portraits of drunkards' livers. To vote for prohibition in the face of the liver portraits means to vote for the good of the other fellow, for even the oldest bibulomaniac always thinks that he himself will escape. This is an act of altruism almost impossible to the mob-man, whose selfishness is but little corrupted by the imagination that shows itself in his betters. His most austere renunciations represent no more than a matching of the joys of indulgence against the pains of hell; religion, to him, is little more than synthesized fear. . . . I venture that many a vote for prohibition comes from gentlemen who look longingly through swinging doors—and pass on in propitiation of Satan and their alert consorts, the lake of brimstone and the corrective broomstick. . . .

→ CHAPTER SEVEN ←

Stable-Names

Why doesn't some patient drudge of a *Privat Dozent* compile a dictionary of the stable-names of the great? All show dogs and race horses, as everyone knows, have stable-names. On the list of entries a fast mare may appear as Czarina Ogla Fedorovna, but in the stable she is not that at all, nor even Czarina or Olga, but maybe Lil or Jennie. And a prize bulldog, Champion Zoroaster or Charlemagne XI on the bench, may be plain Jack or Ponto *en famille*. So with celebrities of the genus Homo. Huxley's official style and appellation was "The Right Hon. Thomas Henry Huxley, P. C., M. D., Ph. D., LL. D., D. C. L., D. Sc., F. R. S.," and his biographer tells us that he delighted in its rolling grandeur—but to his wife he was always Hal. Shakespeare, to his fellows of his Bankside, was Will, and perhaps Willie to Ann Hathaway. The Kaiser is another Willie: the late Czar so addressed him in their famous exchange of telegrams. The Czar himself was Nicky in those days, and no doubt remains Nicky to his intimates today. Edgar Allan Poe was always Eddie to his wife, and Mark Twain was always Youth to his. P. T. Barnum's stable-name was Taylor, his middle name; Charles Lamb's was Guy; Nietzsche's was Fritz; Whistler's was Jimmie; the late King Edward's was Bertie; Grover Cleveland's was Steve; J. Pierpont Morgan's was Jack; Dr. Wilson's is Tom.

Some given names are surrounded by a whole flotilla of stable-names. Henry, for example, is softened variously into Harry, Hen, Hank, Hal, Henny, Enery, On'ry, and Heinie. Which did Ann Boleyn use when she cooed into the suspicious ear of Henry VIII? To which did Henrik Ibsen answer at the domestic hearth? It is difficult to imagine his wife calling him Henrik: the name is harsh, clumsy, razor-edged. But did she make it Hen or Rik, or neither? What was Bismarck to the Fürstin, and to the mother he so vastly feared? Ottchen? Somehow it seems impossible. What was Grant to his wife? Surely not Ulysses! And Wolfgang Amadeus Mozart? And Rutherford B. Hayes? Was Robert Browning ever Bob? Was John Wesley ever Jack? Was Emmanuel Swendenborg ever Manny? Was Tadeusz Kosciusko ever Teddy?

A fair field of inquiry invites. Let some laborious assistant professor explore and chart it. There will be more of human nature in his report than in all the novels ever written.

→ CHAPTER EIGHT ←

THE JEWS

THE JEWS, LIKE THE AMERICANS, LABOR UNDER A PHILOSOPHICAL dualism, and in both cases it is a theological heritage. On the one hand there is the idealism that is lovely and uplifting and will get a man into heaven, and on the other hand there is the realism that works. The fact that the Jews cling to both, thus running, as it were, upon two tracks, is what makes them so puzzling, now and then, to the *goyim.* In one aspect they stand for the most savage practicality; in another aspect they are dreamers of an almost fabulous otherworldiness. My own belief is that the essential Jew is the idealist—that his occasional flashing of hyena teeth is no more than a necessary concession to the harsh demands of the struggle for existence. Perhaps, in many cases, it is due to an actual corruption of blood. The Jews come from the Levant, and their women were exposed for many centuries to the admiration of Greek, Arab, and Armenian. The shark that a Jew can be at his worst is simply a Greek or Armenian at his best.

As a statement of post-mortem and super-terrestrial fact, the religion that the Jews have foisted upon the world seems to me to be as vast a curse as the influenza that we inherit from the Tatars or the democratic fallacies set afloat by the French Revolution. The one thing that can be said in favor of it is that it is not true, and yet we suffer from it almost as much as if it were true. But with it, encasing it and preserving it, there has come something that is positively valuable—something, indeed, that is beyond all price—and that is Jewish poetry. To compare it to the poetry of any other race is wholly impossible; it stands completely above all the rest; it is as far beyond the next best as German music is beyond French music, or French painting beyond English painting, or the English drama beyond the Italian drama. There are single chapters in the Old Testament that are worth all the poetry ever written in the New World and nine-tenths of that written in the Old. The Jews of those ancient days had imagination, they had dignity, they had ears for sweet sound, they had, above all, the faculty of grandeur. The stupendous music that issued from them has swept their barbaric demonology along with it, setting at naught the collective intelligence of the human species; they embalmed their idiotic taboos and fetishes in undying strains, and so gave them some measure of the same immortality. A race of lawgivers? Bosh! Leviticus is as archaic as the Code of Manu, and the Decalogue is a fossil. A race of seers? Bosh again! The God they saw survives only as a bogeyman, a theory, an uneasy and vexatious ghost. A race of traders and sharpers? Bosh a third time! The Jews are as poor as the Spaniards. But a race of poets, my lords, a race of poets! It is a vision of beauty that has ever haunted them. And it has been their destiny to transmit that vision, enfeebled, perhaps, but still distinct, to other and lesser peoples, that life might be made softer for the sons of men, and the goodness of the Lord God—whoever He may be—might not be forgotten.

→ CHAPTER NINE ←

The Comstockian Premiss

It is argued against certain books, by virtuosi of moral alarm, that they depict vice as attractive. This recalls the king who hanged a judge for deciding that an archbishop was a mammal.

CHAPTER TEN

THE LABIAL INFAMY

AFTER FIVE YEARS OF SEARCH I HAVE BEEN ABLE TO DISCOVER BUT one book in English upon the art of kissing, and that is a very feeble treatise by a savant of York, Pa., Dr. R. McCormick Sturgeon. There may be others, but I have been quite unable to find them. Kissing, for all one hears of it, has not attracted the scientists and literati; one compares its meager literature with the endless books upon the other phenomena of love, especially divorce and obstetrics. Even Dr. Sturgeon, pioneering bravely, is unable to get beyond a sentimental and trivial view of the thing he vivisects, and so his book is no more than a compendium of mush. His very description of the act of kissing is made up of sonorous gabble about heaving bosoms, red lips, electric sparks, and such-like imaginings. What reason have we for believing, as he says, that the lungs are "strongly expanded" during the act? My own casual observation inclines me to hold that the opposite is true that the lungs are actually collapsed in a pseudo-asthmatic spasm. Again, what is the ground for arguing that the lips are "full, ripe and red?" The real effect of the emotions that accompany kissing is to empty the superficial capillaries and so produce a leaden pallor. As for such salient symptoms as the temperature, the pulse and the rate of respiration, the learned pundit passes them over without a word.

Mrs. Elsie Clews Parsons would be a good one to write a sober and accurate treatise upon kissing. Her books upon *The Family* and *Fear and Conventionality* indicate her possession of the right sort of learning. Even better would be a work by Havelock Ellis, say, in three or four volumes. Ellis has devoted his whole life to illuminating the mysteries of sex, and his collection of materials is unsurpassed in the world. Surely there must be an enormous mass of instructive stuff about kissing in his card indexes, letter files, book presses, and archives.

Just why the kiss as we know it should have attained to its present popularity in Christendom is probably one of the things past finding out. The Japanese, a very affectionate and sentimental people, do not practise kissing in any form; they regard the act, in fact, with an aversion matching our own aversion to the rubbing of noses. Nor is it in vogue among the Moslems, nor among the Chinese, who countenance it only as between mother and child. Even in parts of Christendom it is girt about by rigid taboos, so that its practise tends to be restricted to a few occasions. Two Frenchmen or Italians, when they meet, kiss each other on both cheeks. One used to see, indeed, many pictures of General Joffre thus bussing the heroes of Verdun; there even appeared in print a story to the effect that one of them objected to the scratching of his moustache. But imagine two Englishment kissing! Or two Germans! As well imagined the former kissing the latter! Such a display of affection is simply impossible to men of Northern blood; they would die with shame if caught at it. The Englishman, like the American, never kisses if he can help it. He even regards it as bad form to kiss his wife in a railway station, or, in fact, anywhere in sight of a third party. The Latin has no such compunctions. He leaps to the business regardless of place or time; his sole concern is with the lady. Once, in driving from Nice to Monte Carlo along the lower Corniche road, I passed a hundred or so open taxicabs containing man and woman, and fully 75 percent of the men had their arms around their companions, and were kissing them. These were not peasants, remember, but well-to-do persons. In England such a scene would have caused a great scandal; in most American States the police would have charged the offenders with drawn revolvers.

The charm of kissing is one of the things I have always wondered at. I do not pretend, of course, that I have never done it; mere politeness forces one to it; there are women who sulk and grow bellicose unless one at least makes the motions of kissing them. But what I mean is that I have never found the act a tenth part as agreeable as poets, the authors of musical comedy librettos, and (on the contrary side) chaperones and the *gendarmerie* make it out. The physical sensation, far from being pleasant, is intensely uncomfortable—the suspension of respiration, indeed, quickly resolves itself into a feeling of suffocation—and the posture necessitated by the approximation of lips and lips is unfailingly a constrained and ungraceful one. Theoretically, a man kisses a woman perpendicularly, with their eyes, those "windows of the soul," synchronizing exactly. But actually, on account of the incompressibility of the nasal cartilages, he has to incline either his or her head to an angle of at least 60 degrees, and the result is that his right eye gazes insanely at the space between her eyebrows, while his left eye is fixed upon some vague spot behind her. An instantaneous photograph of such a maneuvre, taken at the moment of incidence, would probably turn the stomach of even the most romantic man, and force him, in sheer self-respect, to renounce kissing as he has renounced leap-frog and walking on stilts. Only a woman (for women are quite devoid of aesthetic feeling) could survive so damning a picture.

But the most embarrassing moment, in kissing, does not come during the actual kiss (for at that time the sensation of suffocation drives out all purely psychical feelings), but immediately afterward. What is one to say to the woman then? The occasion obviously demands some sort of remark. One has just received (in theory) a great boon; the silence begins to make itself felt; there stands the fair one, obviously waiting. Is one to thank her? Certainly that would be too transparent a piece of hypocrisy, too flaccid a banality. Is one to tell her that one loves her? Obviously, there is danger in such assurances, and beside, one usually doesn't, and a lie is a lie. Or is one to descend to chatty commonplaces—about the weather, literature, politics, the war? The practical impossibility of solving the problem leads almost inevitably to a blunder far worse than any merely verbal one: one kisses her again, and then again, and so on, and so on. The ultimate result is satiety, repugnance, disgust; even the girl herself gets enough.

CHAPTER ELEVEN

A True Ascetic

Herbert Spencer's objection to swearing, of which so much has been made by moralists, was not an objection to its sinfulness but an objection to its charm. In brief, he feared comfort, satisfaction, joy. The boarding houses in which he dragged out his gray years were as bare and cheerless as so many piano boxes. He avoided all the little vices and dissipations which make human existence bearable: good eating, good drinking, dancing, tobacco, poker, poetry, the theatre, personal adornment, philandering, adultery. He was insanely suspicious of everything that threatened to interfere with his work. Even when that work halted him by the sheer agony of its monotony, and it became necessary for him to find recreation, he sought out some recreation that was as unattractive as possible, in the hope that it would quickly drive him back to work again. Having to choose between methods of locomotion on his holidays, he chose going afoot, the most laborious and least satisfying available. Brought to bay by his human need for a woman, he directed his fancy toward George Eliot, probably the most unappetizing woman of his race and time. Drawn irresistibly to music, he avoided the Fifth Symphony and *Tristan und Isolde,* and joined a crowd of old maids singing part songs around a cottage piano. John Tyndall saw clearly the effect of all this and protested against it, saying, "He'd be a much nicer fellow if he had a good swear now and then"—i.e., if he let go now and then, if he yielded to his healthy human instincts now and then, if he went on some sort of debauch now and then. But what Tyndall overlooked was the fact that the meagreness of his recreations was the very element that attracted Spencer to them. Obsessed by the fear—and it turned out to be well-grounded—that he would not live long enough to complete his work, he regarded all joy as a temptation, a corruption, a sin of scarlet. He was a true ascetic. He could sacrifice all things of the present for one thing of the future, all things real for one thing ideal.

→ CHAPTER TWELVE ←

On Lying

Lying stands on a different plane from all other moral offenses, not because it is intrinsically more heinous or less heinous, but simply because it is the only one that may be accurately measured. Forgetting unwitting error, which has nothing to do with morals, a statement is either true or not true. This is a simple distinction and relatively easy to establish. But when one comes to other derelictions the thing grows more complicated. The line between stealing and not stealing is beautifully vague; whether or not one has crossed it is not determined by the objective act, but by such delicate things as motive and purpose. So again, with assault, sex offenses, and even murder; there may be surrounding circumstances which greatly condition the moral quality of the actual act. But lying is specific, exact, scientific. Its capacity for precise determination, indeed, makes its presence or non-presence the only accurate gauge of other immoral acts. Murder, for example, is nowhere regarded as immoral save it involve some repudiation of a social compact, of a tacit promise to refrain from it—in brief, some deceit, some perfidy, some lie. One may kill freely when the pact is formally broken, as in war. One may kill equally freely when it is broken by the victim, as in an assault by a highwayman. But one may not kill so long as it is not broken, and one may not break it to clear the way. Some form of lie is at the bottom of all other recognized crimes, from seduction to embezzlement. Curiously enough, this master immorality of them all is not prohibited by the Ten Commandments, nor is it penalized, in its pure form, by the code of any civilized nation. Only savages have laws against lying per se.

→ CHAPTER THIRTEEN ←

History

It is the misfortune of humanity that its history is chiefly written by third-rate men. The first-rate man seldom has any impulse to record and philosophise; his impulse is to act; life, to him, is an adventure, not a syllogism or an autopsy. Thus the writing of history is left to college professors, moralists, theorists, dunderheads. Few historians, great or small, have shown any capacity for the affairs they presume to describe and interpret. Gibbon was an inglorious failure as a member of Parliament. Thycydides made such a mess of his military (or, rather, naval) command that he was exiled from Athens for twenty years and finally assassinated. Flavius Josephus, serving as governor of Galilee, lost the whole province to the Romans, and had to flee for his life. Momssen, elected to the Prussian Landtag, flirted with the Socialists. How much better we would understand the habits and nature of man if there were more historians like Julius Caesar, or even like Niccolò Machiavelli! Remembering the sharp and devastating character of their rough notes, think what marvelous histories Bismarck, Washington, and Frederick the Great might have written! Such men are privy to the facts; the usual historians have to depend on deductions, rumors, guesses. Again, such men know how to tell the truth, however unpleasant; they are wholly free of that puerile moral obsession which marks the professor. . . . But they so seldom tell it! Well, perhaps some of them have—and their penalty is that they are damned and forgotten.

CHAPTER FOURTEEN

THE CURSE OF CIVILIZATION

A CIVILIZED MAN'S WORST CURSE IS SOCIAL OBLIGATION. THE MOST unpleasant act imaginable is to go to a dinner party. One could get far better food, taking one day with another, at Childs', or even in a Pennsylvania Railroad dining-car; one could find far more amusing society in a bar-room or a bordello, or even at the Y. M. C. A. No hostess in Christendom ever arranged a dinner party of any pretentions without including at least one intensely disagreeable person—a vain and vapid girl, a hideous woman, a follower of baseball, a stockbroker, a veteran of some war or other, a gabbler of politics. And one is enough to do the business.

→ CHAPTER FIFTEEN ←

EUGENICS

THE ERROR OF THE EUGENISTS LIES IN THE ASSUMPTION THAT A physically healthy man is the best fitted to survive. This is true of rats and the *pediculae,* but not of the higher animals, e.g., horses, dogs, and men. In these higher animals one looks for more subtle qualities, chiefly of the spirit. Imagine estimating philosophers by their chest expansions, their blood pressures, their Wassermann reactions!

The so-called social diseases, over which eugenists raise such a pother, are surely not the worst curses that mankind has to bear. Some of the greatest men in history have had them; whole nations have had them and survived. The truth about them is that, save in relatively rare cases, they do very little damage. The horror in which they are held is chiefly a moral horror, and its roots lie in the assumption that they cannot be contracted without sin. Nothing could be more false. Many great moralists have suffered from them: the gods are always up to such sardonic waggeries.

Moreover, only one of them is actually inheritable, and that one is transmitted relatively seldom. But among psychic characters one finds that practically all are inheritable. For example, stupidity, credulity, avarice, pecksniffery, lack of imagination, hatred of beauty, meanness, poltroonry, petty brutality, smallness of soul. . . . I here present, of course, the Puritan complex; there flashes up the image of the "good man," that libel on God and the devil. Consider him well. If you had to choose a sire for a first-rate son, would you choose a consumptive Jew with the fires of eternity in his eyes, or an Iowa right-thinker with his hold full of Bibles and breakfast food?

CHAPTER SIXTEEN

The Jocose Gods

What humor could be wilder than that of life itself? Franz Schubert, on his deathbed, read the complete works of J. Fenimore Cooper. John Millington Synge wrote *Riders to the Sea* on a second-hand $40 typewriter, and wore a celluloid collar. Richard Wagner made a living, during four lean years, arranging Italian opera arias for the cornet. Herbert Spencer sang bass in a barber-shop quartette and was in love with George Eliot. William Shakespeare was a social pusher and bought him a bogus coat-of-arms. Martin Luther suffered from the jim-jams. One of the greatest soldiers in Hungarian history was named Hunjadi Janos. . . .

CHAPTER SEVENTEEN

War

SUPERFICIALLY, WAR SEEMS INORDINATELY CRUEL AND AND WASTEFUL, and yet it must be plain on reflection that the natural evolutionary process is quite as cruel and even more wasteful. Man's chief efforts in times of peace are devoted to making that process less violent and sanguinary. Civilization, indeed, may be defined as a constructive criticism of nature, and Huxley even called it a conspiracy against nature. Man tries to remedy what must inevitably seem the mistakes and to check what must inevitably seem the wanton cruelty of the Creator. In war man abandons these efforts, and so becomes more jovian. The Greeks never represented the inhabitants of Olympus as succoring and protecting one another, but always as fighting and attempting to destroy one another.

No form of death inflicted by war is one-half so cruel as certain forms of death that are seen in hospitals everyday. Besides, these forms of death have the further disadvantage of being inglorious. The average man, dying in bed, not only has to stand the pains and terrors of death; he must also, if he can bring himself to think of it at all, stand the notion that he is ridiculous. . . . The soldier is at least not laughed at. Even his enemies treat his agonies with respect.

→ CHAPTER EIGHTEEN ←

MORALIST AND ARTIST

I DREDGE UP THE FOLLOWING FROM AN ESSAY ON GEORGE BERNARD Shaw by Robert Blatchford, the English Socialist: "Shaw is something much better than a wit, much better than an artist, much better than a politician or a dramatist; he is a moralist, a teacher of ethics, austere, relentless, fiercely earnest."

What could be more idiotic? Then Cotton Mather was a greater man than Johann Sebastian Bach. Then the average college critic of the arts, with his balderdash about inspiration and moral purpose, is greater than Georg Brandes or Saint-Beuve. Then Éugene Brieux, with his Y. M. C. A. platitudinizing, is greater than Molière, with his ethical agnosticism, his ironical determinism.

This childish respect for moralizing runs through the whole of contemporary criticism—at least in England and America. Blatchford differs from the professorial critics only in the detail that he can actually write. What he says about Shaw has been said, in heavy and suffocating words, by almost all of them. And yet nothing could be more untrue. The moralist, at his best, can never be anything save a sort of journalist. Moral values change too often to have any serious validity or interest; what is a virtue today is a sin tomorrow. But the man who creates a thing of beauty creates something that lasts.

CHAPTER NINETEEN

ACTORS

"IN FRANCE THEY CALL AN ACTOR A *M'AS-TU-VU*, WHICH, ANGLICISED, means a have-you-seen-me? . . . The average actor holds the mirror up to nature and sees in it only the reflection of himself." I take the words from a late book on the so-called art of the mime by the editor of a magazine devoted to the stage. The learned author evades plumbing the psychological springs of this astounding and almost invariable vanity, this endless bumptiousness of the *cabotin* in all climes and all ages. His one attempt is banal: "a foolish public makes much of him." With all due respect, Nonsense! The larval actor is full of hot and rancid gases long before a foolish public has had a fair chance to make anything of him at all, and he continues to emit them long after it has tried him, condemned him and bidden him be damned. There is, indeed, little choice in the virulence of their self-respect between a Broadway star who is slobbered over by press agents and fat women, and the poor ham who plays thinking parts in a No. 7 road company. The two are alike charged to the limit; one more ohm, or molecule, and they would burst. Actors begin where militia colonels, Fifth Avenue rectors and Chautauqua orators leave off. The most modest of them (barring, perhaps, a few unearthly traitors to the craft) matches the conceit of the solitary pretty girl on a slow ship. In their lofty eminence of pomposity they are challenged only by Anglican bishops and grand opera tenors. I have spoken of the danger they run of bursting. In the case of tenors it must sometimes actually happen; even the least of them swells visibly as he sings, and permanently as he grows older. . . .

But why are actors, in general, such blatant and obnoxious asses, such arrant posturers and wind-bags? Why is it as surprising to find an unassuming and likable fellow among them as to find a Greek without fleas? The answer is quite simple. To reach it one needs but consider the type of young man who normally gets stage-struck. Is he, taking averages, the intelligent, alert, ingenious, ambitious young fellow? Is he the young fellow with ideas in him, and a yearning for hard and difficult work? Is he the diligent reader, the hard student, the eager inquirer? No. He is, in the overwhelming main, the neighborhood fop and beau, the human clothes-horse, the nimble squire of dames. The youths of more active mind, emerging from adolescence, turn to business and the professions; the men that they admire and seek to follow are men of genuine distinction, men who have actually done difficult and valuable things, men who have fought good (if often dishonest) fights and are respected and envied by other men. The stage-struck youth is of a softer and more shallow sort. He seeks, not a chance to test his mettle by hard and useful work, but an easy chance to shine. He craves the regard, not of men, but of women. He is, in brief, a hollow and incompetent creature, a strutter and poseur, a popinjay, a pretty one. . . .

I thus beg the question, but explain the actor. He is this silly youngster grown older, but otherwise unchanged. An initiate of a profession requiring little more information, culture or capacity for ratiocination than that of the lady of joy, and surrounded in his workshop by men who are as stupid, as vain and as empty as he himself will be in the years to come, he suffers an arrest of development, and the little intelligence that may happen to be in him gets no chance to show itself. The result, in its usual manifestation, is the average bad actor—a man with the cerebrum of a floor-walker and the vanity of a fashionable clergyman. The result, in its highest and holiest form is the actor-manager, with his retinue of press-agents, parasites and worshipping wenches—perhaps the most preposterous and awe-inspiring donkey that civilization has yet produced. To look for sense in a fellow of such equipment and such a history would be like looking for serviettes in a sailors' boarding-house.

By the same token, the relatively greater intelligence of actresses is explained. They are, at their worst, quite as bad as the generality of actors. There are she-stars who are all temperament and balderdash—intellectually speaking, beggars on horseback, servant girls well washed. But no one who knows anything about the stage need be told that it can show a great many more quick-minded and self-respecting women than intelligent men. And why? Simply because its women are recruited, in the main, from a class much above that which furnishes its men. It is, after all, not unnatural for a woman of considerable intelligence to aspire to the stage. It offers her, indeed, one of the most tempting careers that is open to her. She cannot hope to succeed in business, and in the other professions she is an unwelcome and much-scoffed-at intruder, but on the boards she can meet men on an equal footing. It is, therefore, no wonder that women of a relatively superior class often take to the business. . . . Once they embrace it, their superiority to their male colleagues is quickly manifest. All movements against puerility and imbecility in the drama have originated, not with actors, but with actresses—that is, in so far as they have originated among stage folks at all. The Ibsen pioneers were such women as Helena Modjeska, Agnes Sorma and Janet Achurch; the men all hung back. Ibsen, it would appear, was aware of this superior alertness and took shrewd advantage of it. At all events, his most tempting acting parts are feminine ones.

The girls of the stage demonstrate this tendency against great difficulties. They have to carry a heavy handicap in the enormous number of women who seek the footlights merely to advertise their real profession, but despite all this, anyone who has the slightest acquaintance with stagefolk will testify that, taking one with another, the women have vastly more brains than the men and are appreciably less vain and idiotic. Relatively few actresses of any rank marry actors. They find close communion with the strutting brethren psychologically impossible. Stock-brokers, dramatists and even theatrical managers are greatly to be preferred.

CHAPTER TWENTY

THE CROWD

GUSTAVE LE BON AND HIS SCHOOL, IN THEIR DISCUSSIONS OF THE psychology of crowds, have put forward the doctrine that the individual man, cheek by jowl with the multitude, drops down an intellectual peg or two, and so tends to show the mental and emotional reactions of his inferiors. It is thus that they explain the well-known violence and imbecility of crowds. The crowd, as a crowd, performs acts that many of its members, as individuals, would never be guilty of its average intelligence is very low; it is inflammatory, vicious, idiotic, almost simian. Crowds, properly worked up by skilful demagogues, are ready to believe anything, and to do anything.

Le Bon, I daresay, is partly right, but also partly wrong. His theory is probably too flattering to the average numskull. He accounts for the extravagance of crowds on the assumption that the numskull, along with the superior man, is knocked out of his wits by suggestion—that he, too, does things in association that he would never think of doing singly. The fact may be accepted, but the reasoning raises a doubt. The numskull runs amuck in a crowd, not because he has been inoculated with new rascality by the mysterious crowd influence, but because his habitual rascality now has its only chance to function safely. In other words, the numskull is vicious, but a poltroon. He refrains from all attempts at lynching a cappella, not because it takes suggestion to make him desire to lynch, but because it takes the protection of a crowd to make him brave enough to try it.

What happens when a crowd cuts loose is not quite what Le Bon and his followers describe. The few superior men in it are not straightway reduced to the level of the underlying stone-heads. On the contrary, they usually keep their heads, and often make efforts to combat the crowd action. But the stoneheads are too many for them; the fence is torn down or the blackamoor is lynched. And why? Not because the stoneheads, normally virtuous, are suddenly criminally insane. Nay, but because they are suddenly conscious of the power lying in their numbers—because they suddenly realize that their natural viciousness and insanity may be safely permitted to function.

In other words, the particular swinishness of a crowd is permanently resident in the majority of its members—in all those members, that is, who are naturally ignorant and vicious—perhaps 95 percent. All studies of mob psychology are defective in that they underestimate this viciousness. They are poisoned by the prevailing delusion that the lower orders of men are angels. This is nonsense. The lower orders of men are incurable rascals, either individually or collectively. Decency, self-restraint, the sense of justice, courage—these virtues belong only to a small minority of men. This minority never runs amuck. Its most distinguishing character, in truth, is its resistance to all running amuck. The third-rate man, though he may wear the false whiskers of a first-rate man, may always be detected by his inability to keep his head in the face of an appeal to his emotions. A whoop strips off his disguise.

CHAPTER TWENTY-ONE

An American Philosopher

As for William Jennings Bryan, of whom so much piffle, pro and con, has been written, the whole of his political philosophy may be reduced to two propositions, neither of which is true. The first is the proposition that the common people are wise and honest, and the second is the proposition that all persons who refuse to believe it are scoundrels. Take away the two, and all that would remain of Jennings would be a somewhat greasy bald-headed man with his mouth open.

➔ CHAPTER TWENTY-TWO ⟵

CLUBS

MEN'S CLUBS HAVE BUT ONE INTELLIGIBLE PURPOSE: TO AFFORD asylum to fellows who haven't any girls. Hence their general gloom, their air of lost causes, their prevailing acrimony. No man would ever enter a club if he had an agreeable woman to talk to. This is particularly true of married men. Those of them that one finds in clubs answer to a general description: they have wives too unattractive to entertain them, and yet too watchful to allow them to seek entertainment elsewhere. The bachelors, in the main, belong to two classes: (a) those who have been unfortunate in amour, and are still too sore to show any new enterprise, and (b) those so lacking in charm that no woman will pay any attention to them. Is it any wonder that the men one thus encounters in clubs are stupid and miserable creatures, and that they find their pleasure in such banal sports as playing cards, drinking highballs, shooting pool, and reading the barber-shop weeklies? . . . The day a man's mistress is married one always finds him at his club.

CHAPTER TWENTY-THREE

FIDELIS AD URNUM

DESPITE THE COMMON BELIEF OF WOMEN TO THE CONTRARY, FULLY 95 percent of all married men, at least in America, are faithful to their wives. This, however, is not due to virtue, but chiefly to lack of courage. It takes more initiative and daring to start up an extra-legal affair than most men are capable of. They look and they make plans, but that is as far as they get. Another salient cause of connubial rectitude is lack of means. A mistress costs a great deal more than a wife; in the open market of the world she can get more. It is only the rare man who can conceal enough of his income from his wife to pay for a morganatic affair. And most of the men clever enough to do this are too clever to be intrigued.

I have said that 95 percent of married men are faithful. I believe the real proportion is nearer 99 percent What women mistake for infidelity is usually no more than vanity. Every man likes to be regarded as a devil of a fellow, and particularly by his wife. On the one hand, it diverts her attention from his more genuine shortcomings, and on the other hand it increases her respect for him. Moreover, it gives her a chance to win the sympathy of other women, and so satisfies that craving for martyrdom which is perhaps woman's strongest characteristic. A woman who never has any chance to suspect her husband feels cheated and humiliated. She is in the position of those patriots who are induced to enlist for a war by pictures of cavalry charges, and then find themselves told off to wash the general's underwear.

→ CHAPTER TWENTY-FOUR ←

A THEOLOGICAL MYSTERY

THE MORAL ORDER OF THE WORLD RUNS AGROUND ON HAY FEVER. Of what use is it? Why was it invented? Cancer and hydrophobia, at least, may be defended on the ground that they kill. Killing may have some benign purpose, some esoteric significance, some cosmic use. But hay fever never kills; it merely tortures. No man ever died of it. Is the torture, then, an end in itself? Does it break the pride of strutting, snorting man, and turn his heart to the things of the spirit? Nonsense! A man with hay fever is a natural criminal. He curses the gods, and defies them to kill him. He even curses the devil. Is its use, then, to prepare him for happiness to come—for the vast ease and comfort of convalescence? Nonsense again! The one thing he is sure of, the one thing he never forgets for a moment, is that it will come back again next year.

→ CHAPTER TWENTY-FIVE ←

THE TEST OF TRUTH

THE FINAL TEST OF TRUTH IS RIDICULE. VERY FEW RELIGIOUS dogmas have ever faced it and survived. Huxley laughed the devils out of the Gadarene swine. Dowie's whiskers broke the back of Dowieism. Not the laws of the United States but the mother-in-law joke brought the Mormons to compromise and surrender. Not the horror of it but the absurdity of it killed the doctrine of infant damnation. . . . But the razor edge of ridicule is turned by the tough hide of truth. How loudly the barber-surgeons laughed at Harvey—and how vainly! What clown ever brought down the house like Galileo? Or Columbus? Or Jenner? Or Lincoln? Or Darwin? . . . They are laughing at Nietzsche yet. . . .

→ CHAPTER TWENTY-SIX ←

LITERARY INDECENCIES

THE LOW, GRACELESS HUMOR OF NAMES! ON MY SHELF OF POETRY, arranged by the alphabet, Coleridge and J. Gordon Cooglar are next-door neighbors! Mrs. Hemans is beside Laurence Hope! Walt Whitman rubs elbows with Ella Wheeler Wilcox; Robert Browning with Richard Burton; Rossetti with Cale Young Rice; Shelly with Clinton Scollard; Wordsworth with George E. Woodberry; John Keats with Herbert Kaufman!

Ibsen, on the shelf of dramatists, is between Victor Hugo and Jerome K. Jerome. Sudermann follows Harriet Beecher Stowe. Maeterlinck shoulders Percy Mackaye. Shakespeare is between Sardou and Shaw. Euripides and Clyde Fitch! Upton Sinclair and Sophocles! Aeschylus and F. Anstey! D'Annunzio and Richard Harding Davis! Augustus Thomas and Tolstoi!

More alphabetical humor. Gerhart Hauptmann and Robert Hichens; Voltaire and Henry Van Dyke; Flaubert and John Fox, Jr.; Balzac and John Kendrick Bangs; Ostrovsky and E. Phillips Oppenheim; Elinor Glyn and Théophile Gautier; Joseph Conrad and Robert W. Chambers; Zola and Zangwill! . . .

Midway on my scant shelf of novels, between George Moore and Frank Norris, there is just room enough for the two volumes of *Derringford*, by Frank A. Munsey.

→ CHAPTER TWENTY-SEVEN ←

Virtuous Vandalism

A hearing of Schumann's B flat symphony of late, otherwise a very caressing experience, was corrupted by the thought that music would be much the gainer if musicians could get over their superstitious reverence for the mere text of the musical classics. That reverence, indeed, is already subject to certain limitations; hands have been laid, at one time or another, upon most of the immortal oratorios, and even the awful name of Bach has not dissuaded certain German editors. But it still swathes the standard symphonies like some vast armor of rubber and angel food, and so imagination has to come to the aid of the flutes and fiddles when the band plays Schumann, Mozart, and even parts of Beethoven. One discerns, often quite clearly, what the reverend Master was aiming at, but just as often one fails to hear it in precise tones.

This is particularly true of Schumann, whose deficiency in instrumental cunning has passed into proverb. And in the B flat symphony, his first venture into the epic form, his failures are most numerous. More than once, obviously attempting to roll up tone into a moving climax, he succeeds only in muddling his colors. I remember one place—at the moment I can't recall where it is—where the strings and the brass storm at one another in furious figures. The blast of the brass, as the vaudevillains say, gets across—but the fiddles merely scream absurdly. The whole passage suggests the bleating of sheep in the midst of a vast bellowing of bulls. Schumann overestimated the horsepower of fiddle music so far up the E string—or underestimated the full kick of the trumpets. . . . Other such soft spots are well known.

Why, then, go on parroting *gaucheries* that Schumann himself, were he alive today, would have long since corrected? Why not call an ecumenical council, appoint a commission to see to such things, and then forget the sacrilege? As a self-elected delegate from heathendom, I nominate Dr. Richard Strauss as chairman. When all is said and done, Strauss probably knows more about writing for orchestra than any other two men that ever lived, not excluding Wagner. Surely no living rival, as Dr. Sunday would say, has anything on him. If, after hearing a new composition by Strauss, one turns to the music, one is invariably surprised to find how simple it is. The performance reveals so many purple moments, so staggering an array of lusciousness, that the ear is bemused into detecting scales and chords that never were on land or sea. What the exploratory eye subsequently discovers, perhaps, is no more than our stout and comfortable old friend, the highly well-born *hausfrau,* Mme. C Dur—with a vine leaf or two of C sharp minor or F major in her hair. The trick lies in the tone-color—in the flabbergasting magic of the orchestration. There are some moments in "Elektra" when sounds come out of the orchestra that tug at the very roots of the hair, sounds so unearthly that they suggest a caroling of dragons or *bierfisch*—and yet they are made by the same old fiddles that play the Kaiser Quartet, and by the same old trombones that the Valkyrie ride like witch's broomsticks, and by the same old flutes that sob and snuffle in Tit'l's Serenade. And in parts of "Feuersnot"—but Roget must be rewritten by Strauss before "Feuersnot" is described. There is one place where the harps, taking a running start from the scrolls of the violins, leap slambang through (or is it into?) the firmament of Heaven. Once, when I heard this passage played at a concert, a woman sitting beside me rolled over like a log, and had to be hauled out by the ushers.

Yes; Strauss is the man to reorchestrate the symphonies of Schumann, particularly the B flat, the Rhenish and the Fourth. I doubt that he could do much with Schubert, for Schubert, though he is dead nearly a hundred years, yet remains curiously modern. The Unfinished Symphony is full of exquisite color effects—consider, for example, the rustling figure for the strings in the first movement—and as for the C major, it is so stupendous a debauch of melodic and harmonic beauty that one scarcely notices the colors at all. In its slow movement mere loveliness in music probably says all that will ever be said. . . . But what of old Ludwig? Har, har; here we begin pulling the whiskers of Baal Himself. Nevertheless, I am vandal enough to wonder, on sad Sunday mornings, what Strauss could do with the first movement of the C minor. More, if Strauss ever does it and lets me hear the result just once, I'll be glad to serve six months in jail with him. . . . But in Munich, of course! And with a daily visitor's pass for Cousin Pschorr! . . .

The conservatism which shrinks at such barbarities is the same conservatism which demands that the very typographical errors in the Bible be swallowed without salt, and that has thus made a puerile dream-book of parts of Holy Writ. If you want to see how far this last madness has led Christendom astray, take a look at an article by Abraham Mitrie Rihbany, an intelligent Syrian, in the *Atlantic Monthly* of a couple of years ago. The title of the article is "The Oriental Manner of Speech," and in it Rihbany shows how much of mere Oriental extravagance of metaphor is to be found in many celebrated passages, and how little of literal significance. This Oriental extravagance, of course, makes for beauty, but as interpreted by pundits of no imagination it surely doesn't make for understanding. What the Western World needs is a Bible in which the idioms of the Aramaic of thousands of years ago are translated into the idioms of today. The man who undertook such a translation, to be sure, would be uproariously denounced, just as Luther and Wycliffe were denounced, but he could well afford to face the storm. The various Revised Versions, including the Modern Speech New Testament of Richard Francis Weymouth, leave much to be desired. They rectify many naif blunders and so make the whole narrative more intelligible, but they still render most of the tropes of the original literally.

These tropes are not the substance of Holy Writ; they are simply its color. In the same way mere tone-color is not the substance of a musical composition. Beethoven's Eighth Symphony is just as great a work, in all its essentials, in a four-hand piano arrangement as in the original score. Every harmonic and melodic idea of the composer is there; one can trace just as clearly the subtle processes of his mind; every step in the working out of the materials is just as plain. True enough, there are orchestral compositions of which this cannot be reasonably said; their color is so much more important than their form that when one takes away the former the latter almost ceases to exist. But I doubt that many competent critics would argue that they belong to the first rank. Form, after all, is the important thing. It is design that counts, not decoration—design and organization. The pillars of a musical masterpiece are like the pillars of the Parthenon; they are almost as beautiful bleached white as they were in all their original hues.

→ CHAPTER TWENTY-EIGHT ←

A Footnote on the Duel of Sex

If I were a woman I should want to be a blonde, with golden, silky hair, pink cheeks, and sky-blue eyes. It would not bother me to think that this color scheme was mistaken by the world for a flaunting badge of stupidity; I would have a better arm in my arsenal than mere intelligence; I would get a husband by easy surrender while the brunettes attempted it vainly by frontal assault.

Men are not easily taken by frontal assault; it is only strategem that can quickly knock them down. To be a blonde, pink, soft, and delicate, is to be a strategem. It is to be a ruse, a feint, an ambush. It is to fight under the Red Cross flag. A man sees nothing alert and designing in those pale, crystalline eyes; he sees only something helpless, childish, weak; something that calls to his compassion; something that appeals powerfully to his conceit in his own strength. And so he is taken before he knows that there is a war. He lifts his portcullis in Christian charity—and the enemy is in his citadel.

The brunette can make no such stealthy and sure attack. No matter how subtle her art, she can never hope to quite conceal her intent. Her eyes give her away. They flash and glitter. They have depths. They draw the male gaze into mysterious and sinister recesses. And so the male behind the gaze flies to arms. He may be taken in the end—indeed, he usually is—but he is not taken by surprise; he is not taken without a fight. A brunette has to battle for every inch of her advance. She is confronted by an endless succession of Dead Man's Hills, each equipped with telescopes, semaphores, alarm gongs, wireless. The male sees her clearly through her densest smoke-clouds. . . . But the blonde captures him under a flag of truce. He regards her tenderly, kindly, almost pityingly, until the moment the gyves are upon his wrists.

It is all an optical matter, a question of color. The pastel shades deceive him; the louder hues send him to his artillery. God help, I say, the red-haired girl! She goes into action with warning pennants flying. The dullest, blindest man can see her a mile away; he can catch the alarming flash of her hair long before he can see the whites, or even the terrible red-browns, of her eyes. She has a long field to cross, heavily under defensive fire, before she can get into rifle range. Her quarry has a chance to throw up redoubts, to dig himself in, to call for reinforcements, to elude her by ignominious flight. She must win, if she is to win at all, by an unparalleled combination of craft and resolution. She must be swift, daring, merciless. Even the brunette of black and penetrating eye has great advantages over her. No wonder she never lets go, once her arms are around her antagonist's neck! No wonder she is, of all women, the hardest to shake off!

All nature works in circles. Causes become effects; effects develop into causes. The red-haired girl's dire need of courage and cunning has augmented her store of those qualities by the law of natural selection. She is, by long odds, the most intelligent and bemusing of women. She shows cunning, foresight, technique, variety. She always fails a dozen times before she succeeds; but she brings to the final business the abominable expertness of a Ludendorff; she has learnt painfully by the process of trial and error. Red-haired girls are intellectual stimulants. They know all the tricks. They are so clever that they have even cast a false glamour of beauty about their worst defect—their harsh and gaudy hair. They give it euphemistic and deceitful names—auburn, bronze, Titian. They overcome by their hellish arts that deep-seated dread of red which is inborn in all of God's creatures. They charm men with what would even alarm bulls.

And the blondes, by following the law of least resistance, have gone in the other direction. The great majority of them—I speak, of course, of natural blondes; not of the immoral wenches who work their atrocities under cover of a synthetic blondeness—are quite as shallow and stupid as they look. One seldom hears a blonde say anything worth hearing; the most they commonly achieve is a specious, baby-like prattling, an infantile artlessness. But let us not blame them for nature's work. Why, after all, be intelligent? It is, at best, no more than a capaity for unhappiness. The blonde not only doesn't miss it; she is even better off without it. What imaginable intelligence could compensate her for the flat blueness of her eyes, the xanthous pallor of her hair, the doll-like pink of her cheeks? What conceivable cunning could do such execution as her stupendous appeal to masculine vanity, sentimentality, egoism?

If I were a woman I should want to be a blonde. By blondeness might be hideous, but it would get me a husband, and it would make him cherish me and love me.

CHAPTER TWENTY-NINE

Alcohol

Envy, as I have said, is at the heart of the messianic delusion, the mania to convert the happy sinner into a "good" man, and so make him miserable. And at the heart of that envy is fear—the fear to sin, to take a chance, to monkey with the buzzsaw. This ineradicable fear is the outstanding mark of the fifth-rate man, at all times and everywhere. It dominates his politics, his theology, his whole thinking. He is a moral fellow because he is afraid to venture over the fence—and he hates the man who is not.

The solemn proofs, so laboriously deduced from life insurance statistics, that the man who uses alcohol, even moderately, dies slightly sooner than the teetotaler—these proofs merely show that this man is one who leads an active and vigorous life, and so faces hazards and uses himself up—in brief, one who lives at high tempo and with full joy, what Nietzsche used to call the *ja-sager,* or yes-sayer. He may, in fact, die slightly sooner than the teetotaler, but he lives infinitely longer. Moreover, his life, humanly speaking, is much more worth while, to himself and to the race. He does the hard and dangerous work of the world, he takes the chances, he makes the experiments. He is the soldier, the artist, the innovator, the lover. All the great works of man have been done by men who thus lived joyously, strenuously, and perhaps a bit dangerously.

They have never been concerned about stretching life for two or three more years; they have been concerned about making life engrossing and stimulating and a high adventure while it lasts. Teetotalism is as impossible to such men as any other manifestation of cowardice, and, if it were possible, it would destroy their utility and significance just as certainly.

A man who shrinks from a cocktail before dinner on the ground that it may flabbergast his hormones, and so make him die at 69 years, ten months and five days instead of at 69 years, eleven months and seven days—such a man is as absurd a poltroon as the fellow who shrinks from kissing a woman on the ground that she may floor him with a chair leg. Each flees from a purely theoretical risk. Each is a useless encumberer of the earth, and the sooner dead the better. Each is a discredit to the human race, already discreditable enough, God knows.

Teetotalism does not make for human happiness; it makes for the dull, idiotic happiness of the barnyard. The men who do things in the world, the men worthy of admiration and imitation, are men constitutionally incapable of any such pecksniffian stupidity. Their ideal is not a safe life, but a full life; they do not try to follow the canary bird in a cage, but the eagle in the air. And in particular they do not flee from shadows and bugaboos. The alcohol myth is such a bugaboo. The sort of man it scares is the sort of man whose chief mark is that he is always scared.

No wonder the Rockefellers and their like are hot for saving the workingman from John Barleycorn! Imagine the advantage to them of operating upon a flabby horde of timorous and joyless slaves, afraid of all fun and kicking up, horribly moral, eager only to live as long as possible! What mule-like fidelity and efficiency could be got out of such a rabble! But how many Lincolns would you get out of it, and how many Jacksons, and how many Grants?

CHAPTER THIRTY

Thoughts on the Voluptuous

Why has no publisher ever thought of perfuming his novels? The final refinement of publishing, already bedizened by every other art! Barabbas turned Petronius! For instance, consider the bucolic romances of the hyphenated Mrs. Porter. They have a subtle flavor of new-mown hay and daffodils already; why not add the actual essence, or at all events some safe coal-tar substitute, and so help imagination to spread its wings? For Hall Caine, musk and synthetic bergamot. For Mrs. Glyn and her neighbors on the tiger-skin, the fragrant blood of the red, red rose. For the ruffianish pages of Jack London, the pungent, hospitable smell of a first-class bar-room—that indescribable mingling of Maryland rye, cigar smoke, stale malt liquor, radishes, potato salad and *blutwurst*. For the Dartmoor sagas of the interminable Phillpotts, the warm ammoniacal bouquet of cows, poultry and yokels. For the "Dodo" school, violets and Russian cigarettes. For the venerable Howells, lavender and mignonette. For Zola, Rochefort and wet leather. For Mrs. Humphrey Ward, lilies of the valley. For Marie Corelli, tuberoses and embalming fluid. For Chambers, sachet and lip paint. For——

But I leave you to make your own choices. All I offer is the general idea. It has been tried in the theatre. Well do I remember the first weeks of "Florodora" at the old Casino, with a mannikin in the lobby squirting "La Flor de Florodora" upon all us Florodorans. . . . I was put on trial for my life when I got home!

→ CHAPTER THIRTY-ONE ←

The Holy Estate

Marriage is always a man's second choice. It is entered upon, more often than not, as the safest form of intrigue. The caitiff yields quickest; the man who loves danger and adventure holds out longest. Behind it one frequently finds, not that lofty romantic passion which poets hymn, but a mere yearning for peace and security. The abominable hazards of the high seas, the rough humors and pestilences of the forecastle—these drive the timid mariner ashore. . . . The authentic Cupid, at least in Christendom, was discovered by the late Albert Ludwig Siegmund Neisser in 1879.

CHAPTER THIRTY-TWO

Dichtung und Wahrheit

Deponent, being duly sworn, saith: My taste in poetry is for delicate and fragile things—to be honest, for artificial things. I like a frail but perfectly articulated stanza, a sonnet wrought like ivory, a song full of glowing nouns, verbs, adjectives, adverbs, pronouns, conjunctions, prepositions and participles, but without too much hard sense to it. Poetry, to me, has but two meanings. On the one hand, it is a magical escape from the sordidness of metabolism and the class war, and on the other hand it is a subtle, very difficult and hence very charming art, like writing fugues or mixing mayonnaise. I do not go to poets to be taught anything, or to be heated up to indignation, or to have my conscience blasted out of its torpor, but to be soothed and caressed, to be lulled with sweet sounds, to be wooed into forgetfulness, to be tickled under the metaphysical chin. My favorite poem is Lizette Woodworth Reese's "Tears," which, as a statement of fact, seems to me to be as idiotic as the book of Revelation. The poetry I regard least is such stuff as that of Robert Browning and Matthew Arnold, which argues and illuminates. I dislike poetry of intellectual content as much as I dislike women of intellectual content—and for the same reason.

→ CHAPTER THIRTY-THREE ←

Wild Shots

If I had the time, and there were no sweeter follies offering, I should like to write an essay on the books that have quite failed of achieving their original purposes, and are yet of respectable use and potency for other purposes. For example, the book of Revelation. The obvious aim of the learned author of this work was to bring the early Christians into accord by telling them authoritatively what to expect and hope for; its actual effect during eighteen hundred years has been to split them into a multitude of camps, and so set them to denouncing, damning, jailing and murdering one another. Again, consider the autobiography of Benvenuto Cellini. Ben wrote it to prove that he was an honest man, a mirror of all the virtues, an injured innocent; the world, reading it, hails him respectfully as the noblest, the boldest, the gaudiest liar that ever lived. Again, turn to *Gulliver's Travels*. The thing was planned by its rev. author as a devastating satire, a terrible piece of cynicism; it survives as a storybook for sucklings. Yet again, there is *Hamlet*. Shakespeare wrote it frankly to make money for a theatrical manager; it has lost money for theatrical managers ever since. Yet again, there is Caesar's *De Bello Gallico*. Julius composed it to thrill and arouse the Romans; its sole use today is to stupefy and sicken schoolboys. Finally, there is the celebrated book of General F. von Bernhardi. He wrote it to inflame Germany; its effect was to inflame England. . . .

The list might be lengthened almost ad infinitum. When a man writes a book he fires a machine gun into a wood. The game he brings down often astonishes him, and sometimes horrifies him. Consider the case of Ibsen. . . . After my book on Nietzsche I was actually invited to lecture at Princeton.

CHAPTER THIRTY-FOUR

BEETHOVEN

ROMAIN ROLLAND'S *BEETHOVEN*, ONE OF THE CORNERSTONES OF his celebrity as a critic, is based upon a thesis that is of almost inconceivable inaccuracy, to wit, the thesis that old Ludwig was an apostle of joy, and that his music reveals his determination to experience and utter it in spite of all the slings and arrows of outrageous fortune. Nothing could be more absurd. Joy, in truth, was precisely the emotion that Beethoven could never conjure up; it simply was not in him. Turn to *scherzo* of any of his trios, quartets, sonatas or symphonies. A sardonic waggishness is there, and sometimes even a wistful sort of merriment, but joy in the real sense—a kicking up of legs, a light-heartedness, a complete freedom from care—is not to be found. It is in Haydn, it is in Schubert and it is often in Mozart, but it is no more in Beethoven than it is in Tschaikovsky. Even the hymn to joy at the end of the Ninth symphony narrowly escapes being a gruesome parody on the thing itself; a conscious effort is in every note of it; it is almost as lacking in spontaneity as (if it were imaginable at all) a piece of *vers libre* by Augustus Montague Toplady.

Nay; Ludwig was no leaping buck. Nor was it his deafness, nor poverty, nor the crimes of his rascally nephew that pumped joy out of him. The truth is that he lacked it from birth; he was born a

Puritan—and though a Puritan may also become a great man (as witness Herbert Spencer and Beelzebub), he can never throw off being a Puritan. Beethoven stemmed from the Low Countries, and the Low Countries, in those days, were full of Puritan refugees; the very name, in its first incarnation, may have been Barebones. If you want to comprehend the authentic man, don't linger over Rolland's fancies but go to his own philosophizings, as garnered in *Beethoven, the Man and the Artist,* by Friedrich Kerst, Englished by Krehbiel. Here you will find a collection of moral banalities that would have delighted Jonathan Edwards—a collection that might well be emblazoned on gilt cards and hung in Sunday schools. He begins with a naif anthropomorphism that is now almost perished from the world; he ends with a solemn repudiation of adultery. . . . But a great man, my masters, a great man! We have enough biographies of him, and talmuds upon his works. Who will do a full-length psychological study of him?

➔ CHAPTER THIRTY-FIVE ➔

The Tone Art

The notion that the aim of art is to fix the shifting aspects of nature, that all art is primarily representative—this notion is as unsound as the theory that Friday is an unlucky day, and is dying as hard. One even finds some trace of it in Anatole France, surely a man who should know better. The true function of art is to criticise, embellish and edit nature—particularly to edit it, and so make it coherent and lovely. The artist is a sort of impassioned proof-reader, blue-pencilling the *lapsus calami* of God. The sounds in a Beethoven symphony, even the Pastoral, are infinitely more orderly, varied and beautiful than those of the woods. The worst flute is never as bad as the worst soprano. The best violoncello is immeasurably better than the best tenor.

All first-rate music suffers by the fact that it has to be performed by human beings—that is, that nature must be permitted to corrupt it. The performance one hears in a concert hall or opera house is no more than a baroque parody upon the thing the composer imagined. In an orchestra of eighty men there is inevitably at least one man with a sore thumb, or bad kidneys, or a brutal wife, or *katzenjammer*—and one is enough. Some day the natural clumsiness and imperfection of fingers, lips and larynxes will be overcome by mechanical devices, and we shall have

Beethoven and Mozart and Schubert in such wonderful and perfect beauty that it will be almost unbearable. If half as much ingenuity had been lavished upon music machines as has been lavished upon the telephone and the steam engine, we would have had mechanical orchestras long ago. Mechanical pianos are already here. Piano-players, bound to put some value on the tortures of Czerny, affect to laugh at all such contrivances, but that is no more than a pale phosphorescence of an outraged *wille zur macht.* Setting aside half a dozen—perhaps a dozen—great masters of a moribund craft, who will say that the average mechanical piano is not as competent as the average pianist?

When the human performer of music goes the way of the galley-slave, the charm of personality, of course, will be pumped out of the performance of music. But the charm of personality does not help music; it hinders it. It is not a reinforcement to music; it is a rival. When a beautiful singer comes upon the stage, two shows, as it were, go on at once: first the music show, and then the arms, shoulders, neck, nose, ankles, eyes, hips, calves and ruby lips—in brief, the sex-show. The second of these shows, to the majority of persons present, is more interesting than the first—to the men because of the sex interest, and to the women because of the professional or technical interest—and so music is forced into the background. What it becomes, indeed, is no more than a half-heard accompaniment to an imagined anecdate, just as color, line and mass become mere accomplishments to an anecdote in a picture by an English academician, or by a sentimental German of the Boecklin school.

The purified and dephlogisticated music of the future, to be sure, will never appeal to the mob, which will keep on demanding its chance to gloat over gaudy, voluptuous women, and fat, scandalous tenors. The mob, even disregarding its insatiable appetite for the improper, is a natural hero worshiper. It loves, not the beautiful, but the strange, the unprecedented, the astounding; it suffers from an incurable *héliogabalisme.* A soprano who can gargle her way up to G sharp in altissimo interests it almost as much as a contralto who has slept publicly with a grand duke. If it cannot get the tenor who receives $3,000 a night, it will take the tenor who fought the manager with bung-starters last Tuesday. But this is merely saying that the tastes and desires of the mob have nothing to do with music as an art. For its ears, as for its eyes, it demands anecdotes—on the one hand the Suicide symphony, *The Forge in the Forest,* and the general run of Italian opera, and on the other hand such things as *The Angelus, Playing Grandpa,* and the so-called *Mona Lisa.* It cannot imagine art as devoid of moral content, as beauty pure and simple. It always demands something to edify it, or, failing that, to shock it.

These concepts, of the edifying and the shocking, are closer together in the psyche than most persons imagine. The one, in fact, depends upon the other: without some definite notion of the improving it is almost impossible to conjure up an active notion of the improper. All salacious art is addressed, not to the damned, but to the consciously saved; it is Sunday-school superintendents, not bartenders, who chiefly patronize peep-shows, and know the dirty books, and have a high artistic admiration for sopranos of superior gluteal development. The man who has risen above the petty ethical superstitions of Christendom gets little pleasure out of impropriety, for very few ordinary phenomena seem to him to be improper. Thus a Frenchman, viewing the undraped statues which bedizen his native galleries of art, either enjoys them in a purely aesthetic fashion—which is seldom possible save when he is in liquor—or confesses frankly that he doesn't like them at all; whereas the visiting Americano is so powerfully shocked and fascinated by them that one finds him, the same evening, in places where no respectable man ought to go. All art, to this fellow, must have a certain bawdiness, or he cannot abide it. His favorite soprano, in the opera house, is not the fat and middle-aged lady who can actually sing, but the girl with the bare back and translucent drawers. Condescending to the concert hall, he is bored by the posse of enemy aliens in funereal black, and so demands a vocal soloist—that is, a gaudy creature of such advanced corsetting that she can make him forget Bach for a while, and turn his thoughts pleasantly to amorous intrigue.

In all this, of course, there is nothing new. Other and better men have noted the damage that the personal equation does to music, and some of them have even sought ways out. For example, Richard Strauss. His so-called ballet, "Josefs Legend," produced in Paris just before the war, is an attempt to write an opera without singers. All of the music is in the orchestra; the folks on the stage merely go through a pointless pantomime; their main function is to entertain the eye with shifting colors. Thus, the romantic sentiments of Joseph are announced, not by some eye-rolling tenor, but by the first, second, third, fourth, fifth, sixth, seventh and eighth violins (it is a Strauss score!), with the incidental aid of the woodwind, the brass, the percussion and the rest of the strings. And the heroine's reply is made, not by a soprano with a cold, but by an honest man playing a flute. The next step will be the substitution of marionettes for actors. The removal of the orchestra to a sort of trench, out of sight of the audience, is already an accomplished fact at Munich. The end, perhaps, will be music purged of its current ptomaines. In brief, music.

→ CHAPTER THIRTY-SIX ←

Zoos

I OFTEN WONDER HOW MUCH SOUND AND NOURISHING FOOD IS FED to the animals in the zoological gardens of America every week, and try to figure out what the public gets in return for the cost thereof. The annual bill must surely run into millions; one is constantly hearing how much beef a lion downs at a meal, and how many tons of hay an elephant dispatches in a month. And to what end? To the end, principally, that a horde of superintendents and keepers may be kept in easy jobs. To the end, secondarily, that the least intelligent minority of the population may have an idiotic show to gape at on Sunday afternoons, and that the young of the species may be instructed in the methods of amour prevailing among chimpanzees and become privy to the technic employed by jaguars, hyenas and polar bears in ridding themselves of lice.

So far as I can make out, after laborious visits to all the chief zoos of the nation, no other imaginable purpose is served by their existence. One hears constantly, true enough (mainly from the gentlemen they support) that they are educational. But how? Just what sort of instruction do they radiate, and what is its value? I have never been able to find out. The sober truth is that they are no more educational than so many firemen's parades or displays of sky-rockets, and that all they actually offer to the public in return for the taxes wasted upon them is a form of idle and witless amusement, compared to which a visit to a penitentiary, or even to Congress or a state legislature in session, is informing, stimulating and ennobling.

Education your grandmother! Show me a schoolboy who has ever learned anything valuable or important by watching a mangy old lion snoring away in its cage or a family of monkeys fighting for peanuts. To get any useful instruction out of such a spectacle is palpably impossible; not even a college professor is improved by it. The most it can imaginably impart is that the stripes of a certain sort of tiger run one way and the stripes of another sort some other way, that hyenas and polecats smell worse than Greek 'bus boys, that the Latin name of the raccoon (who was unheard of by the Romans) is *Procyon lotor.* For the dissemination of such banal knowledge, absurdly emitted and defectively taken in, the taxpayers of the United States are mulcted in hundreds of thousands of dollars a year. As well make them pay for teaching policemen the theory of least squares, or for instructing roosters in the laying of eggs.

But zoos, it is argued, are of scientific value. They enable learned men to study this or that. Again the facts blast the theory. No scientific discovery of any value whatsoever, even to the animals themselves, has ever come out of a zoo. The zoo scientist is the old woman of zoology, and his alleged wisdom is usually exhibited, not in the groves of actual learning, but in the yellow journals. He is to biology what the late Camille Flammarion was to astronomy, which is to say, its court jester and reductio ad absurdum. When he leaps into public notice with some new pearl of knowledge, it commonly turns out to be no more than the news that Marie Bashkirtseff, the Russian lady walrus, has had her teeth plugged with zinc and is expecting twins. Or that Pishposh, the man-eating alligator, is down with locomotor ataxia. Or that Damon, the grizzly, has just finished his brother Pythias in the tenth round, chewing off his tail, nose and remaining ear.

Science, of course, has its uses for the lower animals. A diligent study of their livers and lights helps to an understanding of the anatomy and physiology, and particularly of the pathology, of man. They are necessary aids in devising and manufacturing many remedial agents, and in testing the virtues of those already devised; out of the mute agonies of a rabbit or a calf may come relief for a baby with diphtheria, or means for an archdeacon to escape the consequences of his youthful follies. Moreover, something valuable is to be got out of a mere study of their habits, instincts and ways of mind—knowledge that, by analogy, may illuminate the parallel doings of the *genus homo,* and so enable us to comprehend the primitive mental processes of Congressmen, morons and the rev. clergy.

But it must be obvious that none of these studies can be made in a zoo. The zoo animals, to begin with, provide no material for the biologist; he can find out no more about their insides than what he discerns from a safe distance and through the bars. He is not allowed to try his germs and specifics upon them; he is not allowed to vivisect them. If he would find out what goes on in the animal body under this condition or that, he must turn from the inhabitants of the zoo to the customary guinea pigs and street dogs, and buy or steal them for himself. Nor does he get any chance for profitable inquiry when zoo animals die (usually of lack of exercise or ignorant doctoring), for their carcasses are not handed to him for autopsy, but at once stuffed with gypsum and excelsior and placed in some museum.

Least of all do zoos produce any new knowledge about animal behavior. Such knowledge must be got, not from animals penned up and tortured, but from animals in a state of nature. A college professor studying the habits of the giraffe, for example, and confining his observations to specimens in zoos, would inevitably come to the conclusion that the giraffe is a sedentary and melancholy beast, standing immovable for hours at a time and employing an Italian to feed him hay and cabbages. As well proceed to a study of the psychology of a juris-consult by first immersing him in Sing Sing, or of a juggler by first cutting off his hands. Knowledge so gained is inaccurate and imbecile knowledge. Not even a college professor, if sober, would give it any faith and credit.

There remains, then, the only true utility of a zoo: it is a childish and pointless show for the unintelligent, in brief, for children, nursemaids, visiting yokels and the generality of the defective. Should the taxpayers be forced to sweat millions for such a purpose? I think not. The sort of man who likes to spend his time watching a cage of monkeys chase one another, or a lion gnaw its tail, or a lizard catch flies, is precisely the sort of man whose mental weakness should be combatted at the public expense, and not fostered. He is a public liability and a public menace, and society should seek to improve him. Instead of that, we spend a lot of money to feed his degrading appetite and further paralyze his mind. It is precisely as if the community provided free champagne for dipsomaniacs, or hired lecturers to convert the army to the doctrines of the Bolsheviki.

Of the abominable cruelties practised in zoos it is unnecessary to make mention. Even assuming that all the keepers are men of delicate natures and ardent zoophiles (which is about as safe as assuming that the keepers of a prison are all sentimentalists, and weep for the sorrows of their charges), it must be plain that the work they do involves an endless war upon the native instincts of the animals, and that they must thus inflict the most abominable tortures every day. What could be a sadder sight than a tiger in a cage, save it be a forest monkey climbing dispairingly up a barked stump, or an eagle chained to its roost? How can man be benefited and made better by robbing the seal of its arctic ice, the hippopotamus of its soft wallow, the buffalo of its open range, the lion of its kingship, the birds of their air?

I am no sentimentalist, God knows. I am in favor of vivisection unrestrained, so long as the vivisectionist knows what he is about. I advocate clubbing a dog that barks unnecessarily, which all dogs do. I enjoy hangings, particularly of converts to the evangelical faiths. The crunch of a cockroach is music to my ears. But when the day comes to turn the prisoners of the zoo out of their cages, if it is only to lead them to the swifter, kinder knife of the *schochet,* I shall be present and rejoicing, and if any one present thinks to suggest that it would be a good plan to celebrate the day by shooting the whole zoo faculty, I shall have a revolver in my pocket and a sound eye in my head.

CHAPTER THIRTY-SEVEN

On Hearing Mozart

The only permanent values in the world are truth and beauty, and of these it is probable that truth is lasting only in so far as it is a function and manifestation of beauty—a projection of feeling in terms of idea. The world is a charnel house of dead religions. Where are all the faiths of the middle ages, so complex and yet so precise? But all that was essential in the beauty of the middle ages still lives. . . .

This is the heritage of man, but not of men. The great majority of men are not even aware of it. Their participation in the progress of the world, and even in the history of the world, is infinitely remote and trivial. They live and die, at bottom, as animals live and die. The human race, as a race, is scarcely cognizant of their existence; they haven't even definite number, but stand grouped together as *x*, the quantity unknown . . . and not worth knowing.

CHAPTER THIRTY-EIGHT

THE ROAD TO DOUBT

THE FIRST EFFECT OF WHAT USED TO BE CALLED NATURAL PHILOSOPHY is to fill its devotee with wonder at the marvels of God. This explains why the pursuit of science, so long as it remains superficial, is not incompatible with the most naïve sort of religious faith. But the moment the student of the sciences passes this stage of childlike amazement and begins to investigate the inner workings of natural phenomena, he begins to see how ineptly many of them are managed, and so he tends to pass from awe of the Creator to criticism of the Creator, and once he has crossed that bridge he has ceased to be a believer. One finds plenty of neighborhood physicians, amateur botanists, high-school physics teachers and other such quasi-scientists in the pews on Sunday, but one never sees a Huxley there, or a Darwin, or an Ehrlich.

CHAPTER THIRTY-NINE

A New Use for Churches

The argument by design, it may be granted, establishes a reasonable ground for accepting the existence of God. It makes belief, at all events, quite as intelligible as unbelief. But when the theologians take their step from the existence of God to the goodness of God they tread upon much less firm earth. How can one see any proof of that goodness in the senseless and intolerable sufferings of man—his helplessness, the brief and troubled span of his life, the inexplicable disproportion between his deserts and his rewards, the tragedy of his soaring aspiration, the worse tragedy of his dumb questioning? Granting the existence of God, a house dedicated to Him naturally follows. He is all-important; it is fit that man should take some notice of Him. But why praise and flatter him for his unspeakable cruelties? Why forget so supinely His failures to remedy the easily remediable? Why, indeed, devote the churches exclusively to worship? Why not give them over, now and then, to justifiable indignation meetings?

Perhaps men will incline to this idea later on. It is not inconceivable, indeed, that religion will one day cease to be a poltroonish acquiescence and become a vigorous and insistent criticism. If God can hear a petition, what ground is there for holding that He would not hear a complaint? It might, indeed, please Him to find

His creatures grown so self-reliant and reflective. More, it might even help Him to get through His infinitely complex and difficult work. Theology has already moved toward such notions. It has abandoned the primitive doctrine of God's arbitrariness and indifference, and substituted the doctrine that He is willing, and even eager, to hear the desires of His creatures—i.e., their private notions, born of experience, as to what would be best for them. Why assume that those notions would be any the less worth hearing and heeding if they were cast in the form of criticism, and even of denunciation? Why hold that the God who can understand and forgive even treason could not understand and forgive remonstrance?

→ CHAPTER FORTY ←

The Root of Religion

The idea of literal truth crept into religion relatively late: it is the invention of lawyers, priests and cheese-mongers. The idea of mystery long preceded it, and at the heart of that idea of mystery was an idea of beauty—that is, an idea that this or that view of the celestial and infernal process presented a satisfying picture of form, rhythm and organization. Once this view was adopted as satisfying, its professional interpreters and their dupes sought to reinforce it by declaring it true. The same flow of reasoning is familiar on lower planes. The average man does not get pleasure out of an idea because he thinks it is true; he thinks it is true because he gets pleasure out of it.

CHAPTER FORTY-ONE

FREE WILL

FREE WILL, IT APPEARS, IS STILL A CHRISTIAN DOGMA. WITHOUT IT the cruelties of God would strain faith to the breaking-point. But outside the fold it is gradually falling into decay. Such men of science as George W. Crile and Jacques Loeb have dealt it staggering blows, and among laymen of inquiring mind it seems to be giving way to an apologetic sort of determinism—a determinism, one may say, tempered by defective observation. The late Mark Twain, in his secret heart, was such a determinist. In his *What Is Man?* you will find him at his farewells to libertarianism. The vast majority of our acts, he argues, are determined, but there remains a residuum of free choices. Here we stand free of compulsion and face a pair or more of alternatives, and are free to go this way or that.

A pillow for free will to fall upon—but one loaded with disconcerting brickbats. Where the occupants of this last trench of libertarianism err is in their assumption that the pulls of their antagonistic impulses are exactly equal—that the individual is absolutely free to choose which one he will yield to. Such freedom, in practise, is never encountered. When an individual confronts alternatives, it is not alone his volition that chooses between them, but also his environment, his inherited prejudices, his race, his color, his condition of servitude. I may kiss a girl or I may not kiss her, but surely it would be absurd to say that I am, in any true sense, a free agent in the matter. The world has even put my helplessness into a proverb. It says that my decision and act depend upon the time, the place—and even to some extent, upon the girl.

Examples might be multiplied ad infinitum. I can scarcely remember performing a wholly voluntary act. My whole life, as I look back upon it, seems to be a long series of inexplicable accidents, not only quite unavoidable, but even quite unintelligible. Its history is the history of the reactions of my personality to my environment, of my behavior before external stimuli. I have been no more responsible for that personality than I have been for that environment. To say that I can change the former by a voluntary effort is as ridiculous as to say that I can modify the curvature of the lenses of my eyes. I know, because I have often tried to change it, and always failed. Nevertheless, it has changed. I am not the same man I was in the last century. But the gratifying improvements so plainly visible are surely not to be credited to me. All of them came from without—or from unplumbable and uncontrollable depths within.

The more the matter is examined the more the residuum of free will shrinks and shrinks, until in the end it is almost impossible to find it. A great many men, of course, looking at themselves, see it as something very large; they slap their chests and call themselves free agents, and demand that God reward them for their virtue. But these fellows are simply idiotic egoists, devoid of a critical sense. They mistake the acts of God for their own acts. Of such sort are the coxcombs who boast about wooing and winning their wives. They are brothers to the fox who boasted that he had made the hounds run. . . .

The throwing overboard of free will is commonly denounced on the ground that it subverts morality and makes of religion a mocking. Such pious objections, of course, are foreign to logic, but nevertheless it may be well to give a glance to this one. It is based upon the fallacious hypothesis that the determinist escapes, or hopes to escape, the consequences of his acts. Nothing could be more untrue. Consequences follow acts just as relentlessly if the latter be involuntary as if they be voluntary. If I rob a bank of my free choice or in response to some unfathomable inner necessity, it is all one; I will go to the same jail. Conscripts in war are killed just as often as volunteers. Men who are tracked down and shanghaied by their wives have just as hard a time of it as men who walk fatuously into the trap by formally proposing.

Even on the ghostly side, determinism does not do much damage to theology. It is no harder to believe that a man will be damned for his involuntary acts than it is to believe that he will be damned for his voluntary acts, for even the supposition that he is wholly free does not dispose of the massive fact that God made him as he is, and that God could have made him a saint if He had so desired. To deny this is to flout omnipotence—a crime at which, as I have often said, I balk. But here I begin to fear that I wade too far into the hot waters of the sacred sciences, and that I had better retire before I lose my hide. This prudent retirement is purely deterministic. I do not ascribe it to my own sagacity; I ascribe it wholly to that singular kindness which fate always shows me. If I were free I'd probably keep on, and then regret it afterward.

→ CHAPTER FORTY-TWO ←

Quid est Veritas?

All great religions, in order to escape absurdity, have to admit a dilution of agnosticism. It is only the savage, whether of the African bush or the American gospel tent, who pretends to know the will and intent of God exactly and completely. "For who hath known the mind of the Lord?" asked Paul of the Romans. "How unsearchable are his judgments, and his ways past finding out!" "It is the glory of God," said Solomon, "to conceal a thing." "Clouds and darkness," said David, "are around him." "No man," said the Preacher, "can find out the work of God." . . . The difference between religions is a difference in their relative content of agnosticism. The most satisfying and ecstatic faith is almost purely agnostic. It trusts absolutely without professing to know at all.

CHAPTER FORTY-THREE

The Doubter's Reward

Despite the common delusion to the contrary the philosophy of doubt is far more comforting than that of hope. The doubter escapes the worst penalty of the man of hope; he is never disappointed, and hence never indignant. The inexplicable and irremediable may interest him, but they do not enrage him, or, I may add, fool him. This immunity is worth all the dubious assurances ever foisted upon man. It is pragmatically impregnable. . . . Moreover, it makes for tolerance and sympathy. The doubter does not hate his opponents; he sympathizes with them. In the end, he may even come to sympathize with God. . . . The old idea of fatherhood here submerges in a new idea of brotherhood. God, too, is beset by limitations, difficulties, broken hopes. Is it disconcerting to think of Him thus? Well, it is any the less disconcerting to think of Him as able to ease and answer, and yet failing? . . .

But he that doubteth—*damnatus est.* At once the penalty of doubt—and its proof, excuse and genesis.

CHAPTER FORTY-FOUR

BEFORE THE ALTAR

A SALIENT OBJECTION TO THE PREVAILING RELIGIOUS CEREMONIAL lies in the attitudes of abasement that it enforces upon the faithful. A man would be thought a slimy and knavish fellow if he approached any human judge or potentate in the manner provided for approaching the Lord God. It is an etiquette that involves loss of self-respect, and hence it cannot be pleasing to its object, for one cannot think of the Lord God as sacrificing decent feelings to mere vanity. This notion of abasement, like most of the other ideas that are general in the world, is obviously the invention of small and ignoble men. It is the pollution of theology by the *sklavmoral.*

→ CHAPTER FORTY-FIVE ←

The Mask

RITUAL IS TO RELIGION WHAT THE MUSIC OF AN OPERA IS TO THE libretto: ostensibly a means of interpretation, but actually a means of concealment. The Presbyterians made the mistake of keeping the doctrine of infant damnation in plain words. As enlightenment grew in the world, intelligence and prudery revolted against it, and so it had to be abandoned. Had it been set to music it would have survived—uncomprehended, unsuspected and unchallenged.

CHAPTER FORTY-SIX

PIA VENEZIANI, POI CRISTIANI

I HAVE SPOKEN OF THE POSSIBILITY THAT GOD, TOO, MAY SUFFER from a finite intelligence, and so know the bitter sting of disappointment and defeat. Here I yielded something to politeness; the thing is not only possible, but obvious. Like man, God is deceived by appearances and probabilities; He makes calculations that do not work out; He falls into specious assumptions. For example, He assumed that Adam and Eve would obey the law in the Garden. Again, He assumed that the appalling lesson of the Flood would make men better. Yet again, He assumed that men would always put religion in first place among their concerns—that it would be eternally possible to reach and influence them through it. This last assumption was the most erroneous of them all. The truth is that the generality of men have long since ceased to take religion seriously. When we encounter one who still does so, he seems eccentric, almost feeble-minded—or, more commonly, a rogue who has been deluded by his own hypocrisy. Even men who are professionally religious, and who thus have far more incentive to stick to religion than the rest of us, nearly always throw it overboard at the first serious temptation. During the past four years, for example, Christianity has been in combat with patriotism all over Christendom. Which has prevailed? How many gentlemen of God, having to choose between Christ and Patrie, have actually chosen Christ?

CHAPTER FORTY-SEVEN

Off Again, on Again

The ostensible object of the Reformation, which lately reached its fourth centenary, was to purge the Church of imbecilities. That object was accomplished; the Church shook them off. But imbecilities make an irresistible appeal to man; he inevitably tries to preserve them by cloaking them with religious sanctions. The result is Protestantism.

CHAPTER FORTY-EIGHT

THEOLOGY

THE NOTION THAT THEOLOGY IS A DULL SUBJECT IS ONE OF THE strangest delusions of a stupid and uncritical age. The truth is that some of the most engrossing books ever written in the world are full of it. For example, the Gospel according to St. Luke. For example, Nietzsche's *Der Antichrist.* For example, Mark Twain's *What Is Man?*, St. Augustine's *Confessions*, Haeckel's *The Riddle of the Universe,* and Huxley's *Essays.* How, indeed, could a thing be dull that has sent hundreds of thousands of men—the very best and the very worst of the race—to the gallows and the stake, and made and broken dynasties, and inspired the greatest of human hopes and enterprises, and embroiled whole continents in war? No, theology is not a soporific. The reason it so often seems so is that its public exposition has chiefly fallen, in these later days, into the hands of a sect of intellectual castrati, who begin by mistaking it for a sub-department of etiquette, and then proceed to anoint it with butter, rose water and talcum powder. Whenever a first-rate intellect tackles it, as in the case of Huxley, or in that of Leo XIII, it at once takes on all the sinister fascination it had in Luther's day.

CHAPTER FORTY-NINE

Exempli Gratia

Do I let the poor suffer, and consign them, as old Friedrich used to say, to statistics and the devil? Well, so does God.

The American Credo

Preface to the Revised and Enlarged Edition

This edition embodies a number of changes, some of omission and some of addition. The imperfections of the original work were obvious to us when we sent it forth, and we are very grateful to those scholars at home and abroad who have contributed so generously to its improvement. In particular, we owe a large debt to Mr. Aubrey Donaldson, M. A., Reader in Comparative Mythology at Oxford, and to Prof. Dr. Gustav Simmelmeyer, of the University of Zürich. Dr. Simmelmeyer printed a long and very learned review of the work in the *Schweizerisches Archiv für Volkskunde,* and it was instrumental in establishing pleasant contacts with distinguished folk-lorists in various European countries, notably Dr. Arnold Letkow of Berlin, Prof. Ledoux of the Sorbonne, Dr. Enrico Forelli of Turin, and Prof. Mendoza of Salamanca, editor of the well-known *Biblioteca de las tradiciones españolas.* Prof. Mendoza was good enough to say that the book showed a revolutionary point of departure in the study of the origin and growth of myths, and to propose that a series of volumes upon the same plan be undertaken by European savants, each dealing with his own country. This proposal has met with a response in Sweden, where Dr. Gothemann, lecturer upon Oral Literatures at Upsala, has undertaken a Swedish work of like character, and in Germany, where various articles dealing with German popular beliefs in the same manner have been printed in the *Beiträge zur Volks- und Völkerkunde,* chiefly from the able pens of Prof. Kuno Goertz and Baron Hereward von Albrechtsein. We are also informed that a Bulgarian ethnologist has undertaken a collection, and that a monograph upon Italian folk-history, by Prof. Forelli, is soon to be published in the *Archivio per lo studio delle tradizioni populari* of Palermo.

From observers nearer home we have received a great deal of aid. In fact, it would fill several pages merely to print the names of those who have kindly favoured us with additions to our collection, and with criticisms of the matter already printed. In the case of the latter we have found it necessary to make few changes. The first edition was incomplete, but we believe that, in the main, it was accurate. In conclusion we have to offer our thanks to the authorities of the Smithsonian Institution and to various members of the American Folk-Lore Society and the American Anthropological Association for important suggestions. Some of the material, of course, is in a state of flux; as the years pass popular beliefs change. We hope, at intervals, to revise the book, and we shall be grateful for contributions and criticisms.

G.J.N.
H.L.M.
New York, January 1, 1922

Preface to the First Edition

I

The superficial, no doubt, will mistake this little book for a somewhat laborious attempt at jocosity. Because, incidentally to its main purpose, it unveils occasional ideas of so inordinate an erroneousness that they verge upon the ludicrous, it will be set down a piece of spoofing, and perhaps denounced as in bad taste. But all the while that main purpose will remain clear enough to the judicious. It is, in brief, the purpose of clarifying the current exchange of rhetorical gas-bombs upon the subject of American ideals and the American character, so copious, so cocksure and withal so ill-informed and inconclusive, by putting into plain propositions some of the notions that lie at the heart of those ideals and enter into the very substance of that character. "For as he thinketh in his heart," said Solomon, "so *is* he." It is a saying, obviously, that one may easily fill with fantastic meanings, as the prevailing gabble of the mental healers, New Thoughters, efficiency engineers, professors of scientific salesmanship and other such mountebanks demonstrates, but nevertheless it is one grounded, at bottom, upon an indubitable fact. Deep down in every man there is a body of congenital attitudes, a corpus of ineradicable doctrines and ways of thinking, that determines his reactions to his ideational environment as surely as his physical activity is determined by the length of his *tibiæ* and the capacity of his lungs. These primary attitudes, in fact, constitute the essential man. It is by recognition of them that one arrives at an accurate understanding of his place and function as a member of human society; it is by a shrewd reckoning and balancing of them, one against another, that one forecasts his probable behaviour in the face of unaccustomed stimuli.

All the arts and sciences that have to do with the management of men in the mass are founded upon a proficient practice of that sort of reckoning. The practical politician, as every connoisseur of ochlocracy knows, is not a man who seeks to inoculate the innumerable caravan of voters with new ideas; he is a man who seeks to search out and prick into energy the basic ideas that are already in them, and to turn the resultant effervescence of emotion to his own uses. And so with the religious teacher, the social and economic reformer, and every other variety of popular educator, down to and including the humblest press-agent of a fifth assistant Secretary of State, moving-picture actor, or Y. M. C. A. boob-squeezing committee. Such adept professors of conviction and enthusiasm, in the true sense, never actually teach anything new; all they do is to give new forms to beliefs already in being, to arrange the bits of glass, onyx, horn, ivory, porphyry and corundum in the mental kaleidoscope of the populace into novel permutations. To change the figure, they may give the medulla oblongata, the cerebral organ of the great masses of simple men, a powerful diuretic or emetic, but they seldom, if ever, add anything to its primary supply of fats, proteids and carbohydrates.

One speaks of the great masses of simple men, and it is of them, of course, that the ensuing treatise chiefly has to say. The higher and more delicately organized tribes and sects of men are susceptible to no such ready anatomizing, for the body of beliefs upon which their ratiocination grounds itself is not fixed but changing, and not artless and crystal-clear but excessively complex and obscure. It is, indeed, the chief mark of a man emerged from the general that he has lost most of his original certainties, and is full of a scepticism which plays like a spray of acid upon all the ideas that come within his purview, including especially his own. One does not become surer as one advances in knowledge, but less sure. No article of faith is proof against the disintegrating effects of increasing information; one might almost describe the acquirement of knowledge as a process of disillusion. But among the humbler ranks of men who make up the great bulk of every civilized people the increase of information is so slow and so arduous that this effect is scarcely to be discerned. If, in the course of long years, they gradually lose their old faiths, it is only to fill the gaps with new faiths that restate the old ones in new terms. Nothing, in fact, could be more commonplace than the observation that the crazes which periodically ravage the proletariat today are, in the main, no more than distorted echoes of delusions cherished centuries ago. The fundamental religious ideas of the lower orders of Christendom have not changed materially in two thousand years, and they were old when they were first borrowed from the heathen of northern Africa and Asia Minor. The Iowa Methodist of today, imagining him competent to understand them at all, would be able to accept the tenets of Augustine without changing more than a few accents and punctuation marks. Every Sunday his raucous ecclesiastics batter his ears with diluted and debased filches from *De Civitate Dei,* and almost every article of his practical ethics may be found clearly stated in the eminent bishop's Ninety-third Epistle. And so in politics. The Bolsheviki of the present not only poll-parrot the balderdash of the French demagogues of 1789; they also mouth what was gospel to every *bête blonde* in the Teutonic forest of the fifth century. Truth shifts and changes like a cataract of diamonds; its aspect is never precisely the same at two successive instants. But error flows down the channel of history like some great stream of lava or infinitely lethargic glacier. It is the one relatively fixed thing in a world of chaos. It is, perhaps, the one thing that gives human society the small stability that it needs, amid all the oscillation of a gelatinous cosmos, to save it from the wreck that ever menaces. Without their dreams men would have fallen upon and devoured one another long ago—and yet every dream is an illusion, and every illusion is a lie.

Nevertheless, this immutability of popular ideas is not quite perfect. The main current, no doubt, goes on unbrokenly, but there are many eddies along the edges and many small tempests on the surface. Thus the aspect changes, if not the substance. What men believe in one century is apparently abandoned in some other century, and perhaps supplanted by something quite to the contrary. Or, at all events, to the contrary in appearance. Off goes the head of the king, and tyranny gives way to freedom. The change seems abysmal. Then, bit by bit, the face of freedom hardens, and by and by it is the old face of tyranny. Then another cycle, and another. But under the play of all these opposites there is something fundamental and permanent—the basic delusion that men may be governed and yet be free. It is only on the surface that there are transformations—and these we must study and make the most of, for of what is underneath men are mainly unconscious. The thing that colours the upper levels is largely the instinctive functioning of race and nationality, the ineradicable rivalry of tribe and tribe, the primary struggle for existence. At bottom, no doubt, the plain men of the whole world are almost indistinguishably alike; a learned anthropologist, Prof. Dr. Boas, has written a book to prove it. But, collected into herds, they gather delusions that are special to herds. Beside the underlying mass thinking there is a superimposed group thinking—a sort of unintelligent class consciousness. This we may prod into. This, in the case of the *Homo americanus,* is what is prodded into in the present work. We perform, it seems to us, a useful pioneering.

Incomplete though our data may be, it is at least grounded upon a resolute avoidance of a priori methods, an absolutely open-minded effort to get at the facts. We pounce upon them as they bob up, convinced that even the most inconsiderable of them may have its profound significance—that the essential may be hidden in the trivial. All we aim at is a first marshalling of materials, an initial running of lines. We are not architects, but furnishers of bricks, nails and laths. But it is our hope that what we thus rake up and pile into a rough heap may yet serve the purposes of an organizer, and so help toward the establishment of the dim and vacillating truth, and rid the scene of, at all events, the worst and most obvious of its present accumulation of errors.

II

In the case of the American of the multitude that accumulation of errors is of astounding bulk and consequence. His ideas are not only grossly misapprehended by all foreigners; they are often misapprehended by his own countrymen of superior education, and even by himself.

This last, at first blush, may seem a mere effort at paradox, but its literal truth becomes patent on brief inspection. Ask the average American what is the salient passion in his emotional armamentarium—what is the idea that lies at the bottom of all his other ideas—and it is very probable that, nine times out of ten, he will nominate his hot and unquenchable rage for liberty. He regards himself, indeed, as the chief exponent of liberty in the whole world, and all its other advocates as no more than his followers, half timorous and half envious. To question his ardour is to insult him as grievously as if one questioned the honour of the republic or the chastity of his wife. And yet it must be plain to any dispassionate observer that this ardour, in the course of a century and a half, has lost a large part of its old burning reality and descended to the estate of a mere phosphorescent superstition. The American of today, in fact, probably enjoys less personal liberty than any other man of Christendom, and even his political liberty is fast succumbing to the new dogma that certain theories of government are virtuous and lawful and others abhorrent and felonious. Laws limiting the radius of his free activity multiply year by year: it is now practically impossible for him to exhibit anything describable as genuine individuality, either in action or in thought, without running afoul of some harsh and unintelligible penalty. It would surprise no impartial observer if the motto, *In God we trust,* were one day expunged from the coins of the republic by the Junkers at Washington, and the far more appropriate word, *Verboten,* substituted. Nor would it astound any save the most romantic if, at the same time, the goddess of liberty were taken off the silver dollars to make room for a bas relief of a policeman in a spiked helmet.

Moreover, this gradual (and, of late, rapidly progressive) decay of freedom goes almost without challenge; the American has grown so accustomed to the denial of his constitutional rights and to the minute regulation of his conduct by swarms of spies, letter-openers, informers and *agents provocateurs* that he no longer makes any serious protest. It is surely a significant fact that, in the face of the late almost incredible proceedings under the so-called Espionage Act and other such laws, the only objections heard of came either from the persons directly affected—nine-tenths of them Socialists, pacifists, or citizens accused of German sympathies, and hence without any rights whatever in American law and equity—or from a small group of professional libertarians, chiefly naturalized aliens. The American people, as a people, acquiesced docilely in all these tyrannies, both during the war and after the war, just as they acquiesced in the invasion of their common rights by the Prohibition Amendment. Worse, they not only acquiesced docilely; they approved actively; they were quite as hotly against the few protestants as they were against the original victims, and gave their hearty approbation to every proposal that the former be punished too. The really startling phenomenon of the war, indeed, was not the grotesque abolition of liberty in the name of liberty, but the failure of that usurpation to arouse anything approaching public indignation. It is impossible to imagine the men of Jackson's army or even of Grant's army submitting to any such absolutism without a furious struggle, but in these latter days it is viewed with the utmost complacency. The descendants of the Americans who punished John Adams so melodramatically for the Alien and Seditions Acts of 1789 failed to raise a voice against the far more drastic legislation of 1917. What is more, they failed to raise a voice against its execution upon the innocent as well as upon the guilty, in gross violation of the most elemental principles of justice and rules of law.

Thus the Americano, put to the test, gave the lie to what is probably his proudest boast, and revealed the chronic human incapacity for accurate self-analysis. But if he thereby misjudged and misjudges himself, he may find some consolation for his error in the lavishness with which even worse misjudgment is heaped upon him by foreigners. To this day, despite the intimate contact of five long years of joint war, the French and the English are ignorant of his true character, and show it in their every discussion of him, particularly when they discuss him in camera. It is the secret but general view of the French, we are informed by confidential agents, that he is a fellow of loose life and not to be trusted with either a wine-pot, a virgin or a domestic fowl—an absurdly inaccurate generalization from the aberrations of soldiers in a far land, cut off from the moral repressions that lie upon them and colour all their acts at home. It is the view of the English, so we hear upon equally reliable authority, that he is an earnest but extremely inefficient oaf, incapable of either the finer technic of war or of its machine-like discipline—another thumping error, for the American is actually extraordinarily adept and ingenious in the very arts that modern war chiefly makes use of, and there is, since the revolt of the Prussian, no other such rigidly regimented man in the world. He has, indeed, reached such a pass in the latter department that it has become almost impossible for him to think of himself save as an obedient member of some vast, powerful and unintelligibly despotic organization—a church, a trades-union, a political party, a tin-pot fraternal order, or what not—, and often he is a member of more than one, and impartially faithful to all. Moreover, as we have seen, he lives under laws which dictate almost every detail of his public and private conduct, and punish every sign of bad discipline with the most appalling rigour; and these laws are enforced by police who supply the chance gaps in them extempore, and exercise that authority in the best manner of prison guards, animal trainers and drill sergeants.

The English and the French, beside these special errors, have a full share in an error that is also embraced by practically every other foreign people. This is the error of assuming, almost as an axiom beyond question, that the Americans are a sordid, money-grubbing people, with no thought above the dollar. You will find it prevailing everywhere on the Continent of Europe. To the German the United States is Dollarica, and the salient American personality, next to the policeman who takes bribes and the snuffling moralist in office, is the Dollarprinzessin. To the Italian the country is a sort of savage wilderness in which everything else, from religion to beauty and from decent repose to human life, is sacrificed to profit. Italians cross the ocean in much the same spirit that our runaway school-boys used to go off to fight the Indians. Some, lucky, return home in a few years with fortunes and gaudy tales; others, succumbing to the natives, are butchered at their labour and buried beneath the cinders of hideous and Godforsaken mining towns. All carry the thought of escape from beginning to end; every Italian hopes to get away with his takings as soon as possible, to enjoy them on some hillside where life and property are reasonably safe from greed. So with the Russian, the Scandinavian, the Balkan hillman, even the Greek and Armenian. The picture of America that they conjure up is a picture of a titanic and merciless struggle for gold, with the stakes high and the contestants correspondingly ferocious. They see the American as one to whom nothing under the sun has any value save the dollar—not truth, or beauty, or philosophical ease, or the common decencies between man and man.

This view, of course, is full of distortion and misunderstanding, despite the fact that even Americans, by hearing it stated so often, have come to allow it a good deal of soundness. The American's concept of himself, as we have seen, is sometimes anything but accurate; in this case he errs almost as greatly as when he venerates himself as the prince of freemen, with gyveless wrists and flashing eyes. As for the foreigner, what he falls into is the typically Freudian blunder of projecting his own worst weakness into another. The fact is that it is he, and not the native American, who is the incorrigible and unimaginative money-grubber. He comes to the United States in search of money, and in search of money alone, and pursuing that single purpose without deviation he makes the mistake of assuming that the American is at the same business, and in the same fanatical manner. From all the complex and colourful life of the country, save only the one enterprise of money-making, he is shut off almost hermetically, and so he concludes that that one enterprise embraces the whole show. Here the unreliable promptings of his sub-conscious passion are helped out by observations that are more logical. Unfamiliar with the language, excluded from all free social intercourse with the native, and regarded as, if actually human at all, then at least a distinctly inferior member of the species, he is forced into the harshest and most ill-paid labour, and so he inevitably sees the American as a pitiless task-master and ascribes the exploitation he is made a victim of to a fabulous exaggeration of his own avarice.

Moreover, the greater success and higher position of the native seem to bear out this notion. In a struggle that is free for all and to the death, the native grabs all the shiniest stakes. *Ergo,* he must love money even more than the immigrant. This logic we do not defend, but there is—and out of it grows the prevailing foreign view of America and the Americans, for the foreigner who stays at home does not derive his ideas from the glittering, lascivious phrases of Dr. Wilson or from the passionate idealism of such superior Americans as Otto H. Kahn, Adolph S. Ochs, S. Stanwood Menken, Jacob H. Schiff, Marcus Loew, Henry Morgenthau, Abram Elkus, Samuel Goldfish, Louis D. Brandeis, Julius Rosenwald, Paul Warburg, Judge Otto Rosalsky, Adolph Zukor, the Hon. Julius Kahn, Simon Guggenheim, Stephen S. Wise and Barney Baruch, but from the hair-raising tales of returned "Americans," i.e., fellow peasants who, having braved the dragons, have come back to the fatherland to enjoy their booty and exhibit their wounds.

The native, as we say, has been so far influenced by this error that he cherishes it himself, or, more accurately, entertains it with shame. Most of his windy idealism is no more than a reaction against it—an evidence of an effort to confute it and live it down. He is never more sweetly flattered than when some politician eager for votes or some evangelist itching for a good plate tells him that he is actually a soaring altruist, and the only real one in the world. This is the surest way to fetch him; he never fails to swell out his chest when he hears that buncombe. In point of fact, of course, he is no more an altruist than any other healthy mammal. His ideals, one and all, are grounded upon self-interest, or upon the fear that is at the bottom of it; his benevolence always has a string tied to it; he could no more formulate a course of action to his certain disadvantage than an Englishman could, or a Frenchman, or an Italian, or a German. But to say that the advantage he pursues is always, or even usually, a monetary one—to argue that he is avaricious, or even, in these later years, a sharp trader—is to spit directly into the eye of the truth. There is probably, indeed, no country in the world in which mere money is held in less esteem than in these United States. Even more than the Russian Bolshevik the American democrat regards wealth with suspicion, and its too eager amassment with a bilious eye. Here alone, west of the Dvina, rich men are *ipso facto* scoundrels and *feræ naturæ,* with no rights that any slanderer is bound to respect. Here alone, the possession of a fortune puts a man automatically upon the defensive, and exposes him to special legislation of a rough and inquisitorial character and to the special animosity of judges, district attorneys and juries. It would be a literal impossibility for an Englishman worth $100,000,000 to avoid public office and public honour; it would be equally impossible for an American worth $100,000,000 to obtain either.

Americans, true enough, enjoy an average of prosperity that is above that witnessed in any other country. Their land, with less labour, yields a greater usufruct than other land; they get more money for their industry; they jingle more coin in their pockets than other peoples. But it is a grievous error to mistake that superior opulence for a sign of money-hunger, for they actually hold money very lightly, and spend a great deal more of it than any other race of men and with far less thought of values. The normal French family, it is often said, could live very comfortably for a week upon what the normal American family wastes in a week. There is, among Americans, not the slightest sign of the unanimous French habit of biting every franc, of calculating the cost of every luxury to five places of decimals, of utilizing every scrap, of sleeping with the bankbook under the pillow. Whatever is showy gets their dollars, whether they need it or not, even whether they can afford it or not. They are, so to speak, constantly on a bust, their eyes alert for chances to get rid of their small change.

Consider, for example, the amazing readiness with which they succumb to the imbecile bait of advertising! An American manufacturer, finding himself with a stock of unsalable goods or encountering otherwise a demand that is less than his production, does not have to look, like his English or German colleague, for foreign dumping grounds. He simply packs his surplus in gaudy packages, sends for an advertising agent, joins an Honest-Advertising club, fills the newspapers and magazines with lying advertisements, and sits down in peace while his countrymen fight their way to his counters. That they will come is almost absolutely sure; no matter how valueless the goods, they will leap to the advertisements; their one desire seems to be to get rid of their money. As a consequence of this almost pathological eagerness, the advertising bill of the American people is greater than that of all other peoples taken together. There is scarcely an article within the range of their desires that does not carry a heavy load of advertising; they actually pay out millions every year to be sold such commonplace necessities as sugar, towels, collars, lead-pencils and corn-meal. The business of thus bamboozling them and picking their pockets enlists thousands and thousands of artists, writers, printers, sign-painters and other such parasites. Their towns are bedaubed with chromatic eye-sores and made hideous with flashing lights; their countryside is polluted; their newspapers and magazines become mere advertising sheets; idiotic slogans and apothegms are invented to enchant them; in some cities they are actually taxed to advertise the local makers of wooden nutmegs. Multitudes of swindlers are naturally induced to adopt advertising as a trade, and some of them make great fortunes at it. Like all other men who live by their wits, they regard themeslves as superior fellows, and every year they hold great conventions, bore each other with learned papers upon the psychology of their victims, speak of one another as men of genius, have themselves photographed by the photographers of newspapers eager to curry favour with them, denounce the government for not spending the public funds for advertising, and summon United States Senators, eminent chautauquans and distinguished vaudeville stars to entertain them. For all this the plain people pay the bill, and never a protest comes out of them.

As a matter of fact, the only genuinely thrifty folks among us, in the sense that a Frenchman, a Scot or an Italian is thrifty, are the immigrants of the most recent invasions. That is why they oust the native wherever the two come into contact—say in New England and in the Middle West. They acquire, bit by bit, the best lands, the best stock, the best barns, not because they have the secret of *making* more money, but because they have the resolution to *spend* less. As soon as they become thoroughly Americanized they begin to show the national prodigality. The old folks wear home-made clothes and stick to the farm; the native-born children order their garments from mail-order tailors and expose themselves in the chautauquas and at the great orgies of Calvinism and Wesleyanism. The old folks put every dollar they can wring from a reluctant environment into real property or the banks; the young folks put their inheritance into phonographs, Fords, boiled shirts, yellow shoes, cuckoo clocks, lithographs of the current mountebanks, oil stock, automatic pianos and the works of Harold Bell Wright, Gerald Stanley Lee and O. Henry.

III

But what, then, is the character that actually marks the American—that is, in chief? If he is not the exalted monopolist of liberty that he thinks he is nor the noble altruist and idealist he slaps upon the chest when he is full of rhetoric, nor the degraded dollar-chaser of European legend, then what is he? We offer an answer in all humility, for the problem is complex and there is but little illumination of it in the literature; nevertheless, we offer it in the firm conviction, born of twenty years' incessant meditation, that it is substantially correct. It is, in brief, this: that the thing which sets off the American from all other men, and gives a peculiar colour not only to the pattern of his daily life but also to the play of his inner ideas, is what, for want of a more exact term, may be called social aspiration. That is to say, his dominant passion is a passion to lift himself by at least a step or two in the society that he is a part of—a passion to improve his position, to break down some shadowy barrier of caste, to achieve the countenance of what, for all his talk of equality, he recognizes and accepts as his betters. The American is a pusher. His eyes are ever fixed upon some round of the ladder that is just beyond his reach, and all his secret ambitions, all his extraordinary energies, group themselves about the yearning to grasp it. Here we have an explanation of the curious restlessness that educated foreigners, as opposed to mere immigrants, always make a note of in the country; it is half aspiration and half impatience, with overtones of dread and timorousness. The American is violently eager to get on, and thoroughly convinced that his merits entitle him to try and to succeed, but by the same token he is sickeningly fearful of slipping back, and out of the second fact, as we shall see, spring some of his most characteristic traits. He is a man vexed, at one and the same time, by delusions of grandeur and an inferiority complex; he is both egotistical and subservient, assertive and politic, blatant and shy. Most of the errors about him are made by seeing one side of him and being blind to the other.

Such a thing as a secure position is practically unknown among us. There is no American who cannot hope to lift himself another notch or two, if he is good; there is absolutely no hard and fast impediment to his progress. But neither is there any American who doesn't have to keep on fighting for whatever position he has; no wall of caste is there to protect him if he slips. One observes everyday the movement of individuals, families, whole groups, in both directions. All of our cities are full of brummagem aristocrats—aristocrats, at all events, in the view of their neighbours—whose grandfathers, or even fathers, were day labourers; and working for them, supported by them, heavily patronized by them, are clerks whose grandfathers were lords of the soil. The older societies of Europe, as every one knows, protect their caste lines a great deal more resolutely. It is as impossible for a wealthy pork packer or company promoter to enter the *noblesse* of Austria, even today, as it would be for him to enter the boudoir of a queen; he is barred out absolutely and even his grandchildren are under the ban. And in precisely the same way it is as impossible for a count of the old Holy Roman Empire to lose caste as it would be for the Dalai Lama; he may sink to unutterable depths within his order, but he cannot get himself out of it, nor can he lose the peculiar advantages that go with membership; he is still a *Graf,* and, as such, above the herd. Once, in a Madrid café, the two of us encountered a Spanish marquis who wore celluloid cuffs, suffered from pediculosis and had been drunk for sixteen years. Yet he remained a marquis in good standing, and all lesser Spaniards, including Socialists, envied him and deferred to him; none would have dreamed of slapping him on the back. Knowing that he was quite as safe within his ancient order as a dog among the *canidæ,* he gave no thought to appearances. But in the same way he knew that he had reached his limit—that no conceivable effort could lift him higher. He was a grandee of Spain and that was all; above glimmered royalty and the hierarchy of the saints, and both royalty and the hierarchy of the saints were as much beyond him as grandeeism was beyond the polite and well-educated head-waiter who laved him with ice-water when he had *mania-a-potu.*

No American is ever so securely lodged. There is always something just ahead of him, beckoning him and tantalizing him, and there is always something just behind him, menacing him and causing him to sweat. Even when he attains to what may seem to be security, that security is very fragile. The English soap-boiler, brewer, shyster attorney or stock-jobber, once he has got into the House of Lords, is reasonably safe, and his children after him; the possession of a peerage connotes a definite rank, and it is as permanent as anything can be in this world. But in America there is no such harbour; the ship is eternally at sea. Money vanishes, official dignity is forgotten, caste lines are as full of gaps as an ill-kept hedge. The grandfather of the Vanderbilts was a bounder; the last of the Washingtons is a petty employé in the Library of Congress.

It is this constant possibility of rising, this constant risk of falling, that gives a barbaric picturesqueness to the panorama of what is called fashionable society in America. The chief character of that society is to be found in its shameless self-assertion, its almost obscene display of its importance and of the shadowy privileges and acceptances on which that importance is based. It is assertive for the simple reason that, immediately it ceased to be assertive, it would cease to exist. Structurally, it is composed in every town of a nucleus of those who have laboriously arrived and a chaotic mass of those who are straining every effort to get on. The effort must be made against great odds. Those who have arrived are eager to keep down the competition of newcomers; on their exclusiveness, as the phrase is, rests the whole of their social advantage. Thus the candidate from below, before horning in at last, must put up with an infinity of rebuff and humiliation; he must sacrifice his self-respect today in order to gain the hope of destroying the self-respect of other aspirants tomorrow. The result is that the whole edifice is based upon fears and abasements, and that every device which promises to protect the individual against them is seized upon eagerly. Fashionable society in America therefore has no room for intelligence; within its fold an original idea is dangerous; it carries regimentation, in dress, in social customs and in political and even religious doctrines, to the last degree. In the American cities the fashionable man or woman must not only maintain the decorum seen among civilized folks everywhere; he or she must also be interested in precisely the right sports, theatrical shows and opera singers, show the right political credulities and indignations, and have some sort of connection with the right church. Nearly always, because of the apeing of English custom that prevails everywhere in America, it must be the so-called Protestant Episcopal Church, a sort of outhouse of the Church of England, with ecclesiastics who imitate the English sacerdotal manner much as small boys imitate the manner of eminent baseball players. Every fashionable Protestant Episcopal congregation in the land is full of ex-Baptists and ex-Methodists who have shed Calvinism, total immersion and the hallelujah hymns on their way up the ladder. The same impulse leads the Jews, whenever the possibility of invading the citadel of the Christians begins to bemuse them (as happened during the late war, for example, when patriotism temporarily adjourned the usual taboos), to embrace Christian Science—as a sort of halfway station, so to speak, more medical than Christian, and hence secure against ordinary derisions. And it is an impulse but little different which lies at the bottom of the much-discussed title-hunt.

A title, however paltry, is of genuine social value, more especially in America; it represents a status that cannot be changed overnight by the rise of rivals, or by personal dereliction, or by mere accident. It is a policy of insurance against dangers that are not to be countered as effectively in any other manner. Miss G——, the daughter of an enormously wealthy scoundrel, may be accepted everywhere, but all the while she is insecure. Her father may lose his fortune tomorrow, or be jailed by newspaper outcry, or marry a prostitute and so commit social suicide himself and murder his daughter, or she herself may fall a victim to some rival's superior machinations, or stoop to fornication of some forbidden variety, or otherwise get herself under the ban. But once she is a duchess, she is safe. No catastrophe short of divorce can take away her coronet, and even divorce will leave the purple marks of it upon her brow. Most valuable boon of all, she is now free to be herself,—a rare, rare experience for an American. She may, if she likes, go about in a Mother Hubbard, or join the Seventh Day Adventists, or declare for the Bolsheviki, or wash her own lingerie, or have her hair bobbed, and still she will remain a duchess, and, as a duchess, irremovably superior to the gaping herd of her political equals.

This social aspiration, of course, is most vividly violent and idiotic on its higher and more gaudy levels, but it is scarcely less earnest below. Every American, however obscure, has formulated within his secret recesses some concept of advancement, however meagre; if he doesn't aspire to be what is called fashionable, then he at least aspires to lift himself in some less gorgeous way. There is not a social organization in this land of innumerable associations that hasn't its waiting list of candidates who are eager to get in, but have not yet demonstrated their fitness for the honour. One can scarcely go low enough to find that pressure absent. Even the tin-pot fraternal orders, which are constantly cadging for members and seem to accept any one not a downright felon, are exclusive in their fantastic way, and no doubt there are hundreds of thousands of proud American freemen, the heirs of Washington and Jefferson, their liberty safeguarded by a million guns, who pine in secret because they are ineligible to membership in the Masons, the Odd Fellows or even the Knights of Pythias. On the distaff side, the thing is too obvious to need exposition. The patriotic societies among women are all machines for the resuscitation of lost superiorities. The plutocracy has shouldered out the old gentry from actual social leadership—that gentry, indeed, presents a prodigious clinical picture of the insecurity of social rank in America—but there remains at least the possibility of insisting upon a dignity which plutocrats cannot boast and may not even buy. Thus the county judge's wife in Smithville or the Methodist pastor's daughter in Jonestown consoles herself for the lack of an opera box with the thought (constantly asserted by badge and resolution) that she had a nobler grandfather, or, at all events, a decenter one, than the Astors, the Vanderbilts and the Goulds.

IV

It seems to us that the genuine characters of the normal American, the characters which set him off most saliently from the men of other nations, are the fruits of all this risk of and capacity for change in status that we have described, and of the dreads and hesitations that go therewith. The American is marked, in fact, by precisely the habits of mind and act that one would look for in a man insatiably ambitious and yet incurably fearful, to wit, the habits, on the one hand, of unpleasant assertiveness, of somewhat boisterous braggardism, of incessant pushing, and, on the other hand, of conformity, caution and subservience. He is forever talking of his rights as if he stood ready to defend them with his last drop of blood, and forever yielding them up at the first demand. Under both the pretension and the fact is the common motive of fear—in brief, the common motive of the insecure and uncertain man, the *average* man, at all times and everywhere, but especially the motive of the average man in a social system so crude and unstable as ours.

"More than any other people," said Wendell Phillips one blue day, "we Amcricans are afraid of one another." The saying seems harsh. It goes counter to the national delusion of uncompromising courage and limitless truculence. It wars upon the national vanity. But all the same there is truth in it. Here, more than anywhere else on earth, the status of an individual is determined by the general consent of the general body of his fellows; here, as we have seen, there are no artificial barriers to protect him against their disapproval, or even against their envy. And here, more than anywhere else, the general consent of that general body of men is coloured by the ideas and prejudices of the inferior majority; here, there is the nearest approach to genuine democracy, the most direct and accurate response to mob emotions. Facing that infinitely powerful but inevitably ignorant and cruel corpus of opinion, the individual must needs adopt caution and fall into timorousness. The desire within him may be bold and forthright, but its satisfaction demands discretion, prudence, a politic and ingratiating habit. The walls are not to be stormed; they must be wooed to a sort of Jerichoan fall. Success thus takes the form of a series of waves of protective colouration; failure is a succession of unmaskings. The aspirant must first learn to imitate exactly the aspect and behaviour of the group he seeks to penetrate. There follows notice. There follows toleration. There follows acceptance.

Thus the hog-murderer's wife picks her way into the society of Chicago, the proud aristocracy of the abbatoir. And thus, no less, the former whiskey drummer insinuates himself into the Elks, and the rising retailer wins the *imprimatur* of wholesalers, and the rich peasant becomes a planter and the father of doctors of philosophy, and the servant girl enters the movies and acquires the status of a princess of the blood, and the petty attorney becomes a legislator and statesman, and Schmidt turns into Smith, and the newspaper reporter becomes a *littérateur* on the staff of the *Saturday Evening Post,* and all of us Yankees creep up, up, up. The business is never to be accomplished by headlong assault. It must be done circumspectly, insidiously, a bit apologetically, *pianissimo;* there must be no flaunting of unusual ideas, no bold prancing of an unaccustomed personality. Above all, it must be done without exciting fear, lest the portcullis fall and the whole enterprise go to pot. Above all, the manner of a Jenkins must be got into it.

That manner, of course, is not incompatible with a certain superficial boldness, nor even with an appearance of truculence. But what lies beneath the boldness is not really an independent spirit, but merely a talent for crying with the pack. When the

American is most dashingly assertive it is a sure sign that he feels the pack behind him, and hears its comforting baying, and is well aware that his doctrine is approved. He is not a joiner for nothing. He joins something, whether it be a political party, a church, a fraternal order or one of the idiotic movements that incessantly ravage the land, because joining gives him a feeling of security, because it makes him a part of something larger and safer than he is himself, because it gives him a chance to work off steam without running any risk. The whole thinking of the country thus runs down the channel of mob emotion; there is no actual conflict of ideas, but only a succession of crazes. It is inconvenient to stand aloof from these crazes, and it is dangerous to oppose them. In no other country in the world is there so ferocious a short way with dissenters; in none other is it socially so costly to heed the inner voice and to be one's own man.

Thus encircled by taboos, the American shows an extraordinary timorousness in all his dealings with fundamentals, and the fact that many of these taboos are self-imposed only adds to their rigour. What every observant foreigner first notices, canvassing the intellectual life of the land, is the shy and gingery manner in which all the larger problems of existence are dealt with. We have, for example, positive laws which make it practically impossible to discuss the sex question with anything approaching honesty. The literature of the subject is enormous, and the general notion of its importance is thereby made manifest, but all save a very small part of that literature is produced by quacks and addressed to an audience that is afraid to hear the truth. So in politics. Almost alone among the civilized nations of the world, the United States pursues critics of the dominant political theory with mediaeval ferocity, condemning them to interminable periods in prison, proceeding against them by clamour and perjury, treating them worse than common blacklegs, and at times conniving at their actual murder by the police. And so, above all in religion. This is the only country of Christendom in which there is no anti-clerical party, and hence no constant and effective criticism of clerical pretension and corruption. The result is that all of the churches reach out for tyranny among us, and that most of them that show any numerical strength already exercise it. In half a dozen of our largest cities the Catholic Church is actually a good deal more powerful than it is in Spain, or even in Austria. Its acts are wholly above public discussion; it makes and breaks public officials; it holds the newspapers in terror; it influences the police and the courts; it is strong enough to destroy and silence any man who objects to its polity. But this is not all. The Catholic Church, at worst, is an organization largely devoted to perfectly legitimate and even laudable purposes, and it is controlled by a class of men who are largely above popular passion, and intelligent enough to see beyond the immediate advantage. More important still, its international character gives it a detached and superior point of view, and so makes it stand aloof from some of the common weaknesses of the native mob. This is constantly revealed by its opposition to Prohibition, vice-crusading and other such crazes of the disinherited and unhappy. The rank and file of its members are ignorant and emotional and are thus almost ideal cannon-fodder for the bogus reformers who operate upon the proletariat, but they are held back by their clergy, to whose superior interest in genuine religion is added a centuries-old heritage of worldly wisdom. Thus the Church of Rome, in America at least, is a civilizing agency, and we may well overlook its cynical alliance with political corruption in view of its steady enmity to that greater corruption which destroys the very elements of liberty, peace and human dignity. It may be a bit too intelligently selfish and harshly realistic, but it is assuredly not swinish.

This adjective, however, fits the opposition as snugly as a coat of varnish—and by the opposition we mean the group of Protestant churches commonly called evangelical, to wit, the Methodist, the Baptist, the Presbyterian and their attendant imitators and inferiors.

It is out of this group that the dominating religious attitude of the American people arises, and, in particular, it is from this group that we get our doctrine that religious activity is not to be challenged, however flagrantly it may stand in opposition to common honesty and common sense. Under cover of that artificial toleration—the product, not of a genuine liberalism, but simply of a mob distrust of dissent—there goes on a tyranny that it would be difficult to match in modern history. Save in a few large cities, every American community lies under a sacerdotal despotism whose devices are disingenuous and dishonourable, and whose power was magnificently displayed in the campaign for Prohibition—a despotism exercised by a body of ignorant, superstitious, self-seeking and thoroughly dishonest men. One may, without prejudice, reasonably defend the Catholic clergy. They are men who, at worst, pursue an intelligible ideal and dignify it with a real sacrifice. But in the presence of the Methodist clergy it is difficult to avoid giving way to the weakness of indignation. What one observes is a horde of uneducated and inflammatory dunderheads, eager for power, intolerant of opposition and full of a childish vanity—a mob of holy clerks but little raised, in intelligence and dignity, above the forlorn half-wits whose souls they chronically rack. In the whole United States there is scarcely one among them who stands forth as a man of sense and information. Illiterate in all save the elementals, untouched by the larger currents of thought, drunk with their power over dolts, crazed by their immunity to challenge by their betters, they carry over into the professional class of the country the spirit of the most stupid peasantry, and degrade religion to the estate of an idiotic phobia. There is not a village in America in which some such preposterous jackass is not in eruption. Worse, he is commonly the leader of its opinion—its pattern in reason, morals and good taste. Yet worse, he is ruler as well as pattern. Wrapped in his sacerdotal cloak, he stands above any effective criticism. To question his imbecile ideas is to stand in contumacy of the revelation of God.

A number of years ago, while engaged in journalism in a large American city, one of us violated all journalistic precedents by printing an article denouncing the local evangelical clergy as, with few exceptions, a pack of scoundrels, and offered in proof their brisk and constant trade in contraband marriages, especially the marriages of girls under the age of consent. He showed that the offer of a two dollar fee was sufficient to induce the majority of these ambassadors of Christ to marry a girl of fourteen or fifteen to a boy a few years older. There followed a great outcry from the accused, with the usual demands that the offending paper print a retraction and discharge the guilty writer from its staff. He thereupon engaged a clipping bureau to furnish him with clippings from the newspapers of the whole country, showing the common activities of the evangelical clergy elsewhere. The result was that he received and reprinted an amazing mass of putrid scandal, greatly to the joy of that moral community. It appeared that these eminent Christian leaders were steadily engaged, North, East, South and West, in doings that would have disgraced so many ward heelers or oyster-shuckers—shady financial transactions, gross sexual irregularities, all sorts of minor crimes. The publication of this evidence from day to day gave the chronicler the advantage of the offensive, and so got him out of a tight place. In the end, as if tickled by his assault, the hierarchy of heaven came to his aid. That is to say, the Lord God Jehovah arranged it that one of the leading Methodist clergymen of the city—in fact, the chronicler's chief opponent—should be taken in an unmentionable sexual perversion at the headquarters of the Young Men's Christian Association, and so be forced to leave town between days. This catastrophe, as we say, the chronicler ascribes to divine intervention. It was entirely unexpected; he knew that the fellow was a liar and a rogue, but he had never suspected that he was also a hog. The episode demoralized the defence to such an extent that it was impossible, in decency, to go on with the war. The chronicler was at once, in fact, forced into hypocritical efforts to prevent the fugitive ecclesiastic's pursuit, extradition, trial and imprisonment, and these efforts, despite their disingenuous character, succeeded. Under another name, he now preaches Christ and Him crucified in the far West, and is, we daresay, a leading advocate of Prohibition, vice-crusading and the other Methodist reforms.

But here we depart from the point. It is not that an eminent Wesleyan should be taken in crim. con. with a member of the Y. M. C. A.; it is that the whole Wesleyan scheme of things, despite the enormous multiplication of such incidents, should still stand above all direct and devastating criticism in America. It is an ignorant and dishonest cult of ignorant and dishonest men, and yet no one has ever had at it from the front. All the newspaper clippings that we have mentioned were extraordinarily discreet. Every offence of a clergyman was presented as if it were an isolated phenomenon, and of no general significance; there was never any challenge of an ecclesiastical organization which bred and sheltered such men, and carried over their curious ethics into its social and political activities. That careful avoidance of the main issue is always observable in These States. Prohibition was saddled upon the country, against the expressed wish of at least two-thirds of the people, by the political chicanery of the same organization, and yet no one, during the long fight, thought to attack it directly; to have done so would have been to violate the taboo described. So when the returning soldiers began to reveal the astounding chicaneries of the Young Men's Christian Association; it was marvelled at for a few weeks, as Americans always marvel at successful pocket-squeezings, but no one sought the cause in the character of the pious brethren primarily responsible. And so, again, when what is called liberal opinion began to revolt against the foreign politics of Dr. Wilson, and in particular, against his apparent repudiation of his most solemn engagements, and his complete insensibility, in the presence of a moral passion, to the most elementary principles of private and public honour. A thousand critics, friendly and unfriendly, sought to account for his amazing shifts and evasions on unintelligible logical grounds, but no one, so far as we know, ventured to point out that his course could be accounted for in every detail, and without any mauling of the facts whatsoever, upon the simple ground that he was a Presbyterian.

We sincerely hope that no one will mistake us here for anarchists who seek to hold the Presbyterian code of ethics, or the Presbyterians themselves, up to derision. We confess frankly that, as private individuals, we are inclined against that code and that all our prejudices run against those who subscribe to it—which is to say, in the direction of toleration, of open dealing, and even of a certain mild snobbishness. We are both opposed to moral enthusiasm, and never drink with a moral man if it can be avoided. The taboos that we personally subscribe to are taboos upon the very things that Presbyterians hold most dear—for example, moral certainty, the proselyting appetite, and what may be described as the passion of the policeman. But we are surely not fatuous enough to cherish our ideas to the point of fondness. In the long run, we freely grant, it may turn out that the Presbyterians are right and we are wrong—in brief, that God loves a moral man more than he loves an amiable and honourable one. Stranger things, indeed, have happened; one might even argue without absurdity that God is actually a Presbyterian Himself. Whether He is or is not we do not presume to say; we simply record the fact that it is our present impression that He is not—and then straightway admit that our view is worth no more than that of any other pair of men.

Meanwhile, however, it is certainly not going too far to notice the circumstance that there is an irreconcilable antithesis between the two sorts of men that we have described—that a great moral passion is fatal to the gentler and more caressing amenities of life, and *vice versa*. The man of morals has a certain character, and the man of honour has a quite different character. No one not an idiot fails to differentiate between the two, or to order his intercourse with them upon an assumption of their disparity. What we know in the United States as a Presbyterian is pre-eminently of the moral type. Perhaps more than any other man among us he regulates his life, and the lives of all who fall under his influence, upon a purely moral plan. In the main, he gets the principles underlying that plan from the Old Testament; if he is to be described succinctly, it is as one who carries over into modern life, with its superior complexity of sin, the simple and rigid ethical concepts of the ancient Jews. And in particular, he subscribes to their theory that it is virtuous to make things hot for the sinner, by which word he designates any person whose conduct violates the ordinances of God as he himself is aware of them and interprets them. Sin is to the Presbyterian the salient phenomenon of this wobbling and nefarious world, and the pursuit and chastisement of sinners the one avocation that is permanently worth while. The product of that simple doctrine is a character of no little vigour and austerity, and one much esteemed by the great masses of men, who are always uneasily conscious of their own weakness in the face of temptation and thus have a sneaking veneration for the man apparently firm, and who are always ready to believe, furthermore, that any man who seems to be having a pleasant time is a rascal and deserving of the fire.

The Presbyterian likewise harbours this latter suspicion. More, he commonly erects it into a certainty. Every single human act, he holds, must be either right or wrong—and the overwhelming majority of them are wrong. He knows exactly what these wrong ones are; he recognizes them instantly and infallibly, by a sort of inspired intuition; and he believes that they should all be punished automatically and with the utmost severity. No one ever heard of a Presbyterian overlooking a fault, or pleading for mercy for the erring. He would regard such an act as the weakness of one ridden by the Devil. From such harsh judgments and retributions, it must be added in fairness, he does not except himself. He detects his own aberration almost as quickly as he detects the aberration of the other fellow, and though he may sometimes seek—being, after all, only human—to escape its consequences, he by no means condones it. Nothing, indeed, could exceed the mental anguish of a Presbyterian who has been betrayed, by the foul arts of some lascivious wench, into any form of adultery, or, by the treason of his senses in some other way, into a voluptuous yielding to the lure of the other *beaux arts*. It has been our fortune, at various times, to be in the confidence of Presbyterians thus seduced from their native virtue, and we bear willing testimony to their sincere horror. Even the least pious of them was as greatly shaken up by what to us, on our lower plane, seemed a mere peccadillo, perhaps in bad taste but certainly not worth getting into a sweat about, as we ourselves would have been by a gross breach of faith.

But, as has been before remarked, the bitter must go with the sweet. In the face of so exalted a moral passion it would be absurd to look for that urbane habit which seeks the well-being of one's self and the other fellow, not in exact obedience to harsh statutes, but in ease, dignity and the more delicate sort of self-respect. That is to say, it would be absurd to ask a thoroughly moral man to be also a man of honour. The two, in fact, are eternal enemies; their endless struggle achieves that happy mean of philosophies which we call civilization. The man of morals keeps order in the world, regimenting its lawless hordes and organizing its governments; the man of honour mellows and embellishes what is thus achieved, giving to duty the aspect of a privilege and making human intercourse a thing of fine faiths and understandings. We trust the former to do what is righteous; we trust the latter to do what is seemly. It is seldom that a man can do both. The man of honour inevitably exalts the punctilio above the law of God; one may trust him, if he has eaten one's salt, to respect one's daughter as he would his own, but if he happens to be under no such special obligation it may be hazardous to trust him with even one's charwoman or one's mother-in-law. And the man of morals, confronted by a moral situation, is usually wholly without honour. Put him on the stand to testify against a woman, and he will tell all he knows about her, even including what he has learned in the purple privacy of her boudoir. More, he will not tell it reluctantly, shame-facedly, apologetically, but proudly and willingly, in response to his high sense of moral duty. It is simply impossible for such a man to lie like a gentleman. He lies, of course, like all of us, and perhaps more often than most of us on the other side, but he does it, not to protect sinners from the moral law, but to make their punishment under the moral law more certain, swift, facile and spectacular.

By this long route we get at our *apologia* for Dr. Wilson, a man from whom we both differ in politics, in theology, in ethics and in epistemology, but one whose great gifts, particularly for moral endeavour in the grand manner, excite our sincere admiration. Both his foes and his friends, it seems to us, do him a good deal of injustice. The former, carried away by that sense of unlikeness which lies at the bottom of most of the prejudices of uncritical men, denounce him out of hand because he is not as they are. A good many of these foes, of course, are not actually men of honour themselves; some of them, in fact, belong to sects and professions—for example, that of intellectual Socialist and that of member of Congress—in which no authentic man of honour could imaginably have a place. But it may be accurately said of them, nevertheless, that if actual honour is not in them, then at least they have something of the manner of honour—that they are moving in the direction of honour, though not yet arrived. Few men, indeed, may be said to belong certainly and irrevocably in either category, that of the men of honour or that of the men of morals. Dr. Wilson, perhaps, is one such man. He is as palpably and exclusively a man of morals as, say, George Washington was a man of honour. He is, in the one category, a great beacon, burning almost blindingly; he is, in the other, no more than a tallow dip, guttering asthmatically.

But the majority of men occupy a sort of twilight zone, and the most that may be said of them is that their faces turn this way or that. Such is the case with Dr. Wilson's chief foes. Their eyes are upon honour, as upon some new and superlatively sweet enchantment, and, bemused to starboard, they view the scene to port with somewhat extravagant biliousness. Thus, when they contemplate His Excellency's long and perhaps unmatchable series of violations of his troth—in the matter of "keeping us out of the war," in the matter of his solemn promises to China, in the matter of his statement of war aims and purposes, in the matter of his shifty dealing with the Russian question, in the matter of his repudiation of the armistice terms offered to the Germans, in the matter of his stupendous lying to the Senate committee on foreign relations, and so on, *ad infinitum*—when they contemplate all that series of evasions, dodgings, hypocrisies, double-dealings and plain mendacities, they succumb to an indignation that is still more than half moral, and denounce him bitterly as a Pecksniff, a Tartuffe and a Pinto. In that judgment, as we shall show, there is naught save a stupid incapacity to understand an unlike man—in brief, no more than the dunderheadedness which makes a German regard every Englishman as a snuffling poltroon, hiding behind his vassals, and causes an Englishman to look upon every German as a fiend in human form, up to his hips in blood.

But one expects a man's foes to misjudge him, and even to libel him deliberately; a good deal of their enmity, in fact, is often no more than a product of their uneasy consciousness that they have dealt unfairly with him; one is always most bitter, not toward the author of one's wrongs, but toward the victim of one's wrongs. Unluckily, Dr. Wilson's friends have had at him even more cruelly. When, seeking to defend what they regard as his honour, they account for his incessant violation of his pledges—to the voters in 1916, to the soldiers drafted for the war, to the Chinese on their entrance, to the Austrians when he sought to get them out, to the

Germans when he offered them his fourteen points, to the country in the matter of secret diplomacy—when his friends attempt to explain his cavalier repudiation of all these pledges on the ground that he could not have kept them without violating later pledges, they achieve, of course, only an imbecility, obvious and damning, for it must be plain that no man is permitted, in honour, to make antagonistic engagements, or to urge his private tranquillity or even the public welfare as an excuse for changing their terms without the consent of the parties of the second part. A man of honour is one who simply does whatever he says he will do, provided the other party holds to the compact too. One cannot imagine him shifting, trimming and making excuses; it is his peculiar mark that he never makes excuses—that the need of making them would fill him with unbearable humiliation. The moment a man of honour faces the question of his honour, he is done for; it can no more stand investigation than the chastity of a woman can stand investigation. In such a character, Dr. Wilson would have been bound irrevocably by all his long series of solemn engagements, from the first to the last, without the slightest possibility of dotting an i or of cutting off the tail of a comma. It would have been as impossible for him to have repudiated a single one of them at the desire of his friends or in the interest of his idealistic enterprises as it would have been for him to have repudiated it to his own private profit.

But here is where both foes and friends go aground; both attempt to inject concepts of honour into transactions predominatingly, and perhaps exclusively, coloured by concepts of morals. The two things are quite distinct, as the two sorts of men are quite distinct. Beside the obligation of honour there is the obligation of morals, entirely independent and often directly antagonistic. And beside the man who yields to the punctilio—the man of honour, the man who keeps his word—there is the man who submits himself, regardless of his personal engagements and the penalties that go therewith, to the clarion call of the moral law, Dr. Wilson is such a man. He is, as has been remarked, a Presbyterian, a Calvinist, a militant moralist. In that rôle, devoted to that high cause, clad in that white garment, he was purged of all obligations of honour to any merely earthly power. His one obligation was to the moral law—in brief, to the ordinance of God, as determined by Christian pastors. Under that moral law, specifically, he was charged to search out and determine its violations by the accused in the dock, to wit, by the German nation, according to the teaching of those pastors and the light within, and to fix and execute a punishment that should be swift, terrible and overwhelming.

To this business, it must be granted by even his most extravagant opponents, he addressed himself with the loftiest resolution and singleness of purpose, excluding all puerile questions of ways and means. He was, by the moral law, no more bound to take into account the process whereby the accused was brought to book and the weight of retribution brought to bear than a detective is bound to remember how any ordinary prisoner is snared for the mill of justice. The detective himself may have been an important factor in that process; he may have taken the prisoner by some stratagem involving the most gross false pretences; he may have even played the *agent provocateur* and so actually suggested, planned and supervised the crime. But surely that would be a ridiculous critic who would argue thereby that the detective should forthwith forget the law violated and the punishment justly provided for it, and go over to the side of the defence on the ground that his dealings with the prisoner involved him in obligations of honour. The world would laugh at such a moral moron, if it did not actually destroy him as an enemy of society. It recognizes the two codes that we have described, and it knows that they are antagonistic. It expects a man sworn to the service of morality to discharge his duty at any cost to his honour, just as it expects a man publicly devoted to honour to keep his word at any cost to his or to the public morals. Moreover, it inclines, when there is a conflict, toward the side of morals; the overwhelming majority of men are men of morals, not men of honour. They believe that it is vastly more important that the guilty should be detected, taken into custody and exposed to the rigour of the law than that the honour of this or that man should be preserved. In truth, there are frequent circumstances under which they positively esteem a man who thus sacrifices his honour, or even their own honour. The man of *dis*honour may actually take on the character of a public hero. Thus, in 1903, when the late Major General Roosevelt, then President, tore up the treaty of 1846, whereby the United States guaranteed the sovereignty of Columbia in the Isthmus of Panama, the great masses of the American plain people not only at once condoned this grave breach of honour, but actually applauded Dr. Roosevelt because his act furthered the great moral enterprise of digging the canal.

These distinctions, of course, are familiar to all men who devote themselves to the study of the human psyche; that morals and honour are not one and the same thing, but two very distinct and even antithetical things, is surely no news to the judicious. But what is thus merely an axiom of ethics, politics or psychology is often kept strangely secret in the United States. We have acquired the habit of evading all the facts of life save those that are most superficial; by long disuse we have almost lost the capacity for thinking analytically and accurately. A thing may be universally known among us, and yet never get itself so much as mentioned. Around scores of elementary platitudes there hangs a shuddering silence as complete as that which hedges in the sacred name of a Polynesian chief. At every election time, in our large cities, most of the fundamental issues are concealed, particularly when they happen to take on a theological colour, which is very often. It is, for example, the timorous public theory, born of this fear of the forthright fact, that when a man sets up as a candidate for, say, a judgeship, the question of his private religious faith is of no practical importance—that it makes no difference whether he is a Catholic or a Methodist. The truth is, of course, that his faith is often of the very first importance—that it will colour his conduct of the forensic combats before him even more than his politics, his capacity to digest proteids or the social aspirations of his wife. One constantly notes, in American jurisprudence, the effects of theological prejudices on the bench; there are at least a dozen controlling decisions, covering especially the new moral legislation, which might almost be mistaken by a layman for sermons by the Rev. Dr. Billy Sunday. The Prohibitionists, during their long and very adroit campaign, shrewdly recognized the importance of controlling the judiciary; in particular, they threw all their power against the election of candidates who were known to be Catholics, or Jews, or free-thinkers. As a result they packed the bench of nearly every state with Methodist, Baptist and Presbyterian judges, and these gentlemen at once upheld all their maze of outrageous statutes. That they would do so if elected was known in advance, and yet, so far as the record shows, it was a rare thing for any one to attack them on the ground of their religion, and rarer still for any such attack to influence many votes. The taboo was working. The majority of voters were eager to avoid that issue. They felt, in some vague and unintelligible way, that it was improper to raise it.

So with all other primary issues. There is surely no country in the world in which the marriage relation is discussed more copiously than in the United States, and yet there is no country in which its essentials are more diligently avoided. Some years ago, seeking to let some sagacity into the prevailing exchange of platitudes, one of us wrote a book upon the subject, grounding it upon the obvious doctrine that women have much more to gain by marriage than men, and that the majority of men are aware of it, and would never marry at all if it were not for women's relentless effort to bring them to it. This banality the writer supported, by dint of great painstaking, in a somewhat novel way. That is to say, he put upon himself the limitation of employing no theory, statement of fact or argument in the book that was not already embodied in a common proverb in some civilized language. Now and then it was a bit hard to find the proverb, but in most cases it was very easy, and in some cases he found, not one, but dozens. Well, this laborious *pastiche* of the obvious made such a sensation that it sold better than any other book that the author had ever written—and the reviews unanimously described it, either with praise or with blame, as an extraordinary collection of heresies, most of them almost too acrid to be bruited about. In other words, this mass of platitudes took Americans by surprise, and somehow shocked them. What was commonplace to even the peasants of the European Continent was so unfamiliar to even the literate minority over here that the book acquired a sort of sinister repute, and the writer himself came to be discussed as a fellow with the habit of arising in decorous society and indelicately blowing his nose.

There is, of course, something of the same shrinking from the elemental facts of life in England; it seems to run with the Anglo-Saxon. This accounts for the shuddering attitude of the English to such platitude-monging foreigners as George Bernard Shaw, the Scotsman disguised as an Irishman, and G. K. Chesterton, who shows all the physical and mental stigmata of a Bavarian. Shaw's plays, which once had all England by the ears, were set down as compendiums of the self-evident by the French, a realistic and plain-spoken people, and were sniffed at in Germany by all save the middle classes, who correspond to the *intelligentsia* of Anglo-Saxondom. But in America, even more than in England, they were viewed as genuinely satanic. We shall never forget, indeed, the tremulous manner in which American audiences first listened to the feeble rattling of the palpable in such pieces as "Man and Superman" and "You Never Can Tell." It was precisely the manner of an old maid devouring "What Every Girl of Forty-Five Should

Know" behind the door. As for Chesterton, his banal arguments in favour of alcohol shocked the country so greatly that his previous high services to religious superstition were forgotten, and today he is seldom mentioned by respectable Americans.

V

It is necessary to repeat that we rehearse all these facts, not in indignation, nor indeed in any spirit of carping whatever, but in perfect serenity and simply as descriptive sociologists. This attitude of mind is but little comprehended in America, where the emotions dominate all human reactions, and even such dismal sciences as paleontology, pathology and comparative philology are gaudily coloured by patriotic and other passions. The typical American learned man suffers horribly from the national disease: he is eternally afraid of something. If it is not that some cheesemonger among his trustees will have him cashiered for receiving a picture post-card from Prof. Dr. Scott Nearing, it is that some sweating and scoundrelly German or Frenchman will discover and denounce his cribs, and if it is not that the foreigner will have at him, it is that he will be robbed of his step from associate to full professor by some rival whose wife is more amiable to the president of the university, or who is himself more popular with the college athletes. Thus surrounded by fears, he translates them, by a familiar psychological process, into indignations. He announces what he has to say in terms of raucous dudgeon, as a negro, having to go past a medical college at night, intones some bellicose gospel-hymn. He is, in brief, vociferously correct. During the late war, at a time of unusual suspicions and hence of unusual hazards, this eagerness to prove orthodoxy by choler was copiously on exhibition. Thus one of the leading American zoölogists printed a work in which, after starting off by denouncing the German naming of new species as ignorant, dishonest and against God, he gradually worked himself up to the doctrine that any American who put a tooth into a slab of *Rinderbrust mit Meerrettig,* or peeped at *Simplicissimus* with the blinds down, or bought his children German-made jumping-jacks, was a traitor to the Constitution and a secret agent of the Wilhelmstrasse. And thus there were American pathologists and bacteriologists who denounced Prof. Dr. Paul Ehrlich as little better than a quack hired by the Krupps to poison Americans, and who displayed their pious horror of the late Prof. Dr. Robert Koch by omitting all acknowledgment of obligation to him from their monographs. And finally there was the posse of "two thousand American Historians" assembled by Mr. Creel to instruct the plain people in the new theory of American history, whereby the Revolution was represented as a lamentable row in an otherwise happy family, deliberately instigated by German intrigue—a posse which reached its greatest height of correct indignation in its approval of the celebrated Sisson documents, to the obscene delight of the British authors thereof.

As we say, we are devoid of all such lofty passions, and hence must present our observations in the flat, unimaginative, unemotional manner of a dentist pulling a tooth. It would not be going too far, in fact, to call us emotional idiots. What ails us is a constitutional suspicion that the other fellow, after all, may be right, or, in any event, partly right. In the present case we by no means reprehend the avoidance of issues that we have described; we merely record it. The fact is that it has certain very obvious uses, and is probably inevitable in a democratic society. It is commonly argued that free speech is necessary to the prosperity of a democracy, but in this doctrine we take no stock. On the contrary, there are plain reasons for holding that free speech is more dangerous to a democracy than to any other form of government, and no doubt these reasons, if only unconsciously, were at the bottom of the extraordinary body of repressive legislation put upon the books during the late war. The essential thing about a democracy is that the men at the head of the state are wholly dependent, for a continuance of their power, upon the good opinion of the popular majority. While they are actually in office, true enough, they are theoretically almost completely irresponsible, but their terms of office are usually so short that they must give constant thought to the imminent canvassing of their acts, and this threat of being judged and turned out commonly greatly conditions their exercise of their power, even while they hold it to the full. Of late, indeed, there has actually arisen the doctrine that they are responsible at all times and must respond to every shift in public sentiment, regardless of their own inclinations, and there has even grown up the custom of subjecting them to formal discipline, as by what is called the recall. The net result is that a public officer under a democracy is bound to regard the popular will during the whole of his term in office, and cannot hope to carry out any intelligible plan of his own if the mob has been set against it.

Now, the trouble with this scheme is that the mob reaches its conclusions, not by logical steps but by emotional steps, and that its information upon all save a very small minority of the questions publicly at issue is always scant and inaccurate. It is thus constantly liable to inflammation by adroit demagogues, or rabble-rousers, and inasmuch as these rabble-rousers are animated as a sole motive by the hope of turning out the existing officers of state and getting the offices for themselves, the man in office must inevitably regard them as his enemies and the doctrines they preach as subversive of good government. This view is not altogether selfish. There is, in fact, sound logic in it, for it is a peculiarity of the mob mind that it always takes in most hospitably what is intrinsically most idiotic—that between two antagonistic leaders it always follows the one who is longest on vague and brilliant words and shortest on sense. Thus the man in office, if he would be free to carry on his duties in anything approaching freedom and comfort, must adopt measures against that tendency to run amuck.

Three devices at once present themselves. One is to take steps against the rabble-rousers by seeking to make it appear that they are traitors, and so arousing the mob against them—in brief, to deny them their constitutional right to free speech under colour of criminal statutes. The second is to combine this plan with that of flooding the country with official news by a corps of press-agents, chautauquans and other such professors of deception. The third is to meet the rabble-rousers on their own ground, matching their appeals to the emotions with appeals even more powerful, and outdoing their vague and soothing words with words even more vague and soothing. All three plans have been in operation since the first days of the republic; the early Federalists employed the first two with such assiduity that the mob of that time finally revolted. All three were brought to the highest conceivable point of perfection by the late Dr. Wilson, a man whose resolute fidelity to his moral ideas was matched only by his magnificent skill at playing upon every prejudice and weakness of the plain people.

But men of such exalted and varied gifts are not common. The average head of a democratic state is not *ipso facto* the best rabble-rouser within that state, but merely one of the best. He may be able, on fair terms, to meet any individual rival, but it is rare for him to be able to meet the whole pack, or even any considerable group. To relieve him from that difficulty, and so prevent the incessant running amuck of the populace, it is necessary to handicap all the remaining rabble-rousers, and this is most effectively done by limitations upon free speech which originate as statutes and gradually take on the form and potency of national customs. Such limitations arose in the United States by precisely that process. They began in the first years of the republic as definite laws. Some of those laws were afterward abandoned, but what was fundamentally sound in them remained in force as custom.

It must be obvious that even Dr. Wilson, despite his tremendous gift for the third of the devices that we have named, would have been in sore case during his second administration if it had not been for his employment of the other two. Imagine the United States during the Summer of 1917 with absolute free speech the order of the day! The mails would have been flooded with Socialist and pacifist documents, every street-corner would have had its screaming soap-box orator, the newspapers would have shaken the very heavens with colossal alarms, and conscientious objection would have taken on the proportions of a national frenzy. In the face of such an avalanche of fears and balderdash, there would have been no work at all for the German propagandists; in fact, it is likely that a great many of them, under suspicion on account of their relative moderation, would have been lynched as agents of the American munitions patriots. For the mob, it must be remembered, infallibly inclines, not to the side of the soundest logic and loftiest purpose, but to the side of the loudest noise, and without the artificial aid of a large and complex organization of press-agents and the power to jail any especially effective opponent forthwith, even a President of the United States would be unable to bawl down the whole fraternity. That it is matter of the utmost importance, in time of war, to avoid any such internal reign of terror must be obvious to even the most fanatical advocate of free speech. There must be, in such emergencies, a resolute pursuit of coherent policies, and that would be obviously impossible with the populace turning distractedly to one bogus messiah after another, and always seeking to force its latest craze upon the government. Thus, while one may perchance drop a tear or two upon the Socialists jailed by a sort of lynch law for trying to exercise their plain constitutional rights, and upon the pacifists tarred and feathered by mobs led by government agents, and upon the conscientious objectors starved and clubbed to death in military dungeons, it must still be plain that such barbarous penalties were essentially necessary. The victims, in the main, were half-wits suffering from the martyr complex; it was their admitted desire to sacrifice themselves for the Larger Good. This desire was gratified—not in the way they hoped for, of course, but nevertheless in a way that must have given any impartial observer a feeling of profound, if discreditable, satisfaction.

What a republic has to fear especially is the rabble-rouser who advocates giving an objective reality to the gaudy theories which lie at the foundations of the prevailing scheme of government. He is far more dangerous than a genuine revolutionist, for the latter comes with ideas that are actually new, or, at all events, new to the mob, and so he has to overcome its congenital hostility to novelty. But the reformer who, under a democracy, bases his case upon the principles upon which democracy is founded has an easy road, for the populace is familiar with those principles and eager to see them put into practical effect. The late Cecil Chesterton, in his penetrating "History of the United States," showed how Andrew Jackson came to power by that route. Jackson, he said, was simply a man so naïve that he accepted the lofty doctrines of the Declaration of Independence without any critical questioning whatever, and "really acted as if they were true." The appearance of such a man, he goes on, was "appalling" to the political aristocrats of 1825. They themselves, of course, enunciated those doctrines daily and based their whole politics upon them—but not to the point of really executing them. So when Jackson came down from the mountains with the same sonorous words upon his lips, but with the addition of a solemn promise to carry them out—when he thus descended upon them, he stole their thunder and spiked their guns, and after a brief struggle he had disposed of them. The Socialists, free-speech fanatics, anti-conscriptionists, anti-militarists and other such democratic maximalists of 1917 and 1918 were, in essence, nothing but a new and formidable horde of Jacksons. Their case rested upon principles held to be true by all good Americans, and constantly reaffirmed by the highest officers of state. It was thus extremely likely that, if they were permitted to woo the public ear, they would quickly amass a majority of suffrages, and so get the conduct of things into their own hands. So it became necessary, in order that the great enterprises then under way might be pushed to a successful issue, that all these marplots be silenced, and it was accordingly done. This proceeding, of course, was theoretically violative of their common rights, and hence theoretically un-American. All the theory, in fact, was on the side of the victims. But war time is no time for theories, and a man with war powers in his hands is not one to parley with them.

As we have said, the menace presented by such unintelligent literalists is probably a good deal more dangerous to a democracy than to a government of any other form. Under an aristocracy, for example, such as prevailed, in one form or another, in England, Germany, Italy and France before the war, it is possible to give doctrinaires a relatively free rein, for even if they succeed in converting the mob to their whim-wham, there remain insuperable impediments to its adoption and execution as law. In England, as every one knows, the impediment was a ruling caste highly skilled in the governmental function and generally trusted by a majority of the populace—a ruling caste firmly intrenched in the House of Lords and scarcely less powerful in the House of Commons. In France it was a bureaucracy so securely protected by law and custom that nothing short of a political cataclysm could shake it. In Germany and Italy it was an aristocracy buttressed by laws cunningly designed to nullify the numerical superiority of the mob, and by a monarchical theory that set up a heavy counterweight to public opinion.

In the face of such adroit checks and balances it is a matter of relative indifference whether the mob blows scalding hot or freezing cold. Whatever the extravagance of its crazes, there remains effective machinery for holding them in check until they spend themselves, which is usually soon enough. Thus the English government, though theoretically as much opposed to anarchists as the American government, gave them cheerful asylum before the war and permitted them to preach their lamentable notions almost without check, whereas in America they early aroused great fears and were presently put under such disabilities that their propaganda became almost impossible. Even in France, where they had many converts and were frequently in eruption, there was far more hospitality to them than in the United States. And thus in the Germany of Bismarck's day, the Socialists, after a brief and aberrant attempt to suppress them, were allowed to run free, despite the fact that their doctrine was quite as abhorrent to German official doctrine as anarchism was to American official doctrine. The German ruling caste of those days was sheltered behind laws and customs which enabled it to pull the teeth of Socialism, even in the face of enormous Socialist majorities. But under a democracy it is difficult, and often downright impossible, to oppose the popular craze of the moment with any effect, and so there must be artificial means of disciplining the jake-fetchers who seek to set such enthusiasms in motion. The shivering fear of Bolshevism, visible of late among the capitalists of America, is based upon a real danger. These capitalists have passed through the burning fires of Rooseveltian trust-busting and Bryanistic populism, and they know very well that half a dozen Lenines and Trotskis, turned loose upon the plain people, would quickly recruit a majority of them for a holy war upon capital, and that they have the political power to make such a holy war devastating.

The amateur of popular psychology may wonder why it is that the mob, in the face of the repressions constantly practised in the United States, does not occasionally rise in revolt, and so get back its right to be wooed and ravished by all sorts of mountebanks. Theoretically it has that right, and what is more, it has the means of regaining it; nothing could resist it if it made absolute free speech an issue in a national campaign and voted for the candidate advocating it. But something is overlooked here, and that is the fact that the mob has no liking for free speech per se. Some of the grounds of its animosity we have rehearsed. Others are not far to seek. One of them lies in the mob's chronic suspicion of all advocates of ideas, born of its distaste for ideas themselves. The mob-man cannot imagine himself throwing up his job and deserting his home, his lodge and his speak-easy to carry a new gospel to his fellows, and so he is inclined to examine the motives of any other man who does so. The one motive that is intelligible to him is the desire for profit, and he commonly concludes at once that this is what moves the propagandist before him. His reasoning is defective, but his conclusion is usually not far from right. In point of fact, idealism is not a passion in America, but a trade; all the salient idealists make a living at it, and some of them, for example, Dr. Bryan and the Rev. Dr. Sunday, are commonly believed to have amassed large fortunes. For an American to advocate a cause without any hope of private usufruct is almost unheard of; it would be difficult to find such a man who was not plainly insane. The most eloquent and impassioned of American idealists are candidates for public office; on the lower levels idealism is no more than a handmaiden of business, like advertising or belonging to the Men and Religion Forward Movement.

Another and very important cause of the proletarian's failure to whoop for free speech is to be found in his barbarous delight in persecution, regardless of the merits of the cause. The spectacle of a man exercising the right of free speech yields, intrinsically, no joy, for there is seldom anything dramatic about it. But the spectacle of a man being mobbed, jailed, beaten and perhaps murdered for trying to exercise it is a good show like any other good show, and the populace is thus not only eager to witness it but even willing to help it along. It is therefore quite easy to set the mob upon, say, the Bolsheviki, despite the fact that the Bolsheviki have the professed aim of doing the mob an incomparable service. During the war-time jinks of the Post office and the Department of Justice, popular opinion was always on the side of the raiding parties. It applauded every descent upon a Socialist or pacifist meeting, not because it was very hotly in favour of war—in fact, it was lukewarm about war, and resisted all efforts to heat it up until overwhelming swarms of yokel-yankers were turned upon it—but because it was in favour of a safe and stimulating form of rough-house, with the police helping instead of hindering. It never stopped to inquire about the merits of the matter. All it asked for was a melodramatic raid, followed by a noisy trial of the accused in the newspapers, and the daily publication of sensational (and usually bogus) evidence about the discovery of compromising literature in his wife's stockings, including records of his receipt of $100,000 from von Bernstorff, Carranza or some other transient hobgoblin. The celebrated O'Leary trial was typical. After months of blood-curdling charges in the press, it turned out when the accused got before a court that the evidence against him, on which it was sought to convict him of a capital offence, was so feeble that it would have scarcely sufficed to convict him of an ordinary misdemeanor, and that most of this feeble testimony was palpably perjured. Nevertheless, public opinion was nearly unanimously against him from first to last, and the jury which acquitted him was almost apologetic about its inability to give the populace the crowning happiness of a state hanging.

Under cover of the war, of course, the business of providing such shows prospered extraordinarily, but it is very active even in time of peace. The surest way to get on in politics in America is to play the leading part in a prosecution which attracts public notice. The list of statesmen who have risen in that fashion includes the names of many of the highest dignity, e.g., Hughes, Folk, Whitman, Heney, Baker and Palmer. Every district attorney in America prays nightly that God will deliver into his hands some Thaw, or Becker, or O'Leary, that he may get upon the front pages and so become a governor, a United States senator, or a justice of the Supreme Court of the United States. The late crusade against W. R. Hearst, which appeared to the public as a great patriotic movement, was actually chiefly managed by a subordinate prosecuting officer who hoped to get high office out of it.

This last aspirant failed in his enterprise largely because he had tackled a man who was himself of superb talents as a rouser of the proletariat, but nine times out of ten the thing succeeds. Its success is due almost entirely to the factor that we have mentioned, to wit, to the circumstance that the sympathy of the public is always on the side of the prosecution. This sympathy goes so far that it is ready to condone the most outrageous conduct in judges and prosecuting officers, providing only they give good shows. During the late war upon Socialists, pacifists, anti-conscriptionists and other such heretics, judges theoretically employed to insure fair trials engaged in the most amazing attacks upon prisoners before them, denouncing them without hearing them, shutting out evidence on their side and making stump speeches to the jury against them. That conduct aroused no public indignation; on the contrary, such judges were frequently praised in the newspapers and a good many of them were promoted to higher courts. Even in time of peace there is no general antipathy to that sort of thing. At least two-thirds of our judges, federal, state and municipal, colour their decisions with the newspaper gabble of the moment; even the Supreme Court has shown itself delicately responsive to the successive manias of the Uplift, which is, at bottom, no more than an organized scheme for inventing new crimes and making noisy pursuit of new categories of criminals. Some time ago an intelligent Mexican, after studying our courts, told us that he was surprised that, in a land ostensibly of liberty, so few of the notorious newspaper-wooers and blacklegs upon the bench were assassinated. It is, in fact, rather curious. The thing happens very seldom, and then it is usually in the South, where the motive is not altruistic but political. That is to say, the assassin merely desires to remove one blackleg in order to make a place for some other blackleg. He has no objection to systematized injustice; all he desires is that it be dispensed in favour of his own side.

VI

The mob delight in melodramatic and cruel spectacles, thus constantly fed and fostered by the judicial arm in the United States, is also at the bottom of another familiar American phenomenon, to wit, lynching. A good part of the enormous literature of lynching is devoted to a discussion of its causes, but most of that discussion is ignorant and some of it is deliberately mendacious. The majority of Southern commentators argue that the motive of the lynchers is a laudable yearning to "protect Southern womanhood," despite the plain fact that only a very small proportion of the blackamoors hanged and burned are even so much as accused of molesting Southern womanhood. On the other hand, some of the negro intellectuals of the North ascribe the recurrent butcheries to the Southern white man's economic jealousy of the Southern black, who is fast acquiring property and reaching out for the prerogatives that go therewith. Finally, certain white Northerners seek a cause in mere political animosity, arguing that the Southern white hates the negro because the latter is his theoretical equal at the polls, though actually not permitted to vote.

All of these notions seem to us to be fanciful. Lynching is popular in the South simply because the Southern populace, like any other populace, delights in thrilling shows, and because no other sort of show is provided by the backward culture of the region. The introduction of prize-fighting down there, or baseball on a large scale, or amusement places like Coney Island, or amateur athletic contests, or picnics like those held by the more truculent Irish fraternal organizations, or any other such wholesale devices for shocking and diverting the proletariat would undoubtedly cause a great decline in lynching. The art is practised, in the overwhelming main, in remote and God-forsaken regions, in which the only rival entertainment is offered by one-sided political campaigns, third-rate chautauquas and Methodist revivals. When it is imitated in the North, it is always in some drab factory or mining town. Genuine race riots, of course, sometimes occur in the larger cities, but these are always economic in origin, and have nothing to do with lynching, properly so-called. One could not imagine an actual lynching at, say, Atlantic City, with ten or fifteen bands playing, blind pigs in operation up every alley, a theatre in every block or two, and the boardwalk swarming with ladies of joy. Even a Mississippian, transported to such scenes, succumbs to the atmosphere of pleasure, and so has no seizures of moral rage against the poor darkey. Lynching, in brief, is a phenomenon of isolated and stupid communities, a mark of imperfect civilization; it follows the hookworm and malaria belt; it shows itself in inverse proportion to the number of shoot-the-chutes, symphony orchestras, roof gardens, theatres, horse races, yellow journals and automatic pianos. No one ever heard of a lynching in Paris, at Newport, or in London. But there are incessant lynchings in the remoter parts of Russia, in the backwoods of Serbia, Bulgaria and Herzegovina, in Mexico and Nicaragua, and in such barbarous American states as Alabama, Georgia and South Carolina.

The notion that lynching in the South is countenanced by the gentry or that they take an actual hand in it is libelous and idiotic. The well-born and well-bred Southerner is no more a savage than any other man of condition. He may live among savages, but that no more makes him a savage than an English gentleman is made one by having a place in Wales, or a Russian by living on his estate in the Ukraine. What Northern observers mistake for the gentry of the South, when they report the participation of "leading citizens" in a lynching, is simply the office-holding and commercial bourgeoisie—the offspring of the poor white trash who skulked at home during the Civil War, robbing the widows and orphans of the soldiers at the front, and so laying the foundations of the present "industrial prosperity" of the section, i.e., its conversion from a region of large landed estates and urbane life into a region of stinking factories, filthy mining and oil towns, child-killing cotton mills, vociferous chambers of commerce and other such swineries. It is, of course, a fact that the average lynching party in Mississippi or Alabama is led by the mayor and that the town judge climbs down from his bench to give it his official support, but it is surely not a fact that these persons are of the line of such earlier public functionaries as Pickens, Troup and Pettus. On the contrary, they correspond to the lesser sort of Tammany officeholders and to the vermin who monopolize the public functions in such cities as Boston and Philadelphia. The gentry, with few exceptions, have been forced out of the public service everywhere south of the Potomac, if not out of politics. The Democratic victory in 1912 flooded all the governmental posts at Washington with Southerners, and some of them remain in office to this day, and are among the chief functionaries of the nation. But in the whole vast corps there are, we believe, but ten who would be accepted as gentlemen by Southern standards, and only three of these are in posts of any importance. In the two houses of Congress there is but one.

It is thus absurd to drag the gentry of the South—the Bourbons of New England legend—into a discussion of the lynching problem. They represent, in fact, what remains of the only genuine aristocracy ever visible in the United States, and lynching, on the theoretical side, is far too moral a matter ever to engage an aristocracy. The true lynchers are the plain people, and at the bottom of the sport there is nothing more noble than the mob man's chronic and ineradicable poltroonery. Cruel by nature, delighting in sanguinary spectacles, and here brought to hatred of the negro by the latter's increasing industrial, (*not* political, capitalistic, or social) rivalry, he naturally diverts himself in his moments of musing with visions of what he would do to this or that Moor if he had the courage. Unluckily, he hasn't, and so he is unable to execute his dream a cappella. If, inflamed by liquor, he attempts it, the Moor commonly gives him a beating, or even murders him. But what thus lies beyond his talents as an individual at once becomes feasible when he joins himself with other men in a like situation. This is the genesis of a mob of lynchers. It is composed primarily of a few men with definite grievances, sometimes against the negro lynched but often against quite different negroes. It is composed secondarily of a large number of fifth-rate men eager for a thrilling show, involving no personal danger. It is composed in the third place of a few rabble-rousers and politicians, all of them hot to exhibit themselves before the populace at a moment of public excitement and in an attitude of leadership. It is the second element that gives life to the general impulse. Without its ardent appetite for a rough and shocking spectacle there would be no lynching. Its influence is plainly shown by the frequent unintelligibility of the whole proceeding; all its indignation over the crime alleged to be punished is an afterthought; any crime will answer, once its blood is up. Thus the most characteristic lynchings in the South are not those in which a confessed criminal is done to death for a definite crime, but those in which, in sheer high spirits, some convenient African is taken at random and lynched, as the newspapers say, "on general principles." That sort of lynching is the most honest and normal, and we are also inclined to think that it is also the most enjoyable, for the other sort brings moral indignation with it, and moral indignation is disagreeable. No man can be both indignant and happy.

But here, seeking to throw a feeble beam or two of light into the mental processes of the American proletarian, we find ourselves entering upon a discussion that grows narrow and perhaps also dull. Lynching, after all, is not an American institution, but a peculiarly Southern institution, and even in the South it will die out as other more seemly recreations are introduced. It would be quite easy, we believe, for any Southern community to get rid of it by establishing a good brass band and having concerts every evening. It would be even easier to get rid of it by borrowing a few professional scoundrels from the Department of Justice, having them raid the "study" of the local Methodist archdeacon, and forthwith trying him publicly—with a candidate for governor as prosecuting officer—for seduction under promise of salvation. The trouble down there is not a special viciousness. The Southern poor white, taking him by and large, is probably no worse and no better than the anthropoid proletarian of the North. What ails the whole region is Philistinism. It has lost its old aristocracy of the soil and has not yet developed an aristocracy of money. The result is that its cultural ideas are set by stupid and unimaginative men—Southern equivalents of the retired Iowa steer sniffers and grain sharks who pollute Los Angeles, American equivalents of the rich English nonconformists. These men, though they have accumulated wealth, have not yet acquired the capacity to enjoy civilized recreations. Worse, most of them are still so barbarous that they regard such recreations as immoral. The dominating opinion of the South is thus against most of the devices that would diminish lynching by providing substitutes for it. In every Southern town some noisy clown of a Methodist or Presbyterian clergyman exercises a local tyranny. These men are firmly against all the divertissements of more cultured regions. They oppose prize-fighting, horse-racing, Sunday baseball and games of chance. They are bitter prohibitionists. By their incessant vice-crusades they reduce the romance of sex to furtiveness and piggishness. They know nothing of music or the drama, and view a public library merely as something to be rigorously censored. We are convinced that their ignorant moral enthusiasm is largely to blame for the prevalence of lynching. No doubt they themselves are sneakingly conscious of the fact, or at least aware of it subconsciously, for lynching is the only public amusement that they never denounce.

Their influence reveals strikingly the readiness of the inferior American to accept ready-made opinions. He seems to be pathetically eager to be told what to think, and he is apparently willing to accept any instructor who takes the trouble to tackle him. This, also, was brilliantly revealed during the late war. The powers which controlled the press during that fevered time swayed the populace as they pleased. So long as the course of Dr. Wilson was satisfactory to them he was depicted as a second Lincoln, and the plain people accepted the estimate without question. To help reinforce it the country was actually flooded with lithographs showing Lincoln and Wilson wreathed by the same branch of laurel, and copies of the print got into millions of humble homes. But immediately Dr. Wilson gave offence to his superiors, he began to be depicted as an idiot and a scoundrel, and this judgment promptly displaced the other one in the popular mind. The late Major General Roosevelt was often a victim of that sort of boob-bumping. A man of mercurial temperament, constantly shifting his position on all large public questions, he alternately gave great joy and great alarm to the little group of sagaciously wilful men which exercises genuine sovereignty over the country, and this alternation of emotions showed itself, by way of the newspapers and other such bawdy agencies, in the vacillation of public opinion. The fundamental platitudes of the nation were used both for him and against him, and always with immense effect. One year he was the last living defender of the liberties fought for by the Fathers; the next year he was an anarchist. Roosevelt himself was much annoyed by this unreliability of the mob. Now and then he sought to overcome it by direct appeals, but in the long run he was usually beaten. Toward the end of his life he resigned himself to a policy of great discretion, and so withheld his voice until he was sure what hymn was being lined out.

The newspapers and press associations, of course, do not impart the official doctrine of the moment in terms of forthright instructions; they get it over, as the phrase is, in the form of delicate suggestions, most of them under cover of the fundamental platitudes aforesaid. Their job is not to inspire and inform public discussion, but simply to colour it, and the task most frequently before them is that of giving a patriotic and virtuous appearance to whatever the proletariat is to believe. They do this, of course, to the tune of deafening protestations of their own honesty and altruism. But there is really no such thing as an honest newspaper in America; if it were set up tomorrow it would perish within a month. Every journal, however rich and powerful, is the trembling slave of higher powers, some financial, some religious and some political. It faces a multitude of censorships, all of them very potent. It is censored by the Postoffice, by the Jewish advertisers, by the Catholic Church, by the Methodists, by the Prohibitionists, by the banking oligarchy of its town, and often by even more astounding authorities, including the Sinn Fein. Now and then a newspaper makes a valiant gesture of revolt, but it is only a gesture. There is not a single daily in the United States that would dare to discuss the problem of Jewish immigration honestly. Nine tenths of them, under the lash of snobbish Jewish advertisers, are even afraid to call a Jew a Jew; their orders are to call him a Hebrew, which is regarded as sweeter. During the height of the Bolshevist scare not one American paper ventured to direct attention to the plain and obtrusive fact that the majority of Bolshevists in Russia and Germany and at least two-thirds of those taken in the United States were of the faith of Moses, Mendelssohn and Gimbel. But the Jews are perhaps not the worst. The Methodists, in all save a few big cities, exercise a control over the press that is far more rigid and baleful. In the Anti-Saloon League they have developed a machine for terrorizing office-holders and the newspapers that is remarkably effective, and they employed it during the long fight for Prohibition to throttle all opposition save the most formal.

In this last case, of course, the idealists who thus forced the speak-easy upon the country had an easy task, for all of the prevailing assumptions and prejudices of the mob were in their favour.

No doubt it is true, as has been alleged, that a majority of the voters of the country were against Prohibition and would have defeated it at a plebiscite, but equally without doubt a majority of them were against the politicians so brutally clubbed by the Anti-Saloon League, and ready to believe anything evil of them, and eager to see them manhandled. Moreover, the League had another thing in its favour: it was operated by strictly moral men, oblivious to any notion of honour. Thus it advocated and procured the abolition of legalized liquor selling without the slightest compensation to the men who had invested their money in the business under cover of and even at the invitation of the law—a form of repudiation and confiscation unheard of in any other civilized country. Again, it got through the constitutional amendment by promising the liquor men to give them one year to dispose of their lawfully accumulated stocks—and then broke its promise under cover of alleged war necessity, despite the fact that the war was actually over. Both proceedings, so abhorrent to any man of honour, failed to arouse any indignation among the plain people. On the contrary the plain people viewed them as, in some vague way, smart and creditable, and as, in any case, thoroughly justified by the superior moral obligation that we have hitherto discussed.

Thus the *Boobus americanus* is lead and watched over by zealous men, all of them highly skilled at training him in the way that he should think and act. The Constitution of his country guarantees that he shall be a free man and assumes that he is intelligent, but the laws and customs that have grown up under that Constitution give the lie to both the guarantee and the assumption. It is the fundamental theory of all the more recent American law, in fact, that the average citizen is half-witted, and hence not to be trusted to either his own devices or his own thoughts. If there were not regulations against the saloon (it seems to say) he would get drunk every day, dissipate his means, undermine his health and beggar his family. If there were not postal regulations as to his reading matter, he would divide his time between Bolshevist literature and pornographic literature and so become at once an anarchist and a guinea pig. If he were not forbidden under heavy penalites to cross a state line with a wench, he would be chronically unfaithful to his wife. Worse, if his daughter were not protected by statutes of the most draconian severity, she would succumb to the first Italian she encountered, yield up her person to him, enroll herself upon his staff and go upon the streets. So runs the course of legislation in this land of freemen. We could pile up example upon example, but will defer the business for the present. Perhaps it may be resumed in a work one of us is now engaged upon—a full length study of the popular mind under the republic. But that work will take years. . . .

VII

No doubt we should apologize for writing, even so, so long a preface to so succinct a book. The one excuse we can think of is that, having read it, one need not read the book. That book, as we have said, may strike the superficial as jocular, but in actual fact it is a very serious and even profound composition, not addressed to the casual reader, but to the scholar. Its preparation involved a great diligence, and its study is not to be undertaken lightly. What the psychologist will find to admire in it, however, is not its learning and painstaking, its laborious erudition, but its compression. It establishes, we believe, a new and clearer method for a science long run to turgidity and flatulence. Perhaps it may be even said to set up an entirely new science, to wit, that of descriptive sociological psychology. We believe that this field will attract many men of inquiring mind hereafter and yield a valuable crop of important facts. The experimental method, intrinsically so sound and useful, has been much abused by orthodox psychologists; it inevitably leads them into a trackless maze of meaningless tables and diagrams; they keep their eyes so resolutely upon the intellectual process that they pay no heed to the primary intellectual materials. Nevertheless, it must be obvious that the conclusions that a man comes to, the emotions that he harbours and the crazes that sway him are of much less significance than the fundamental assumptions upon which they are all based.

There has been, indeed, some discussion of those fundamental assumptions of late. We have heard, for example, many acute discourses upon the effects produced upon the whole thinking of the German people, peasants and professors alike, by the underlying German assumption that the late Kaiser was anointed of God and hence above all ordinary human responsibility. We have heard talk, too, of the curious Irish axiom that there is a mysterious something in the nature of things, giving the Irish people an indefeasible right to govern Ireland as they please, regardless of the safety of their next-door neighbours. And we have heard many outlandish principles of the same sort from political theorists, e.g., regarding the inalienable right of democracy to prevail over all other forms of government and the inalienable right of all national groups, however small, to self-determination. Well, here is an attempt to assemble in convenient form, without comment or interpretation, some of the fundamental beliefs of the largest body of human beings now under one flag in Christendom. It is but a beginning. The field is barely platted. It must be explored to the last furlong and all its fantastic and fascinating treasures unearthed and examined before ever there can be any accurate understanding of the mind of the American people.

GEORGE JEAN NATHAN
H. L. MENCKEN
New York, 1920

THE AMERICAN CREDO

§ 1

THAT THE PHILOPROGENITIVE INSTINCT IN RABBITS IS SO INTENSE that the alliance of two normally assiduous rabbits is productive of 265 offspring in one year.

§ 2

That there are hundreds of letters in the Dead Letter Office whose failure to arrive at their intended destinations was instrumental in separating as many lovers.

§ 3

That the Italian who sells bananas on a push-cart always takes the bananas home at night and sleeps with them under his bed.

§ 4

That a man's stability in the community and reliability in business may be measured by the number of children he has.

§ 5

That in Japan an American can buy a beautiful geisha for two dollars and that, upon being bought, she will promptly fall madly in love with him and will run his house for him in a scrupulously clean manner.

§ 6

That all sailors are gifted with an extraordinary propensity for amour, but that on their first night of shore leave they hang around the water-front blind-pigs and are given knock-out drops.

§ 7

That when a comedian, just before the rise of the curtain, is handed a telegram announcing the death of his mother or only child, he goes out on the stage and gives a more comic performance than ever.

§ 8

That the lions in the cage which a lion-tamer enters are always sixty years old and have had all their teeth pulled.

§ 9

That the Siamese Twins were joined together by gutta percha moulded and painted to look like a shoulder blade.

§ 10

That if a woman about to become a mother plays the piano every day, her baby will be born a Victor Herbert.

§ 11

That all excursion boats are so old that if they ran into a drifting beer-keg they would sink.

§ 12

That a doctor knows so much about women that he can no longer fall in love with one of them.

§ 13

That when one takes one's best girl to see the monkeys in the zoo, the monkeys invariably do something that is very embarrassing.

§ 14

That firemen, awakened suddenly in the middle of the night, go to fires in their stocking feet.

§ 15

That something mysterious goes on in the rooms back of chop suey restaurants.

§ 16

That oil of pennyroyal will drive away mosquitoes.

§ 17

That the old ladies on summer hotel verandas devote themselves entirely to the discussion of scandals.

§ 18

That a bachelor, expecting a feminine visitor, by way of subtle preliminary strategy smells up his rooms with Japanese punk.

§ 19

That all one has to do to gather a large crowd in New York is to stand on the curb a few moments and gaze intently at the sky.

§ 20

That one can get an excellent bottle of wine in France for a franc.

§ 21

That it is dangerous to drink out of a garden hose, since if one does one is likely to swallow a snake.

§ 22

That all male negroes can sing.

§ 23

That when a girl enters a hospital as a nurse, her primary object is always to catch one of the doctors.

§ 24

That the postmasters in small towns read all the postcards.

§ 25

That a young girl ought to devote herself sedulously to her piano lessons since, when she is married, her playing will be a great comfort to her husband.

§ 26

That all theater box-office employés are very impolite and hate to sell a prospective patron a ticket.

§ 27

That all great men have illegible signatures.

§ 28

That all iron-moulders and steam-fitters, back in the days of freedom, used to get drunk every Saturday night.

§ 29

That if a man takes a cold bath regularly every morning of his life he will never be ill.

§ 30

That ginger snaps are made of the sweepings of the floor in the bakery.

§ 31

That every circus clown's heart is breaking for one reason or another.

§ 32

That a bullfighter always has so many women in love with him that he doesn't know what to do.

§ 33

That George M. Cohan spends all his time hanging around Broadway cafés and street-corners making flip remarks.

§ 34

That one can never tell accurately what the public wants.

§ 35

That every time one sat upon an old-fashioned horse-hair sofa one of the protruding sharp hairs would stab one through the union suit.

§ 36

That when an ocean vessel collides with another vessel or hits an iceberg and starts to sink, the ship's band promptly rushes up to the top deck and begins playing "Nearer, My God, to Thee."

§ 37

That in no town in America where it has played has *Uncle Tom's Cabin* ever failed to make money.

§ 38

That the tenement districts are the unhealthy places they are because the dwellers hang their bed-clothing out on the fire-escapes.

§ 39

That, in small town hotels, the tap marked "hot water" always gives forth cold water and that the tap marked "cold" always gives forth hot.

§ 40

That every lieutenant in the American army who went to France had an affair with a French comtesse.

§ 41

That when cousins marry, their children are born blind, deformed, or imbecile.

§ 42

That a cat falling from the twentieth story of the Singer Building will land upon the pavement below on its feet, uninjured and as frisky as ever.

§ 43

That the accumulation of great wealth always brings with it great unhappiness.

§ 44

That it is unlucky to count the carriages in a funeral.

§ 45

That the roulette wheel at Monte Carlo is controlled by a wire as thin as a hair which is controlled in turn by a button hidden beneath the rug near the operator's great toe.

§ 46

That Polish women are so little human that one of them can have a baby at 8 AM and cook her husband's dinner at noon.

§ 47

That Henry James never wrote a short sentence.

§ 48

That it is bad luck to kill a spider.

§ 49

That German peasants are possessed of a profound knowledge of music.

§ 50

That every coloured cook has a lover who never works, and that she feeds him by stealing the best part of every dish she cooks.

§ 51

That George Bernard Shaw doesn't really believe anything he writes.

§ 52

That the music of Richard Wagner is all played *fortissimo,* and by cornets.

§ 53

That the Masonic order goes back to the days of King Solomon.

§ 54

That swearing is forbidden by the Bible.

§ 55

That all newspaper reporters carry notebooks.

§ 56

That whiskey is good for snake-bite.

§ 57

That surgeons often kill patients for the sheer pleasure of it.

§ 58

That ten drops of camphor in half a glass of water will prevent a cold.

§ 59

That the first thing a country jake does when he comes to New York is to make a bee line for Grant's Tomb and the Aquarium.

§ 60

That if one's nose tickles it is a sign that one is going to meet a stranger or kiss a fool.

§ 61

That if one's right ear burns, it is a sign that some one is saying nice things about one.

§ 62

That if one's left ear burns, it is a sign that some one is saying mean things about one.

§ 63

That French women use great quantities of perfume in lieu of taking a bath.

§ 64

That a six-footer is invariably a virtuoso of amour superior to a man of, say, five feet seven.

§ 65

That a soubrette is always fifteen or twenty years older than she looks.

§ 66

That what impels most men to have their fingernails manicured is a vanity for having manicured fingernails.

§ 67

That water rots the hair and thus causes baldness.

§ 68

That when one twin dies, the other twin becomes exceedingly melancholy and soon also dies.

§ 69

That one may always successfully get a cinder out of the eye by not touching the eye, but by rolling it in an outward direction and simultaneously blowing the nose.

§ 70

That if one wears light weight underwear winter and summer the year 'round, one will never catch a cold.

§ 71

That a drunken man is invariably more bellicose than a sober man.

§ 72

That all prize-fighters and baseball players have their hair cut round in the back.

§ 73

That the work of a detective calls for exceptionally high sagacity and cunning.

§ 74

That on the first day of the season in the pleasure parks many persons, owing to insufficiently tested apparatus, are regularly killed on the roller-coasters.

§ 75

That a play, a novel, or a short story with a happy ending is necessarily a commercialized and inartistic piece of work.

§ 76

That a person who follows up a cucumber salad with a dish of ice-cream will inevitably be the victim of cholera morbus.

§ 77

That a Sunday School superintendent is always carrying on an intrigue with one of the girls in the choir.

§ 78

That it is one of the marks of a gentleman that he never speaks evil of a woman.

§ 79

That a member of the Masons cannot be hanged.

§ 80

That a policeman can eat *gratis* as much fruit and as many peanuts off the street-corner stands as he wants.

§ 81

That the real President of the United States is J. P. Morgan.

§ 82

That onion breath may be promptly removed by drinking a little milk.

§ 83

That onion breath may be promptly removed by eating a little parsley.

§ 84

That Catholic priests conduct their private conversations in Latin.

§ 85

That John Drew is a great society man.

§ 86

That all Swedes are stupid fellows, and have very thick skulls.

§ 87

That all the posthumously printed stories of David Graham Phillips and Jack London have been written by hacks hired by the magazine editors and publishers.

§ 88

That a man like Charles Schwab, who has made a great success of the steel business, could in the same way easily have become a great composer like Bach or Mozart had he been minded thus to devote his talents.

§ 89

That the man who doesn't hop promptly to his feet when the orchestra plays "The Star Spangled Banner" as an overture to Hurtig and Seamon's "Hurly-Burly Girlies" must have either rheumatism or pro-Bolshevik sympathies.

§ 90

That every workman in Henry Ford's factory owns a pretty house in the suburbs and has a rose garden in the backyard.

§ 91

That all circus people are very pure and lead domestic lives.

§ 92

That if a spark hits a celluloid collar, the collar will explode.

§ 93

That when a bachelor who has hated children for twenty years gets married and discovers he is about to become a father, he is delighted.

§ 94

That drinking three drinks of whiskey a day will prevent pneumonia.

§ 95

That every negro who went to France with the army had a liaison with a white woman and won't look at a nigger wench any more.

§ 96

That all Russians have unpronounceable names.

§ 97

That awnings keep rooms cool.

§ 98

That it is very difficult to decipher a railroad time-table.

§ 99

That gamblers may always be identified by their habit of wearing large diamonds.

§ 100

That when a man embarks in a canoe with a girl, the chances are two to one that the girl will move around when the boat is in mid-stream and upset it.

§ 101

That German babies are brought up on beer in place of milk.

§ 102

That a man with two shots of cocaine in him could lick Jack Dempsey.

§ 103

That fully one half the repertoire of physical ailments is due to uric acid.

§ 104

That a woman, when buying a cravat for a man, always picks out one of green and purple with red polka-dots.

§ 105

That a negro's vote may always be readily bought for a dollar.

§ 106

That cripples always have very sunny dispositions.

§ 107

That if one drops a crust of bread into one's glass of champagne, one can drink indefinitely without getting drunk.

§ 108

That a brass band always makes one feel like marching.

§ 109

That, when shaving on a railway train, a man invariably cuts himself.

§ 110

That the male Spaniard is generally a handsome, flashing-eyed fellow, possessed of fiery temper.

§ 111

That after drinking a glass of absinthe one has peculiar hallucinations and nightmares.

§ 112

That since the Indians were never bald, baldness comes from wearing tight hats.

§ 113

That all wine-agents are very loose men.

§ 114

That the editor of a woman's magazine is always a lizzie.

§ 115

That what is contained in the pitcher on the speakers' platform is always ice-water.

§ 116

That all Senators from Texas wear sombreros, chew tobacco, expectorate profusely, and frequently employ the word "maverick."

§ 117

That the meters on taxicabs are covertly manipulated by the chauffeurs by means of wires hidden under the latters' seats.

§ 118

That Lillian Russell is as beautiful today as she was thirty-five years ago.

§ 119

That if a young woman can hold a lighted match in her fingers until it completely burns up, it is a sign that her young man really loves her.

§ 120

That if a young woman accidentally puts on her lingerie wrong side out, it is a sign that she will be married before the end of the year.

§ 121

That if a bride wears an old garter with her new finery, she will have a happy married life.

§ 122

That a sudden chill is a sign that somebody is walking over one's grave.

§ 123

That some ignoble Italian is at the bottom of every Dorothy Arnold *fugax*.

§ 124

That a tarantula will not crawl over a piece of rope.

§ 125

That millionaires always go to sleep at the opera.

§ 126

That Paderewski can get all the pianos he wants for nothing.

§ 127

That a bloodhound never makes a mistake.

§ 128

That celery is good for the nerves.

§ 129

That the jokes in *Punch* are never funny.

§ 130

That the Mohammedans are heathens.

§ 131

That a sudden shock may cause the hair to turn grey over night.

§ 132

That the farmer is an honest man, and greatly imposed upon.

§ 133

That all the antique furniture sold in America is made in Grand Rapids, Mich., and that the holes testifying to its age are made either with gimlets or by trained worms.

§ 134

That if a dog is fond of a man it is an infallible sign that the man is a good sort, and one to be trusted.

§ 135

That blondes are flightier than brunettes.

§ 136

That a nurse, however ugly, always looks beautiful to the sick man.

§ 137

That bookkeepers are always round-shouldered.

§ 138

That if one touches a hop-toad, one will get warts.

§ 139

That a collar-button that drops to the floor when one is dressing invariably rolls into an obscure and inaccessible spot and eludes the explorations of its owner.

§ 140

That an American ambassador has the French, German, Italian, Spanish, Portuguese, Russian, and Japanese languages at his finger tips, and is chummy with royalty.

§ 141

That the ready-made mail order blue serge suits for men are put together with mucilage, and turn green after they have been in the sunlight for a day or two.

§ 142

That if one has only three matches left, the first two will invariably go out, but that the third and last will remain lighted.

§ 143

That all Chinamen smoke opium.

§ 144

That every country girl who falls has been seduced by a man from the city.

§ 145

That an intelligent prize-fighter always triumphs over an ignorant prize-fighter, however superior the latter in agility and strength.

§ 146

That a doctor's family never gets sick.

§ 147

That nature designed a horse's tail primarily as a flicker-off of flies.

§ 148

That nicotine keeps the teeth in a sound condition.

§ 149

That when an Odd Fellow dies he is always given a magnificent funeral by his lodge, including a band and a parade.

§ 150

That the man who is elected president of the Senior Class in a college is always the most popular man in his class.

§ 151

That a minor actress in a theatrical company always considers the leading man a superb creature, and loves him at a distance.

§ 152

That a Southern levee is a gay place.

§ 153

That when a dog whines in the middle of the night, it is a sure sign that some one is going to die.

§ 154

That the stenographer in a business house is always coveted by her employer, who invites her to luncheon frequently, gradually worms his way into her confidence, keeps her after office hours one day, accomplishes her ruin, and then sets her up in a magnificently furnished apartment in Riverside Drive and appeases her old mother by paying the latter's expenses for a summer holiday with her daughter at the seashore.

§ 155

That the extinction of the Indian has been a deplorable thing.

§ 156

That everybody has a stomach-ache after Thanksgiving dinner.

§ 157

That, in summer, tan shoes are much cooler on the feet than black shoes.

§ 158

That every man who calls himself Redmond is a Jew whose real name is Rosenberg.

§ 159

That General Grant never directed a battle save with a cigar in his mouth.

§ 160

That there is something slightly peculiar about a man who wears spats.

§ 161

That the more modest a young girl is, the more innocent she is.

§ 162

That what a woman admires above everything else in a man is an upright character.

§ 163

That seafaring men drink nothing but rum.

§ 164

That no family in the slums has less than six children.

§ 165

That a piece of camphor worn on a string around the neck will ward off disease.

§ 166

That a saloon with a sign reading "Family Entrance" on its side door invariably has a bawdy house upstairs.

§ 167

That the wife of a rich man always wistfully looks back into the past and wishes she had married a poor man.

§ 168

That all persons prominent in smart society are very dull.

§ 169

That when ordering a drink of whiskey at a bar, a man always used to instruct the bartender as to the size of the drink he desired by saying "two fingers" or "three fingers."

§ 170

That all the wine formerly served in Italian restaurants was made in the cellar, and was artificially coloured with some sort of dye that was very harmful to the stomach.

§ 171

That all criminals get caught sooner or later.

§ 172

That stokers on ocean liners are from long service so used to the heat of the furnaces that they don't notice it.

§ 173

That what draws men to horse races is love of the sport.

§ 174

That tarantulas often come from the tropics in bunches of bananas, and that when one of them stings a negro on the wharf he swells up, turns green and dies within three hours.

§ 175

That a man will do anything for the woman he loves.

§ 176

That the reason William Gillette, who has been acting for over forty years, always smokes cigars in the parts he plays is because he is very nervous when on the stage.

§ 177

That the doughnut is an exceptionally indigestible article.

§ 178

That one captive balloon in every two containing persons on pleasure bent breaks away from its moorings, and drifts out to sea.

§ 179

That a workingman always eats what is in his dinnerpail with great relish.

§ 180

That children were much better behaved twenty years ago than they are today.

§ 181

That the cashier of a restaurant in adding up a customer's cheque always adds a dollar which is subsequently split between himself and the waiter.

§ 182

That it is impossible to pronounce the word "statistics" without stuttering.

§ 183

That the profession of white slaving, in 1900 controlled exclusively by Chinamen, has since passed entirely under the control of Italians.

§ 184

That every person in the Riviera lives in a "villa."

§ 185

That the chief form of headgear among the Swiss is the Alpine hat.

§ 186

That each year a man volunteers to take his children to the circus merely as a subterfuge to go himself.

§ 187

That all marriages with actresses turn out badly.

§ 188

That San Francisco is a very gay place, and full of opium joints.

§ 189

That an elevator operator never succeeds in stopping his car on a level with the floor.

§ 190

That they don't make any pianos today as good as the old square ones.

§ 191

That a man who habitually clears his throat before he speaks is generally a self-important hypocrite and a bluffer.

§ 192

That Maurice Maeterlinck, the Belgian Dr. Frank Crane, leads a monastic life.

§ 193

That whenever a vaudeville comedian quotes a familiar commercial slogan, such as "His Master's Voice," or "Eventually, why not now?", he is paid $50 a performance for doing so.

§ 194

That all Asiatic idols have large precious rubies in their foreheads.

§ 195

That when the foe beheld Joan of Arc leading the French army against them, a look of terror froze their features and that, casting their arms from them, they broke into a frenzied and precipitate flight.

§ 196

That the late King Edward VII as Prince of Wales easily got every girl he wanted.

§ 197

That the penitentiaries of the United States contain a great number of hapless prisoners possessed of a genuine gift for poetry.

§ 198

That if a cat gets into a room where a baby is sleeping, the cat will suck the baby's breath and kill it.

§ 199

That all men named Clarence, Claude or Percy are sissies.

§ 200

That a street car conductor steals every fifth nickel.

§ 201

That the security of a bank is to be estimated in proportion to the solidity of the bank building.

§ 202

That seventy-five percent of all taxicab drivers have at one time or another been in Sing Sing.

§ 203

That one can buy a fine suit of clothes in London for twelve dollars.

§ 204

That the chicken salad served in restaurants is always made of veal.

§ 205

That a play without a bed in it never makes any money in Paris.

§ 206

That Conan Doyle would have made a wonderful detective.

§ 207

That an oyster-shucker every month or so discovers a pearl which he goes out and sells for five hundred dollars.

§ 208

That a napkin is always wrapped around a champagne bottle for the purpose of hiding the label, and that the quality of the champagne may be judged by the amount of noise the cork makes when it is popped.

§ 209

That because a married woman remains loyal to her husband she loves him.

§ 210

That every time one blows oneself to a particularly expensive cigar and leans back to enjoy oneself with a good smoke after a hearty and satisfying dinner, the cigar proceeds to burn down the side.

§ 211

That when a police captain goes on a holiday he always gets boilingly drunk.

§ 212

That an Italian puts garlic in everything he eats, including coffee.

§ 213

That if one hits a negro on the head with a cobblestone, the cobblestone will break.

§ 214

That all nuns have entered convents because of unfortunate love affairs.

§ 215

That, being surrounded by alcoholic beverages and believing the temptation would be irresistible once he began, a bartender in the old days never took a drink.

§ 216

That all millionaires are born in small ramshackle houses situated near railroad tracks.

§ 217

That farmers afford particularly easy prey for book-agents and are the largest purchasers of cheap sets of Guy de Maupassant, Rudyard Kipling and O. Henry.

§ 218

That George Washington never told a lie.

§ 219

That a dark cigar is always a strong one.

§ 220

That the night air is poisonous.

§ 221

That a hair from a horse's tail, if put into a bottle of water, will turn into a snake.

§ 222

That champagne is the best of all wines.

§ 223

That it snowed every Christmas down to fifteen years ago.

§ 224

That if a young woman finds a piece of tea leaf floating around the top of her tea cup, it is a sign that she will be married before the end of the year.

§ 225

That if, after one lusty blow, a girl's birthday cake reveals nine candles still burning, it is a sign that it will be nine years before she gets married.

§ 226

That if, while promenading, a girl and her escort walk on either side of a water hydrant or other obstruction instead of both walking 'round it on the same side, they will have a misunderstanding before the month is over.

§ 227

That it is unlikely that a man and woman who enter a hotel without baggage after 10 PM and register are man and wife.

§ 228

That all country girls have clear, fresh, rosy complexions.

§ 229

That chorus girls spend the time during the entr'-actes sitting around naked in their dressing-rooms telling naughty stories.

§ 230

That many soldiers' lives have been saved in battle by bullets lodging in Bibles which they have carried in their breast pockets.

§ 231

That each year the Fourth of July exodus to the bathing beaches on the part of persons from the city establishes a new record.

§ 232

That women with red hair or wide nostrils are possessed of especially passionate natures.

§ 233

That three-fourths of the inhabitants of Denver are lungers who have gone there for the mountain air.

§ 234

That, when sojourning in Italy, one always feels very lazy.

§ 235

That the people of Johnstown, Pa., still talk of nothing but the flood.

§ 236

That there is no finer smell in the world than that of burning autumn leaves.

§ 237

That Jules Verne anticipated all the great modern inventions.

§ 238

That a man is always a much heartier eater than a woman.

§ 239

That all the girls in Mr. Ziegfeld's "Follies" are extraordinarily seductive, and that at least 40 head of bank cashiers are annually guilty of tapping the till in order to buy them diamonds and Russian sables.

§ 240

That a college sophomore is always a complete ignoramus.

§ 241

That rubbers in wet weather are a preventive of colds.

§ 242

That if one eats oysters in a month not containing an "r," one is certain to get ptomaine poisoning.

§ 243

That a woman with a 7½-C foot always tries to squeeze it into a 4½-A shoe.

§ 244

That no shop girl ever reads anything but Laura Jean Libbey and the cheap sex magazines.

§ 245

That there is something peculiar about a man who wears a red tie.

§ 246

That all Bolsheviki and Anarchists have whiskers.

§ 247

That all the millionaires of Pittsburgh are very loud fellows, and raise merry hell with the chorus girls every time they go to New York.

§ 248

That a man of fifty-five is always more experienced than a man of thirty-five.

§ 249

That new Bermuda potatoes come from Bermuda.

§ 250

That the boy who regularly stands at the foot of his class in school always turns out in later life to be very successful.

§ 251

That the ornamental daggers fashioned out of one hundred dollars' worth of Chinese coins strung together, which one buys in Pekin or Hong Kong for three dollars and a quarter, are fashioned out of one hundred dollars' worth of Chinese coins.

§ 252

That it is hard to find anyone in Hoboken, N. J., who can speak English.

§ 253

That the headwaiter in a fashionable restaurant has better manners than any other man in the place.

§ 254

That a girl always likes best the man who is possessed of a cavalier politeness.

§ 255

That the most comfortable room conceivable is one containing a great big open fireplace.

§ 256

That brunettes are more likely to grow stout in later years than blondes.

§ 257

That a sepia photograph of the Coliseum, framed, is a work of art.

§ 258

That every time one crosses the English Channel one encounters rough weather and is very sea-sick.

§ 259

That the Navajo blankets sold to trans-continental tourists by the Indians on the station platform at Albuquerque, New Mexico, are made by the Elite Novelty M'f'g. Co. of Passaic, N. J., and are bought by the Indians in lots of 1,000.

§ 260

That appendicitis is an ailment invented by surgeons twelve years ago for money-making purposes and that, in the century before that time, no one was ever troubled with it.

§ 261

That a theatrical matineé performance is always inferior to an evening performance, the star being always eager to hurry up the show in order to get a longer period for rest before the night performance.

§ 262

That John D. Rockefeller would give his whole fortune for a digestion good enough to digest a cruller.

§ 263

That a clergyman leads an easy and lazy life, and spends most of his time visiting women parishioners while their husbands are at work.

§ 264

That it is almost sure death to eat cucumbers and drink milk at the same meal.

§ 265

That all bank cashiers, soon or late, tap the till.

§ 266

That the members of fashionable church choirs, during the sermon, engage in kissing and hugging behind the pipe-organ.

§ 267

That women who are in society never pay any attention to their children, and wish that they would die.

§ 268

That if one gets one's feet wet, one is sure to catch cold.

§ 269

That all French women are very passionate, and will sacrifice everything to love.

§ 270

That when a drunken man falls he never hurts himself.

§ 271

That all Chinese laundrymen sprinkle their laundry by taking a mouthful of water and squirting it out at their wash in a fine spray; and that, whatever the cost of living to a white man, the Chinese laundryman always lives on eight cents a day.

§ 272

That if one fixes a savage beast with one's eye, the beast will remain rooted to the spot and presently slink away.

§ 273

That if one eats cucumbers and then goes in swimming, one will be seized with a cramp.

§ 274

That hiccoughs may be stopped by counting slowly up to one hundred.

§ 275

That newspaper reporters hear, every day, a great many thumping scandals that they fail to print, and that they refrain through considerations of honour.

§ 276

That the young East Side fellow who plays violin solos at the moving-picture theatre around the corner is so talented that, if he had the money to go to Europe to study, he would be a rival to Kreisler within three years.

§ 277

That Paderewski, during the piano-playing days, wore a wig, and was actually as bald as a coot.

§ 278

That lightning never strikes twice in the same place.

§ 279

That when a doctor finds there is nothing the matter with a man who has come to consult him, he never frankly tells the man there's nothing wrong with him, but always gives him bread pills.

§ 280

That, in a family crisis, the son always sticks to the mother and the daughter to the father.

§ 281

That beer is very fattening.

§ 282

That no man of first-rate mental attainments ever goes in for dancing.

§ 283

That a woman can't sharpen a lead pencil.

§ 284

That on every trans-Atlantic steamer there are two smooth gamblers who, the moment the ship docks, sneak over the side with the large sum of money they have won from the passengers.

§ 285

That if one gets out of bed on the left side in the morning, one has a mean disposition for the rest of the day.

§ 286

That a woman who has led a loose life is so grateful for the respect shown her by the man who asks her to marry him that she makes the best kind of wife.

§ 287

That fish is a brain food.

§ 288

That street-corner beggars have a great deal of money hidden away at home under the kitchen floor.

§ 289

That it is advisable for a young woman who takes gas when having a tooth pulled to be accompanied by some one, by way of precaution against the dentist.

§ 290

That all girls educated in convents turn out in later life to be hell-raisers.

§ 291

That a young girl may always safely be trusted with the kind of man who speaks of his mother.

§ 292

That a nine-year-old boy who likes to play with toy steam engines is probably a born mechanical genius and should be educated to be an engineer.

§ 293

That all celebrated professional humourists are in private life heavy and witless fellows.

§ 294

That when one stands close to the edge of a dizzy altitude, one is seized peculiarly with an impulse to jump off.

§ 295

That if one eats an apple every night before retiring, one will never be ill.

§ 296

That all negroes born south of the Potomac can play the banjo and are excellent dancers.

§ 297

That whenever a negro is educated he refuses to work and becomes a criminal.

§ 298

That whenever an Italian begins to dress like an American and to drive a Dodge car, it is a sign he has taken to black-handing or has acquired an interest in the white-slave trust.

§ 299

That, in the days when there were breweries, the men who drove beer-wagons drank 65 glasses of beer a head a day, and that it didn't hurt them because it came direct from the wood.

§ 300

That, until the time of American intervention, the people of the Philippines were all cannibals, and displayed the heads of their fallen enemies on poles in front of their houses.

§ 301

That whenever a crowd of boys goes camping in summer two or three of them are drowned, and the rest come home suffering from poison ivy.

§ 302

That whenever a will case gets into the courts, the lawyers gobble all the money, and the heirs come out penniless.

§ 303

That every female moving-picture star carries on an intrigue with her leading man, and will marry him as soon as he can get rid of his poor first wife, who took in washing in order to pay for his education in the art of acting.

§ 304

That all theatrical managers are Jews, and that most of them can scarcely speak English.

§ 305

That a great many of women's serious diseases are due to high French heels.

§ 306

That if one does not scratch a mosquito bite, it will stop itching.

§ 307

That when a girl gives a man a pen-knife for a present, their friendship will come to an unhappy end unless he exercises the precaution to ward off bad luck by giving her a penny.

§ 308

That whenever one takes an umbrella with one, it doesn't rain.

§ 309

That the cloth used in suits made in England is so good that it never wears out.

§ 310

That cinnamon drops are coloured red with a dye-stuff manufactured out of the dried bodies of cochineal insects.

§ 311

That the missionaries in China and Africa make fortunes robbing the natives they are sent out to convert.

§ 312

That there is a revolution in Central America every morning before breakfast, and that the sole object of all the revolutionary chiefs is to seize the money in the public treasury and make off to Paris.

§ 313

That whenever there is a funeral in an Irish family the mourners all get drunk and proceed to assault one another with clubs.

§ 314

That all immigrants come to America in search of liberty, and that when they attempt to exercise it they should be immediately sent back.

§ 315

That whenever a rich American girl marries a foreign nobleman, he at once gets hold of all her money, then beats her and then runs away with an actress.

§ 316

That if one begins eating peanuts one cannot stop.

§ 317

That a bachelor never has any one to sew the buttons on his clothes.

§ 318

That whenever a dog wags his tail it is a sign that he is particularly happy.

§ 319

That an Italian street labourer can do a hard day's work on one large plate of spaghetti a day.

§ 320

That if one breaks a mirror one will have bad luck for seven years.

§ 321

That two men seldom agree that the same girl is good-looking.

§ 322

That in the infinitesimal space of time between the springing of the trap-door and his dropping through it, a hanged man sees his entire life pass in panorama before him.

§ 323

That when Washington crossed the Delaware, he stood up in the bow of the boat holding aloft a large American flag.

§ 324

That whereas a man always hopes his first child will be a boy, his wife always hopes that it will be a girl.

§ 325

That the first time a boy smokes a cigar he always becomes deathly sick.

§ 326

That a woman always makes a practice of being deliberately late in keeping an appointment with a man.

§ 327

That if, encountering a savage beast in the jungle, one falls upon the ground, lies still and pretends that one is dead, the savage beast will promptly make off and not hurt one.

§ 328

That if one sits in front of the Café de la Paix, in Paris, one will soon or late see everybody in the world that one knows.

§ 329

That it is always twice as hard to get rid of a summer cold as to get rid of a winter cold.

§ 330

That a soft speaking voice is the invariable mark of a well bred man.

§ 331

That the persons who most vociferously applaud the playing of *Dixie* in restaurants are all Northerners who have never been further South than Allentown, Pa.

§ 332

That the larger the dog, the safer he is for children.

§ 333

That Catholic priests never solicit money from their parishioners, but merely assess them so much a head, and make them pay up instantly.

§ 334

That nine times in ten when one is in pain, and a doctor assures one that he is squirting morphine into one's arm, what he is really squirting in is only warm water.

§ 335

That a German civilian, before the war, had to get off the sidewalk whenever an army lieutenant approached him on the street, and that, if he failed to do so instantly, the lieutenant was free to run him through with his sword.

§ 336

That while it may be possible, in every individual case of spiritualist communication with the dead, to prove fraud by the medium, the accumulated effect of such communications is to demonstrate the immortality of the soul.

§ 337

That an Italian who earns and saves $1,000 in America can take the money home, invest it in an estate, and live like a rich man thereafter.

§ 338

That all Mormons, despite the laws against it, still practise polygamy, and that they have agents all over the world recruiting cuties for their harems.

§ 339

That when a man goes to a photographer's to have his picture taken, the knowledge that he is having his picture taken always makes him very self-conscious, thus causing him to assume an expression which results in the photograph being an inaccurate likeness.

§ 340

That if the lower line on the palm of one's hand is a long one, it is a sign that one is going to live to a ripe old age.

§ 341

That Italian counts, before the war, always used to make their expenses when they came to America by acting as wine agents.

§ 342

That a Russian peasant, in the days of the czar, drank two quarts of vodka a day.

§ 343

That a German farmer can raise more produce on one acre of land than an American can raise on a hundred.

§ 344

That a boil on the neck purifies the blood and is worth $1,000.

§ 345

That whenever a Frenchman comes home unexpectedly, some friend of the family makes a quick sneak out of the back door.

§ 346

That every negro servant girl spends at least half of her wages on preparations for taking the kink out of her hair.

§ 347

That the licorice candy sold in cheap candy stores is made of old rubber boots.

§ 348

That if a boy is given all he wants to drink at home he will not drink when he is away from home.

§ 349

That the second-class passengers on a trans-Atlantic steamship always have more fun than the first-class passengers.

§ 350

That a drunken man always pronounces every "s" as "sh."

§ 351

That champagne will prevent seasickness.

§ 352

That thin wrists and slender ankles are unmistakable signs of aristocratic breeding.

§ 353

That when one asks a girl to go canoeing she always brings along a bright red or yellow sofa cushion.

§ 354

That when a woman buys cigars for a man she always judges the quality of the cigars by the magnificence of the cigar-bands.

§ 355

That candle light makes a woman forty-five years old look fifteen years younger.

§ 356

That the winters in the United States are a good deal less cold than they used to be, and that the change has been caused by the Gulf Stream.

§ 357

That the Thursday matinées given by Chauncey Olcott are attended only by Irish servant girls.

§ 358

That the reason the British authorities didn't lock up Bernard Shaw during the war was because they were afraid of his mind.

§ 359

That Professor Garner was able to carry on long and intimate conversations with monkeys in their own language.

§ 360

That oysters are a great aphrodisiac.

§ 361

That if one sleeps with one's head on a high pillow one will be round-shouldered.

§ 362

That coal miners get so dirty that they have to wash so often that they are the cleanest working-men in the world.

§ 363

That the average French housewife can make such a soup out of the contents of a garbage-can that the eater will think he is at the Ritz.

§ 364

That such authors as Dr. Frank Crane and Herbert Kaufman do not really believe what they write, but print it simply for the money that is in it.

§ 365

That the average newspaper cartoonist makes $100,000 a year.

§ 366

That when a play is given in an insane asylum the inmates always laugh at the tragic moments and cry at the humorous moments.

§ 367

That if a girl takes the last cake off a plate she will die an old maid.

§ 368

That men high in public affairs always read detective stories for diversion.

§ 369

That the wireless news bulletins posted daily on ocean liners are made up on board.

§ 370

That the Swiss, when they sing, always yodel.

§ 371

That all German housewives are very frugal.

§ 372

That if one holds a buttercup under a person's chin and a yellow light is reflected upon that person's chin, it is a sign that he likes butter.

§ 373

That all penny-in-the-slot weighing machines make a fat woman lighter and a thin woman heavier.

§ 374

That in the period just before a woman's baby is born the woman's face takes on a peculiar spiritual and holy look.

§ 375

That when a Chinese laundryman hands one a slip for one's laundry, the Chinese letters which he writes on the slip have nothing to do with the laundry but are in reality a derogatory description of the owner.

§ 376

That an old woman with rheumatism in her leg can infallibly predict when it is going to rain.

§ 377

That Philadelphia is a very sleepy town.

§ 378

That it is impossible for a man to learn how to thread a needle.

§ 379

That there is something unmanly about a grown man playing the piano, save only when he plays it in a bordello.

§ 380

That a couple of quinine pills, with a chaser of rye whiskey, will cure a cold.

§ 381

That all Congressmen who voted for Prohibition are secret lushers and have heavy stocks of all sorts of liquors in their cellars.

§ 382

That a recent President of the United States was a great fellow with the gals, and used to carry on with a stock-company actress.

§ 383

That all the best cooks are men.

§ 384

That all Japanese butlers are lieutenants in the Japanese Navy and that they read and copy all letters received by the folks they work for.

§ 385

That the best way to stop nose-bleed is to drop a door-key down the patient's back.

§ 386

That a thunder-storm will cause milk to turn sour.

§ 387

That if a man drinks three glasses of buttermilk everyday he will never be ill.

§ 388

That whenever two Indians meet they greet each other with the word "How!"

§ 389

That the Justices of the Supreme Court of the United States all chew tobacco while hearing cases, but that they are very serious men otherwise, and never laugh, or look at a pretty girl, or get tight.

§ 390

That all negro prize-fighters marry white women, and that they afterward beat them.

§ 391

That New Orleans is a very gay town and full of beautiful French creoles.

§ 392

That gin is good for the kidneys.

§ 393

That the English lower classes are so servile that they say "Thank you, sir," if one kicks them in the pantaloons.

§ 394

That the gipsies who go about the country are all horse-thieves, and that they will put a spell upon the cattle of any farmer who has them arrested for stealing his mare.

§ 395

That every bachelor of easy means has an illicit affair with a grass widow in a near-by city and is the father of several illegitimate children.

§ 396

That a country editor receives so many presents of potatoes, corn, rutabagas, asparagus, country ham, carrots, turnips, etc., that he never has to buy any food.

§ 397

That whenever news reached him of another Federal disaster Abraham Lincoln would laugh it off with a very funny and often somewhat smutty story, made up on the spot.

§ 398

That George Washington died of a heavy cold brought on by swimming the Potomac in the heart of winter to visit a yellow girl on the Maryland shore.

§ 399

That all negroes who show any intelligence whatever are actually two-thirds white, and the sons of United States Senators.

§ 400

That the late King Leopold of Belgium left 350 illegitimate children.

§ 401

That Senator Henry Cabot Lodge is a very brainy man, though somewhat stuck up.

§ 402

That if one eats ice-cream after lobster one will be doubled up by belly-ache.

§ 403

That Quakers, for all their religion, are always very sharp traders and have a great deal of money hidden away in banks.

§ 404

That old baseball players always take to booze, and so end their days either as panhandlers, as night watchmen or as janitors of Odd Fellows' halls.

§ 405

That the object of the players, in college football, is to gouge out one another's eyes and pull off one another's ears.

§ 406

That the sort of woman who carries around a Pomeranian dog, if she should ever have a child inadvertently, would give the midwife $500 to make away with it.

§ 407

That a woman likes to go to a bargain sale, fight her way to the counter, and have pins stuck into her and her feet mashed by other women.

§ 408

That, if one swallows an ounce of olive oil before going to a banquet, one will not get drunk.

§ 409

That a mud-turtle is so tenacious of life that if one cuts off his head a new one will grow in its place.

§ 410

That the only things farmers read are government documents and patent-medicine almanacs.

§ 411

That if one's ear itches it is a sign that some one is talking of one.

§ 412

That Italian children, immediately they leave the cradle, are sewed into their underclothes, and that they never get a bath thereafter until they are confirmed.

§ 413

That all Catholic priests are very hearty eaters, and have good wine cellars.

§ 414

That politics in America would be improved by turning all the public offices over to business men.

§ 415

That department store sales are always fakes, and that they mark down a few things to attract the women and then swindle them by lifting the prices on things they actually want.

§ 416

That 100,000 abortions are performed in Chicago every year.

§ 417

That John D. Rockefeller has a great mind, and would make a fine President if it were not for his craze for money.

§ 418

That all the Jews who were drafted during the late war were put into the Quartermaster's Department on account of their extraordinary business acumen.

§ 419

That a jury never convicts a pretty woman.

§ 420

That chorus girls in the old days got so tired of drinking champagne that the sound of a cork popping made them shudder.

§ 421

That the Massachusetts troops, after the first battle of Bull Run, didn't stop running until they reached Harrisburg, Pa.

§ 422

That General Grant was always soused during a battle, and that on the few occasions when he was sober he got licked.

§ 423

That the late King Edward used to carry on in Paris at such a gait that he shocked even the Parisians.

§ 424

That it takes an Englishman two days to see a joke, and that he always gets it backward even then.

§ 425

That headwaiters in fashionable hotels make $100 a day.

§ 426

That if a bat flies into a woman's hair, the hair must be cut off to get it out.

§ 427

That all the women in Chicago have very large feet.

§ 428

That on cold nights policemen always sneak into stables on their beats and go to sleep.

§ 429

That all the schoolboys in Boston have bulged brows, wear large spectacles and can read Greek.

§ 430

That all dachshunds come from Germany.

§ 431

That nine out of every ten Frenchmen have syphilis.

§ 432

That the frankfurters sold at circuses and pleasure parks are made of dog meat.

§ 433

That all the cheaper brands of cigarettes are sophisticated with drugs, and in time cause those who smoke them to get softening of the brain.

§ 434

That rock-and-rye will cure a cold.

§ 435

That a country boy armed with a bent pin can catch more fish than a city angler with the latest and most expensive tackle.

§ 436

That red-haired girls are especially virulent.

§ 437

That all gamblers eventually go broke.

§ 438

That the worst actress in the company is always the manager's wife.

§ 439

That an elephant in a circus never forgets a person who gives him a chew of tobacco or a rotten peanut, but will single him out from a crowd years afterward and bash in his head with one colossal blow.

§ 440

That it is unlucky to put your hat on a bed.

§ 441

That an old sock makes the best wrapping for a sore throat.

§ 442

That lighting three cigarettes with one match will bring some terrible calamity upon one or other of the three smokers.

§ 443

That milking a cow is an operation demanding a special talent that is possessed only by yokels, and that a person born in a large city can never hope to acquire it.

§ 444

That whenever there is a rough-house during a strike, it is caused by foreign anarchists who are trying to knock out American idealism.

§ 445

That, whatever the demerits of Jews otherwise, they are always very kind to their old parents.

§ 446

That the Swiss army, though small, is so strong that not even the German army in its palmy days could have invaded Switzerland, and that it is strong because all Swiss are patriots to the death.

§ 447

That when two Frenchmen fight a duel, whether with pistols or with swords, neither of them is ever hurt half so much as he would have been had he fought an honest American wearing boxing-gloves.

§ 448

That whenever Prohibition is enforced in a region populated by negroes, they take to morphine, heroin and other powerful drugs, and begin murdering all of the white inhabitants.

§ 449

That all the great writers of the world now use typewriters.

§ 450

That all Presidents of the United States get many hot tips on the stock-market, but that they are too honourable to play them, and so turn them over to their wives, who make fortunes out of them.

§ 451

That Elihu Root is an intellectual giant, and that it is a pity the suspicion of him among farmers makes it impossible to elect him President.

§ 452

That no man not a sissy can ever learn to thread a needle or darn a sock.

§ 453

That all glass blowers soon or late die of consumption.

§ 454

That all women who go in bathing at the French seaside resorts affect very naughty one-piece bathing suits.

§ 455

That George M. Cohan and Irving Berlin can only play the piano with one finger.

§ 456

That farmers always go into gold mine swindles because of the magnificently embossed stock certificates.

§ 457

That the Germans eat six regular meals a day, and between times stave off their appetite with numerous Schweitzer cheese sandwiches, blutwurst and beer.

§ 458

That David Belasco teaches his actresses how to express emotion by knocking them down and pulling them around the stage by the hair.

§ 459

That only Americans travel in the first class carriages of foreign railway trains, and that fashionable Englishmen always travel third class.

§ 460

That the whiskey sold in blind pigs contains wood alcohol and causes those who drink it to go blind.

§ 461

That wealthy society women never wear their pearl necklaces in public, but always keep them at home in safes and wear indistinguishable imitations instead.

§ 462

That the late Charles Yerkes had no less than twenty girls, for each of whom he provided a Fifth Avenue mansion and a yearly income of $50,000.

§ 463

That when one goes to a railroad station to meet someone, the train is never on time.

§ 464

That the theatregoers in the Scandinavian countries care for nothing but Ibsen and Strindberg.

§ 465

That all doctors write prescriptions illegibly.

§ 466

That Englishwomen are very cold.

§ 467

That when the weather man predicts rain it always turns out fair, and that when he predicts fair it always rains.

§ 468

That lemon juice will remove freckles.

§ 469

That if a woman wears a string of amber beads she will never get a sore throat.

§ 470

That no well-bred person ever chews gum.

§ 471

That all actors sleep till noon, and spend the afternoon calling on women.

§ 472

That the men who make sauerkraut press it into barrels by jumping on it with their bare feet.

§ 473

That the moment a nigger gets eight dollars, he goes to a dentist and has one of his front teeth filled with gold.

§ 474

That one never sees a Frenchman drunk, all the souses whom one sees in Paris being Americans.

§ 475

That a daughter is always a much greater comfort to a mother in after life than a son.

§ 476

That a man with a weak, receding chin is always a nincompoop.

§ 477

That English butlers always look down on their American employers, and frequently have to leave the room to keep from laughing out loud.

§ 478

That the most faithful and loving of all dogs is the Newfoundland.

§ 479

That a man always dislikes his mother-in-law, and goes half-crazy everytime she visits him.

§ 480

That St. Louis in summer is the hottest place in the world.

§ 481

That all the men in the moving picture business were formerly cloak and suit merchants, and that they are now all millionaires.

§ 482

That the accumulation of money makes a man hard, and robs him of all his finer qualities.

§ 483

That, in an elevator, it is always a man who usurps the looking-glass.

§ 484

That it is very unlucky to wear an opal.

§ 485

That if a man's eyebrows meet, it is a sign that he has a very unpleasant nature.

§ 486

That a negro ball always ends up in a grand free-for-all fight, in which several coons are mortally slashed with razors.

§ 487

That if Houdini were locked up in Sing Sing, he would manage to make his get-away in less than half an hour's time.

§ 488

That Bob Ingersoll is in hell.

§ 489

That monkey-glands will restore a man of 85 to the vigor of 21, and cause him to elope with a Swedish servant-girl and become the father of twins.

§ 490

That the Pullman conductor always has a lower berth in reserve and can fix it for you if he is properly approached.

§ 491

That if an understudy makes a hit, the regular actor or actress immediately gets well and never misses another performance.

§ 492

That Aaron Burr possessed an irresistible charm for all the women with whom he came in contact, and that the virtue of even the most strait-laced was a very poor risk if left in a room alone with him as long as ten minutes.

§ 493

That whenever Stonewall Jackson prayed before a battle, it was a sure sign that the fighting was going to be very sanguinary and that lots of Yankees would be out of luck.

§ 494

That all schoolchildren are inordinately happy but don't know it.

§ 495

That a goat will wax fat on a diet of tin cans and back numbers of the *Saturday Evening Post.*

§ 496

That a little girl who is markedly pretty between the years of six and ten will probably lose all of her physical charms before she is grown; and that one who, at the same age, is hideously ugly will probably develop into a rare beauty.

§ 497

That no atheist has ever seriously contemplated the stars or the growth of a jimpson weed.

§ 498

That all English schoolboys call their fathers "pater" and write excellent Latin verse.

§ 499

That very ugly people are usually fascinating.

§ 500

That any English naval officer can easily drink a quart of whiskey in an evening and show no signs of intoxication.

§ 501

That the movie editors steal all of the good plots from the scenarios which amateurs have submitted.

§ 502

That it takes the united efforts of a large Persian family forty years to make one dining-room rug.

§ 503

That whenever grown people talk scandal in the presence of children, the little tots promptly rush off to the neighbours and repeat it.

§ 504

That only about one out of every hundred American citizens has any idea of the real issues of the campaign when he votes on election day.

§ 505

That the chief duty of a fireman, when not engaged in answering alarms, is to sit next to a warm fire in the hose-house and play checkers.

§ 506

That paper-hangers leave a room in a complete mess after they have finished their work.

§ 507

That an illegitimate child is always more or less gifted with artistic promptings, and usually turns out to be a poet or a violinist.

§ 508

That a circus is never as good as its posters lead one to believe.

§ 509

That candy ruins the teeth.

§ 510

That buttermilk is excellent for the complexion.

§ 511

That one can infallibly tell a cigar is a good one if the ashes remain on the end and don't fall off.

§ 512

That all press-agents are liars.

§ 513

That jewellers, in cleaning or repairing costly baubles, invariably remove the original stones and insert others made of paste.

§ 514

That all moving pictures of English country life are staged in Fort Lee, New Jersey.

§ 515

That if one steps on a rusty tack one will inevitably get lock-jaw.

§ 516

That it helps a young man in business if he grows a moustache.

§ 517

That barbers are inordinately loquacious.

§ 518

That having a baby interferes with an actress' career.

§ 519

That when one takes one's best girl buggy riding the horse never respects the situation.

§ 520

That when one buys a promising looking package at a sale of unclaimed freight, it always contains a set of burglar tools or the collected works of F. Marion Crawford.

§ 521

That the French steamship lines serve excellent wine gratis.

§ 522

That a policeman is never around when he is wanted.

§ 523

That the negro is absolutely unreliable, and that it is impossible to count upon him doing what he promises to do.

§ 524

That Theda Bara was born in Arabia.

§ 525

That the invariable dessert in a third-rate boarding house is stewed prunes.

§ 526

That Clara Morris was so good in "Camille" because she used to go around to the hospitals and study the way women suffering from tuberculosis died.

§ 527

That one can buy practically everything in Kokomo that is on sale in the Rue de la Paix.

§ 528

That home-cooking is far more appetizing than that in the best restaurant.

§ 529

That all graduates of Harvard wear horn-rimmed spectacles and speak with a marked English accent.

§ 530

That before the Volstead act nobody ever attempted a round of golf without drinking ten cocktails, and that since national prohibition the average player has reduced his record for the course by at least five strokes.

§ 531

That a young man who fails in business invariably dances the tango with great skill.

§ 532

That no traveller ever remembers anything of Rome except the fact that he paid $7 a day for his room and had to walk down the hallway to get a bath.

§ 533

That neither of the parties to a stage kiss derives any enjoyment from it.

§ 534

That no college professor understands baseball, but that every college professor sneaks off at periodic intervals to enjoy a good hot burlesque show.

§ 535

That all insane people insist that they are sane.

§ 536

That all patent-medicines are hooch in disguise.

§ 537

That seagulls fly around and around, never alighting until they drop dead from exhaustion.

§ 538

That motion-picture directors always throw away the working 'script after the first scene, and make up the action as the play progresses.

§ 539

That country garage-keepers sprinkle the nearby roads with crushed glass.

§ 540

That revenue officials imbibe at least three-fourths of the booze that they confiscate.

§ 541

That no matter how badly she wants to be kissed, a girl will demur for a time just to make things interesting.

§ 542

That clergymen slip on store collars with ties attached whenever they leave their sacred duties, and raise hell in general.

§ 543

That any dish which has a French name is covered with a sauce that looks like glue.

§ 544

That a young man who inherits $100,000 invariably squanders his fortune before he is thirty-five.

§ 545

That all the most successful sirens are blondes.

§ 546

That rich women invariably dress in dowdy fashion and are mistaken for the servants of their French maids.

§ 547

That women who are able to afford servants wear kimonos during the greater part of the day and read best sellers.

§ 548

That deacons drive hard bargains.

§ 549

That farm hands begin each day by eating three dozen pancakes.

§ 550

That New Yorkers are the most provincial people in the world.

§ 551

That men who commute finally grow not to mind it.

§ 552

That suburbanites always leave a play before it is over so that they can catch the last train home.

§ 553

That steamer acquaintances never become real friends.

§ 554

That trapeze performers often fall on purpose, in order to convince the audience of the difficulties of their profession.

§ 555

That all the poetry in magazines is bad, and is accepted merely to fill up blank spaces at the bottom of a page.

§ 556

That the woman writer on an evening newspaper who gives advice to the lovelorn is invariably a man with a flowing beard.

§ 557

That all moving picture scenarios fetch fabulous prices.

§ 558

That tailors do not mind how long you keep them waiting for their money.

§ 559

That, if a woman constantly bleaches her hair, she is in danger of going insane.

§ 560

That garrulous people never have anything worth saying.

§ 561

That most people would steal a million dollars if they were sure they'd never be caught.

§ 562

That Maude Adams and David Warfield almost go mad because they are forced to play one part so long.

§ 563

That only millionaires go to Newport.

§ 564

That no one ever gets a full night's sleep in a sleeping-car.

§ 565

That lots of fashionable people eat at Childs' restaurants simply because they like good griddle cakes and coffee.

§ 566

That it is possible to overcome seasickness by sucking the juice of a lemon.

§ 567

That all men who wear beards do so in order to conceal weak chins.

§ 568

That the futurist painters are all insane.

§ 569

That, if you lend money, you lose the friendship of the recipient of your kindness.

§ 570

That any play by a Russian author is sordid and certain to give one the blues.

§ 571

That newspaper reporters can write without difficulty, no matter how much noise and confusion is around them.

§ 572

That the beer you brew at home is just as good as that made in Munich.

§ 573

That as soon as the American Army landed in France half of the men in each French company were allowed to go home to help their wives swindle the Americans.

§ 574

That a man who has five children stands more chance of being elected President than a man who has none.

§ 575

That all artists are impractical.

§ 576

That opportunity comes at least once to every man.

§ 577

That people who live in New York never have a moment to themselves.

§ 578

That the reason bachelors hate to visit happily married couples is that it makes them miserable with envy.

§ 579

That widows are far more dangerous than débutantes.

§ 580

That women who worry about losing their beauty age much faster than those who don't.

§ 581

That whenever a group of men get together they immediately begin discussing booze and women.

§ 582

That if a woman gives a man a letter to mail, it will remain in his pocket for a week.

§ 583

That all long-haired men are effeminate, and all short-haired women are masculine.

§ 584

That prohibition, whatever its faults, is a good thing for the workingman.

§ 585

That being in love with a beautiful woman is a great inspiration to an artist.

§ 586

That it is always necessary to tie ribbons on the wrists of twins to keep Beulah from being confused with Otto.

§ 587

That there is something the matter with a man who can tell a Louis XV clock from a salt cellar by Benvenuto Cellini.

§ 588

That Abraham Lincoln was the originator of the smoking car story.

§ 589

That all young widows prolong the period of mourning if they think black becoming.

§ 590

That all negroes have perfect white teeth.

§ 591

That the editorial staff of *The Liberator* is composed entirely of anarchists, who are very violent characters.

§ 592

That if a sailor dies on board a ship, a shark becomes promptly cognizant of the fact and proceeds to follow the ship all the way across the ocean.

§ 593

That the *Boston Transcript* is written entirely by college professors, and that its English is so good that common people can't understand it.

§ 594

That no woman can throw straight, and that if she aims a brick at the mantelpiece it will hit the bookcase behind her.

§ 595

That all of Woodrow Wilson's shortcomings were due to his having been a college professor.

§ 596

That dramatic critics get many invitations from beautiful actresses to dine with them alone in their boudoirs, and that the beautiful actresses there make love to them in order to get good notices.

§ 597

That a sharp man may for ten cents often pick up in a second-hand book-store a book that is worth a hundred dollars.

§ 598

That while the days in California are very warm, the evenings are always so cool that one has to wear an overcoat.

§ 599

That Ruth Law was in reality a German boy shrewdly disguised.

§ 600

That the mutual confidences of boarding-school girls are very racy.

§ 601

That the late Grover Cleveland was a great booze-fighter, and used to carry on like a drunken sailor at the White House.

§ 602

That if one sleeps with the moonlight shining full in one's face, one will go insane.

§ 603

That if one's nose itches, it is a sign that someone is coming to visit.

§ 604

That both Abraham Lincoln and Jefferson Davis were the illegitimate sons of Henry Clay.

§ 605

That a negro who wears gold-rimmed spectacles never actually needs them, but affects them because they make him look intelligent.

§ 606

That the liquid contained in the centre of many golf balls will cause instant total blindness.

§ 607

That when one asks a bell-boy in a hotel in Buda-Pest to get one's suit pressed, he reappears in a few minutes with a large blonde.

§ 608

That the description of the Battle of the Marne in "The Four Horsemen of the Apocalypse" is a wonderful piece of writing.

§ 609

That all the officers of the United States Navy, before the day of Josephus Daniels, were terrific boozers, and that it was a common thing for them to run a battleship ashore, at a cost to the taxpayers of $9,000,000.

§ 610

That if one spills salt, one should throw a pinch over one's left shoulder to ward off ill luck.

§ 611

That when some one walks between a couple, each of them should say "bread and butter" to ward off a quarrel.

§ 612

That when one sees a red-headed woman, one is sure to see a white horse within a block.

§ 613

That it is bad luck to see the new moon over one's left shoulder.

§ 614

That carrying a nutmeg in one's pocket will prevent rheumatism.

§ 615

That a piece of bread and butter, if dropped, will always fall butter side down.

§ 616

That before the war whenever the American ambassador in Berlin attended a diplomatic function he would be insulted by German high officials who would crack jokes about the United States.

§ 617

That rapping on wood will ward off calamity.

§ 618

That if one's corns hurt, it is a sign that it is going to rain.

§ 619

That if one dreams of falling and dreams that one lands, one will never awaken and will be dead.

§ 620

That if one saves the pennies, the dollars will save themselves.

§ 621

That to have a black cat cross one's path means bad luck.

§ 622

That when a man consults his watch he always forgets what time it is the instant after he has replaced it in his pocket.

§ 623

That cockroaches born in the morning are great-grandfathers before evening.

§ 624

That thunder sours fresh milk.

§ 625

That when one of the ultra-fashionable set gives a house-party the guests do nothing but lounge around, drink cocktails, and engage in a great deal of very witty repartee.

§ 626

That there are a vast number of desperate underworld characters who will engage to murder anybody for a sum not exceeding one dollar and fifty cents.

§ 627

That French ladies' maids during their idle moments amuse themselves by peeping through the key-holes of bedroom doors.

§ 628

That women search their husbands' pants pockets at night and appropriate all the loose change.

§ 629

That to drop a dish-rag signifies that company is coming.

§ 630

That one can greatly increase one's chest expansion by standing in front of an open window every morning and taking twenty-five deep breaths.

§ 631

That at every fashionable wedding there are present no less than a dozen detectives who are engaged to watch the valuable gifts, and that nobody can ever distinguish the detectives from the guests.

§ 632

That people who live far away from New York know far more about the town than the natives do.

§ 633

That if one is having bad luck in a card game a great change of fortune is effected by walking around one's chair.

§ 634

That all policemen have unduly large feet.

§ 635

That people suffering from tuberculosis are always very optimistic and feel sure that there is nothing the matter with them.

§ 636

That old ladies enjoy attending a funeral and that they always obtain front-row seats.

§ 637

That when a man on the streets gazes at a woman wearing abbreviated skirts his evil nature is awakened, but that if he were to see the same woman in a bathing suit the sight of her would leave him cold.

§ 638

That when one swallows a needle it travels through the body for years and years and ultimately emerges somewhere in the region of the little toe.

§ 639

That if a young swain can watch his girl eat corn on the cob and still have any love for her, his affection is genuine.

§ 640

That the cooks who prepare griddle cakes in the front windows of Childs' restaurants are all expert jugglers.

§ 641

That a man who lives to be a hundred years old always takes a glass of whiskey a day and uses tobacco freely.

§ 642

That if a demi-rep really falls in love with a man she is always faithful to him to the bitter end.

§ 643

That if China could organize an army in proportion to its population it could conquer the world in about three weeks.

§ 644

That when an old maid retires at night she always looks under the bed for a burglar, and that if she were to discover one she would immediately lock the door and throw the key out of the window.

§ 645

That when a Frenchman gets in a free-for-all fight he always strikes out with his feet instead of his fists.

§ 646

That it is extremely hazardous to drink well-water in the dark since one is likely to swallow a pollywog.

§ 647

That the director of an orchestra makes a great many gestures merely to show off and that the music would be almost as good if there were no leader at all.

§ 648

That when a small boy is having his photograph taken he will remain very quiet if one tells him that a little bird is about to emerge from the camera.

§ 649

That people of Oriental blood always have very wily natures and that they glide about without making a sound.

§ 650

That when a military spy is caught he always has in his possession a small but extremely valuable piece of paper which he immediately proceeds to chew up and swallow.

§ 651

That middle-aged widows are very fond of college boys.

§ 652

That the headwaiter in every fashionable restaurant owns a block of apartments and a Rolls-Royce.

§ 653

That the first thing the Bolsheviks did in Russia was to nationalize the women, and that all of the most toothsome cuties were reserved for Trotsky and Lenin.

§ 654

That no matter how angry a woman may be at her husband he can always appease her wrath by giving her enough money to buy a new hat.

§ 655

That during the late war a great many society girls who acted as nurses cut up high jinks with the young soldiers.

§ 656

That when people who are unaccustomed to money inherit a fortune their existence is likely to become very miserable.

§ 657

That before long all the money in the country will be in the hands of the Jews.

§ 658

That if the man in the end seat of a trolley car yawns, every one else in the car will soon also be yawning.

§ 659

That a person's sensations while drowning are rather agreeable and that on the whole it is a very pleasant death.

§ 660

That cows have very sad eyes.

§ 661

That raspberries taste better when eaten off the bush.

§ 662

That acrobats could not do their stunts if they had not had their bones scientifically broken a few moments after they were born.

§ 663

That when two women enter a street car they always have a loud argument as to which one will stand the fare, but that as a matter of fact they are both bluffing and neither one wants to pay.

§ 664

That Chinese labourers work sixteen hours a day and are paid a weekly stipend of approximately eleven cents.

§ 665

That football is a very fine thing and greatly improves the moral character of college boys and that they never neglect an opportunity in the heat of a game to surreptitiously kick an opponent in the back of the head.

§ 666

That the men who pass the collection plates in Fifth Avenue churches always have a lot of loose change in their pockets on Monday morning.

§ 667

That the nurses in maternity hospitals are often careless and that the babies frequently get mixed up.

§ 668

That a youth who goes to Harvard, though he may learn nothing, is given a high polish.

§ 669

That many women who live in fashionable apartment houses have liaisons with the elevator boys.

§ 670

That the liquor problem is entirely due to corner saloons and that if there had never been such places nobody would have ever got drunk.

§ 671

That most women begin a street flirtation by dropping their handerchiefs.

§ 672

That a German never spends less than one hour consuming a single glass of beer.

§ 673

That women of the half world always carry all their money in their stockings.

§ 674

That American men have more respect for women than the men of any other country.

§ 675

That a flea is a very intelligent insect.

§ 676

That all the chorus girls in the Hippodrome are over forty years of age and have false teeth.

§ 677

That in a photoplay a motion picture actress brings tears to her eyes by concealing an onion in her handkerchief.

§ 678

That it is very dangerous to sleep in a folding bed since it is liable to close up in the middle of the night and smother one to death.

§ 679

That the Indians in wild west shows are in reality not Indians at all but painted Chinamen.

§ 680

That a man who is sitting in front of one will turn around if one concentrates one's attention on the back of his head.

§ 681

That a dexterous pickpocket can actually extract a roll of bills from the inside of one's undershirt without one being the wiser.

§ 682

That a young man who holds a position of trust in the financial world is constantly shadowed by detectives and that if he were to dine with a chorus girl he would immediately lose his job.

§ 683

That women who loll about the beaches in stunning bathing costumes never go near the water.

§ 684

That whenever a bank fails the president is always a venerable grey-haired man who either commits suicide or goes to jail.

§ 685

That French actresses never hesitate to appear on the stage perfectly nude.

§ 686

That people who sit in the gallery at a play are more discriminating than those in the orchestra.

§ 687

That when a man falls from a great height he always loses consciousness before he hits the ground.

§ 688

That most men, when dressed in evening clothes, can hardly be distinguished from waiters.

§ 689

That convicts like their existence in the new reformed prisons so much that they often refuse to leave when their terms have expired.

§ 690

That a Mason who reveals the secrets of the order will mysteriously disappear and never be heard of again.

§ 691

That Daniel Webster delivered his greatest orations when he was so drunk that he had to hold on to a table to stand up.

§ 692

That when Italians make wine they always press the grapes with their bare feet.

§ 693

That all star intercollegiate sprinters die of enlargement of the heart.

§ 694

That the most beneficial sleep is that which comes before midnight.

§ 695

That people with red hair are more directly descended from monkeys than the rest of mankind.

§ 696

That professors are absent-minded, that they often come to their classes minus collar or tie, and that they sometimes walk into other people's homes by mistake while engrossed in deep thought.

§ 697

That a pitcher on a baseball team is not expected to hit.

§ 698

That when they drop anything on the floor in a canning factory they put it into the can without washing it, no matter how dirty the floor is.

§ 699

That a Chinaman may kill his wife for less than nothing, and need never even go into court to explain his conduct.

§ 700

That a negro will not work so long as he has a nickel in his pocket.

§ 701

That when a man tells you that he was born in Virginia it is a sign that he will try to sell you a gold brick or some oil stock.

§ 702

That all Irishmen are very witty, and when engaged in an argument invariably crush their opponents with a final excruciatingly funny remark.

§ 703

That all professors at German universities spend their evenings in beer-gardens, and that each one slowly sips from twenty-five to forty steins of lager before retiring.

§ 704

That all French poets stay hooched up on absinthe and produce their most sublime works when in a semi-demented condition.

§ 705

That the capacity of any negro boy for watermelon is unlimited.

§ 706

That laundry wagon drivers are mostly college graduates.

§ 707

That if an Irishman were shipwrecked on a cannibal island he would be married to the chief's daughter and running the joint inside of a week.

§ 708

That all Methodist deacons, when they visit a city, get hilariously drunk and spend their time at leg shows and disreputable resorts.

§ 709

That people who are born rich are never vain, and that people who are born poor and later become rich are always vain.

§ 710

That when a hard boiled guy gets married he usually becomes so respectable that it hurts.

§ 711

That Edgar Allan Poe wrote all his stuff while sobering up after sprees.

§ 712

That England always persuades some other country to do her fighting for her, and that, when both her ally and her enemy are exhausted, she comes in strong at the finish and reaps all the benefits from the war.

§ 713

That when an Indian falls in love with a white woman and she refuses to marry him he never loses his self-possession, but goes back to his own people and lies around in the sun wrapped in a blanket.

§ 714

That summer romances are forgotten with the first frost.

§ 715

That in the days of chivalry all the Knights Errant were gallant to all the women they met, said their prayers every night before retiring, drank a little, but did not swear.

§ 716

That if you are familiar with a negro once, he will shove you off the sidewalk into the gutter the next time he meets you.

§ 717

That only a small percentage of Americans know more than a few lines of "The Star-Spangled Banner," and that they are so unfamiliar with the tune that they are always getting to their feet when the band plays "How Dry I am."

§ 718

That the French and English were eager to give up and make peace on the Kaiser's terms when the United States horned in and forced them to go on.

§ 719

That if one tries on a suit of clothes in a Jewish clothing store one is always told that it is a perfect fit, no matter if it hangs like a coat upon a rack or clings like the paper to the wall.

§ 720

That old negro mammies, now fast becoming extinct, always refer to their "white folks" as "honey chile."

§ 721

That a piece of asafœtida worn about the neck will ward off various diseases.

§ 722

That born and bred Virginians and South Carolinians are very proud of their origin and are given to excessive braggadocio.

§ 723

That in spite of the fact that all negroes make a great holiday of July the Fourth only about five percent of them know why they are celebrating.

§ 724

That when you've made up your mind to have a tooth extracted it always stops aching just as you place your hand on the dentist's doorknob.

§ 725

That persons with exceedingly high foreheads are always possessed of remarkable intelligence.

§ 726

That it is almost impossible to find a person living in New York who was born there.

§ 727

That drinking vinegar or the juice of a lemon will reduce one's weight.

§ 728

That all negroes love funerals and circuses, and turn out in great numbers to attend them both, arrayed in their best clothes.

§ 729

That a fortune-teller invariably says that you are going on a long journey, will cross water, and had better beware of a certain dark person who is trying to make trouble.

§ 730

That nowhere is such hospitality found as south of the Mason and Dixon line.

§ 731

That the quivering cry of a screech owl heard just outside a house is a sign that some one in the house will shortly die.

§ 732

That seaside building lots are under the water a greater part of the time.

§ 733

That it is impossible to learn a foreign language at college.

§ 734

That when people read a patent medicine pamphlet they immediately become convinced that they are suffering from all the diseases described therein.

§ 735

That a husband is tickled to death when his wife goes away to the country.

§ 736

That a negro eats nothing but pork chops and chicken, and that he always has a razor handy.

§ 737

That popular song writers always steal their melodies from well known operas.

§ 738

That a clever Central Office detective knows the face of every crook in town.

§ 739

That only a millionaire can afford to play polo.

§ 740

That when one is taking a bath it is very difficult to keep the soap under control.

§ 741

That a Jew always outwits a Christian in a business deal.

§ 742

That one always gets tired of a blonde quicker than a brunette.

§ 743

That the chief purpose of music in hotel dining-rooms is to drown the noise of people eating soup.

§ 744

That people go abroad and visit historic places for the sole purpose of being able to brag about it.

§ 745

That a married man never enjoys kissing his wife.

§ 746

That a man's wife is never as good a cook as his mother.

§ 747

That the women of backwoods communities have learned how to dress as a result of watching motion pictures.

§ 748

That when a girl who has been raised in poor circumstances marries, she demands a lot of expensive jewelry, four automobiles, three country houses, and a large staff of servants; but that when a girl who is accustomed to every luxury marries, she is perfectly willing to sew, cook, wash, take care of the baby, and darn her husband's socks.

§ 749

That people with a strong physique are more likely to succumb to an illness than those who look delicate.

§ 750

That as a result of prohibition all wealthy Americans who like to tipple will go abroad and spend the rest of their lives there.

§ 751

That all of the Americans taken prisoner by the Bolsheviki were innocent.

§ 752

That in Japan all the positions of trust in the banks are held by Chinamen.

§ 753

That in English families of title, the younger sons always cut up high jinks, and have to be sent out of the country because of gambling debts or escapades with women.

§ 754

That you can judge a man by what newspaper he reads.

§ 755

That a few minutes before an atheist dies he usually changes his mind and becomes deeply religious, and that if he fails to do so he dies in great agony.

§ 756

That at every girls' boarding school there are several female rakes who do nothing but smoke cigarettes, tell risqué stories, and put the other girls hep to a lot of things they should not know.

§ 757

That some day Canada will become a part of the United States.

§ 758

That artists' models, while posing, frequently faint from exhaustion.

§ 759

That, in the old days, whenever a millionaire gave a midnight supper party a semi-clad chorus girl would dance on the table, and the guests would drink champagne out of her slipper.

§ 760

That people in the theatrical profession never take marriage seriously.

§ 761

That indigent men always pawn their winter overcoats when the warm weather begins.

§ 762

That the crowned heads of Continental Europe have vast quantities of illegitimate children.

§ 763

That when a man is suffering from misfortune he is always greatly cheered up by meeting a friend who is also in woe.

§ 764

That up until twenty years ago all physicians affected beards, but that they no longer do so because it is considered unsanitary.

§ 765

That at the time of the American Revolution everybody in England was in favour of giving the colonies their liberty and that the war only took place because of the obstinacy of the king, who was very pro-German.

§ 766

That finger bowls are really of no value and are merely used as a matter of form.

§ 767

That when a bride and groom arrive at an hotel resort they never are able to disguise the fact that they have just been married.

§ 768

That if an undertaker were to discover that a supposedly dead person was still alive, he would immediately inject poison into the body in order not to lose the job.

§ 769

That a man who loudly declares that he intends always to remain a bachelor always marries the first pretty girl he meets.

§ 770

That there is no future for a man who works in a bank.

§ 771

That when a subway conductor calls out the names of the stations nobody can understand him.

§ 772

That no matter how courageous a man may be he is always afraid to visit a dentist.

§ 773

That parents suffer great mental anguish when they whip their children.

§ 774

That people who offer one a firm handclasp are very upright and honest.

§ 775

That a high-minded man and woman never kiss each other until the man proposes marriage.

§ 776

That a man who follows horse-racing goes broke sooner or later.

§777

That a minister's son usually grows up to be a drunkard or a thief.

§ 778

That most people who own automobiles cannot afford them.

§ 779

That when a man of little breeding attends a banquet he never knows what spoon or fork to use.

§ 780

That no matter how happy a bride may be she always weeps on her wedding day.

§ 781

That in London all clerks go to work at ten AM, quit at 3 PM, and wear silk hats.

§ 782

That when one drops a penny in a chewing gum slot machine, the chances are that nothing will come out.

§ 783

That the chief pastime of young medical students is hurling human arms and legs at each other in the dissecting room.

§ 784

That you can get the best seat in the Grand Opera House at Milan for twenty cents.

§ 785

That if Theodore Roosevelt had been president when the War began he would have ended it within three weeks.

§ 786

That a man who falls in love with a married woman is rotten to the core and is capable of any crime from murder to petty larceny.

§ 787

That a beautiful woman never has any brains.

§ 788

That if a waiter in a restaurant has a grudge against one he will surreptitiously spit into one's food.

§ 789

That the Haitians still practise cannibalism.

§ 790

That young girls only smoke cigarettes because they think it looks smart.

§ 791

That the only people who really appreciate opera are Italian barbers.

§ 792

That if one is in a great hurry to get some place, one is always greatly delayed en route.

§ 793

That a great many society women use very profane language.

§ 794

That a tremendous amount of sickness is caused by drinking ice water.

§ 795

That a person who has little to say is very wise and a profound thinker.

§ 796

That people who live in Brooklyn have a great many babies.

§ 797

That to pay a bill in cash causes one a great deal more anguish than to pay it with a cheque.

§ 798

That people who purloin spoons from hotel dining-rooms and keep them as souvenirs are honest in every other way.

§ 799

That when two young girls who room together return from a party they always lie awake all night and talk about it.

§ 800

That when a woman has a row with her husband she always cries and threatens to return to her mother.

§ 801

That at a wedding nobody ever pays any attention to the bridegroom.

§ 802

That every small village has a haunted house.

§ 803

That a human being's heart stops beating one instant in the middle of the night.

§ 804

That up to fifteen years ago people always went to Niagara Falls for their honeymoon.

§ 805

That professional card sharps always dress immaculately and have very ingratiating manners.

§ 806

That in a crowded car a man never offers his seat to a woman unless she is very beautiful.

§ 807

That a young man must engage in a certain amount of deviltry before he settles down.

§ 808

That people who go to church a great deal are either fanatics or hypocrites.

§ 809

That a bride always looks very pretty.

§ 810

That people who receive complimentary seats for the theatre always roast the play.

§ 811

That battleships are of no further fighting value, and that they are only constructed for the convenience of admirals who use them as they would private yachts.

§ 812

That the Germans never invent anything themselves, but that they appropriate the most ingenious inventions of other people.

§ 813

That it is easier to teach a mongrel dog tricks than a thoroughbred.

§ 814

That whether a New Englander is in Siberia, Hindustan, Alaska or Flatbush, he always returns home for Thanksgiving.

§ 815

That an after-dinner speech is always very tiresome.

§ 816

That most women's diseases are the result of modern fashions in dress.

§ 817

That everybody who signed the Declaration of Independence was a great man.

§ 818

That the late war was decided upon years ago by Bismarck, who, in formulating his plans, freely consulted Nietzsche.

§ 819

That when Lee surrendered to Grant there was a very touching scene; that Lee offered Grant his sword, which Grant declined and that Grant then offered Lee a cigar and a swig out of a pint of whiskey, which Lee accepted.

§ 820

That hasty marriages are bound to end disastrously.

§ 821

That the men who own the hat-checking privileges in New York restaurants are all millionaires.

§ 822

That there is a strange and mysterious difference between people who live in Manhattan and people who live in Brooklyn.

§ 823

That it makes no difference when one drops tobacco ashes on the carpet, because the ashes help to preserve it.

§ 824

That when one of the houris in a Turkish seraglio misbehaves, she is immediately sewn up in a sack and dropped through a trap-door into a subterranean river.

§ 825

That if one goes out wearing new clothes it is sure to rain.

§ 826

That a tremendous amount of kidney trouble is due to motorcycles and jitney automobiles.

§ 827

That when a woman driving an automobile gets into a tight place she promptly loses her head and causes an accident.

§ 828

That if one were to read the dictionary ten minutes each day one would become very learned.

§ 829

That the Rev. Dr. Billy Sunday has made $1,000,000 out of his gospel business.

§ 830

That when a Spaniard is in love he hangs around all night beneath the window of his inamorata and serenades her with a guitar.

§ 831

That London women have beautiful complexions, which they owe entirely to the fogs.

§ 832

That young people become especially amorous in the springtime.

§ 833

That Isaac Newton discovered the law of gravity because, as a boy, an apple fell off a tree and fetched him a bang on the coco.

§ 834

That Edgar Allan Poe was always drunk except when he took morphine.

§ 835

That in every family the father is partial to the girl and the mother to the son.

§ 836

That if a man tries to flirt with a woman at a little distance and she looks with curiosity at his feet, he will be so overcome by embarrassment that he will retreat.

§ 837

That the current craze for spiritualism is the result of propaganda financed by the men who manufacture ouija boards.

§ 838

That the monocle worn by an Englishman is made of cheap window glass, and that whenever he wants to see anything he has to drop it out of his eye.

§ 839

That the late J. Pierpont Morgan was the easiest mark the fake antique dealers of Europe had discovered in 250 years, and that a syndicate of Italians actually built five factories in Italy for the sole purpose of manufacturing fake Rembrandts to sell to him.

§ 840

That when peroxide of hydrogen is applied to an open wound, the ensuing bubbling shows that the wound is being efficaciously disinfected.

§ 841

That since the war all the French atheists have become devout Catholics.

§ 842

That England entered the war in order to discharge an obligation of honour to Belgium.

§ 843

That Southerners are chivalrous.

§ 844

That all college girls wear glasses and are very ugly.

§ 845

That all men who want to work very little and get a lot of money for it are Bolsheviki.

§ 846

That the life of a young man who marries an old woman for her money is always a very miserable and unhappy one.

§ 847

That prize-fighters are very good to their mothers, and that they are drunk all the time they are not training for a match.

§ 848

That in all the battles of the late war, both on the eastern front and on the western front, the German hordes enormously outnumbered the small and gallant bands of Russians, Frenchmen, Italians, Rumanians, Portuguese, Sikhs, Cambodians, Irishmen, Scotchmen, Welchmen, Canadians, Australians, New Zealanders, Somalis, Greeks, Singalese and Americans who opposed them.

§ 849

That water drunk from the washstand faucet is not as pure as water drunk from the kitchen faucet.

§ 850

That if a child eats snow he will get diphtheria.

§ 851

That all professional strong men are muscle-bound.

§ 852

That men who are good to animals are often wife-beaters.

§ 853

That a baby knows instinctively whether a man is good or bad.

§ 854

That there are a lot of things which are very good in theory but wont work in practice.

§ 855

That if all the money in the world were to be divided, within a year the same men would have it again.

§ 856

That although 200 percent of Washington's army deserted at one time or another, the patriotism and valour of the Continentals should set us a great example.

§ 857

That the late Theodore Roosevelt got a dollar a word for all his magazine writings.

§ 858

That the French make great soldiers; that the English Tommy is a great soldier; that the Canadians make great soldiers; that the Australians, Germans, Belgians and Americans make great soldiers; that the Cossacks are great soldiers; that the Japs make great little soldiers, etc., etc.

§ 859

That the French, Dutch, Belgians, Jews, Scotch and Germans are very thrifty peoples; that the Italians save every cent they make; that the New England Yankee is very economical; that the Chinese and Japanese live on rice and are extraordinarily thrifty; that, in fact, no one is improvident and extravagant except Americans in New York and Paris, and all Irishmen.

§ 860

That if all the coal in the world should suddenly give out, science would quickly devise something in its stead.

§ 861

That it always takes a woman at least an hour and a half to dress, whereas a man finishes the job in three minutes.

§ 862

That Henry Ford is against the Jews because he tried to borrow $50,000,000 from them and they demanded 10 percent a month.

§ 863

That all the girls in Richmond, Va., are great beauties, but that they will not look at a Yankee.

§ 864

That Baltimore is the place to eat oysters, and that the folks down there are all epicures and live on the fat of the land.

§ 865

That the Pennsylvania Dutch are all very rich, but that they can't speak English and never take a bath.

§ 866

That the late war was caused by the Kaiser single-handed, and that his plan was to seize all of Europe, reduce the inhabitants to slavery, and then conquer the United States.

§ 867

That every dollar-a-year man during the war swindled the government out of at least $1,000,000.

§ 868

That President Harding was nominated at Chicago as a result of a clever trick arranged by Col. George W. Harvey, and that Harvey was made Ambassador to England as a reward.

§ 869

That a war with England would probably be a good thing, inasmuch as the English would be afraid to cross the ocean, and so the United States would have a chance to grab both Canada and Mexico.

ENDNOTES

A BOOK OF PREFACES
CHAPTER I

[1] Joseph Conrad: A short study of his intellectual and emotional attitude toward his work and of the chief characteristics of his novels, by Wilson Follett; New York, Doubleday, Page & Co. (1915).

[2] The Advance of the English Novel. New York, Dodd, Mead & Co., 1916, p. 215.

[3] Conrad, in the *Forum,* May, 1915.

[4] New York and London. G. P. Putnam's Sons, 1907.

[5] The Intelligence of Woman. Boston, Little, Brown & Co., 1916, p. 6–7.

[6] In *The New Review,* Dec., 1897.

[7] Printed in the United States as Children of the Sea, but now restored to its original title.

[8] Here are some actual prices from booksellers' catalogues:

	1914	1916	1920
Almayer's Folly (1895)	$12.00	$24.00	$40.00
An Outcast of the Islands (1896)	11.50	20.00	35.00
The Nigger of the Narcissus (1898)	7.50	20.00	35.00
Tales of Unrest (1898)	12.50	20.00	35.00
Lord Jim (1900)	7.50	22.50	25.00
The Inheritors (1901)	12.00	20.00	30.00
Youth (1902)	5.00	7.50	25.00
Typhoon (1903)	4.00	5.50	16.00
Romance (1903)	5.00	7.50	9.00
Nostromo (1904)	2.50	4.50	7.50
The Mirror of the Sea (1906)	5.00	11.00	15.00
A Set of Six (1908)	3.00	7.50	10.00
Under Western Eyes (1911)	4.50	4.50	6.00
Some Reminiscences (1912)	4.50	9.00	15.00
Chance (1913)	2.00	5.00	15.00
Victory (1915)	2.00	2.50	4.25

[9] New York, Chas. Scribner's Sons, 1915, pp. 1–21.
[10] New York, Dodd, Mead & Co., 1916, pp. 192–217.
[11] Some English Story Tellers: A Book of the Younger Novelists; New York, Henry Holt & Co., 1912, pp. 1–30.
[12] A Disquisition on Conrad, *Fortnightly Review,* April, 1908.
[13] The Genius of Mr. Joseph Conrad, *North American Review,* June, 1904.
[14] Joseph Conrad: A Study; New York, Doubleday, Page & Co., 1914.
[15] Joseph Conrad; London, Nisbet & Co. (1916).

CHAPTER II

[1] Fuller's comparative obscurity is one of the strangest phenomena of American letters. Despite his high achievement, he is seldom discussed, or even mentioned. Back in 1899 he was already so far forgotten that William Archer mistook his name, calling him Henry Y. Puller. *Vide* Archer's pamphlet, The American Language; New York, 1899.
[2] For example, in The Cambridge History of English Literature, which runs to fourteen large volumes and a total of nearly 10,000 pages, Huxley receives but a page and a quarter of notice, and his remarkable mastery of English is barely mentioned in passing. His two debates with Gladstone, in which he did some of the best writing of the century, are not noticed at all.
[3] A Brief History of German Literature; New York, Chas. Scribner's Sons, 1909.
[4] New York, 1917; reprinted from *The Seven Arts* for Feb., 1917.
[5] Life, Art and America, p. 5.
[6] The episode is related in A Hoosier Holiday.
[7] A Princess of Arcady, published in 1900.
[8] New York, The Century Co., 1916.
[9] In *The Seven Arts,* May, 1917.
[10] The *Nation,* Dec. 2, 1915.
[11] 1186–1189. So translated by Floyd Dell: "O ye deathward-going tribes of man, what do your lives mean except that they go to nothingness?"
[12] The New York *Evening Post,* Dec. 31, 1915.
[13] Despite the comstockian attack, Dreiser is still fairly well represented on the shelves of American public libraries. A canvas of the libraries of the 25 principal cities gives the following result, an X indicating that the corresponding book is catalogued, and a—that is not:

	Sister Carrie	*Jennie Gerhardt*	*The Financier*	*The Titan*	*A Traveler at Forty*	*The "Genius"*	*Plays of the Natural*	*A Hoosier Holiday*
New York	×	–	–	×	×	×	×	×
Boston	–	–	–	–	×	–	×	–
Chicago	×	×	×	×	×	×	×	×
Philadelphia	×	×	×	×	×	×	×	×
Washington	–	–	–	–	×	–	×	–
Baltimore	–	–	–	–	×	–	–	–
Pittsburgh	–	–	×	×	×	×	–	×
New Orleans	–	–	–	–	–	–	–	–
Denver	×	×	×	×	×	×	×	×
San Francisco	×	×	×	×	×	–	–	×
St. Louis	×	×	×	×	×	–	×	–
Cleveland	×	×	×	×	–	×	×	–
Providence	–	–	–	–	–	–	–	–
Los Angeles	×	×	×	×	×	×	×	×
Indianapolis	×	×	×	–	×	–	×	×
Louisville	×	×	–	×	×	×	×	×
St. Paul	×	×	–	–	×	–	×	×
Minneapolis	×	×	×	–	×	–	×	–
Cincinnati	×	×	×	–	×	–	×	×
Kansas City	×	×	×	×	×	×	×	×
Milwaukee	–	–	–	–	×	–	×	×
Newark	×	×	×	×	×	×	×	×
Detroit	×	×	×	–	×	×	×	×
Seattle	×	×	–	–	×	–	×	×
Hartford	–	–	–	–	–	–	–	×

This table shows that but two libraries, those of Providence and New Orleans, bar Dreiser altogether. The effect of alarms from newspaper reviewers is indicated by the scant distribution of the *The "Genius,"* which is barred by 14 of the 25. It should be noted that some of these libraries issue certain of the books only under restrictions. This I know to be the case in Louisville, Los Angeles, Newark and Cleveland. The Newark librarian informs me that Jennie Gerhardt is to be removed altogether, presumably in response to some protest from local Comstocks. In Chicago The "Genius" has been stolen, and on account of the withdrawal of the book the Public Library has been unable to get another copy.

[14] The *North American Review,* Feb., 1916.

[15] Another competent valuation, by Randolph Bourne, is in *The Dial,* June 14, 1917.

CHAPTER III

[1] The Science of English Verse; New York, Scribner, 1880.

[2] Masks and Minstrels of New Germany; Boston, John W. Luce & Co., 1911.

[3] New York, Doubleday, Page & Co., 1913.

[4] The Drift of Romanticism; Boston, Houghton Mifflin Co., 1913.

[5] New York, Dodd, Mead & Co., 1916.

[6] New York, Chas. Scribner's Sons, 1917.

[7] New York, The Macmillan Co., 1917.

CHAPTER IV

[1] American Literature, tr. by Julia Franklin; New York, Doubleday, Page & Co., 1915.

[2] New York, Dodd, Mead & Co., 1916.

[3] The first edition for public sale did not appear until June, 1917, and in it the preface was suppressed.

[4] Second edition; Boston, Little, Brown & Co., 1859, xxvi.

[5] *Cf.* The Puritan, by Owen Hatteras, *The Smart Set,* July, 1916; and The Puritan's Will to Power, by Randolph S. Bourne, *The Seven Arts,* April, 1917.

[6] An instructive account of the organization and methods of the Anti-Saloon League, a thoroughly typical Puritan engine, is to be found in Alcohol and Society, by John Koren; New York, Henry Holt & Co., 1916.

[7] U.S. Rep., vol. 242, No. 7, p. 502.

[8] The majority opinion, written by Mr. Justice Day, is given in U.S. Rep., vol. 242, no. 7, pp. 482–496.

[9] New York, (1914).

[10] I quote from page 157 of Anthony Comstock, Fighter, the official biography. On page 239 the number of his prosecutions is given as 3,646, with 2,682 convictions, which works out to but 73 percent He is credited with having

destroyed 50 tons of books, 28,425 pounds of stereotype plates, 16,900 photographic negatives, and 3,984,063 photographs—enough to fill "sixteen freight cars, fifteen loaded with ten tons each, and the other nearly full."

[11] By Charles Gallaudet Trumbull; New York, Fleming H. Revell Co. (1913).

[12] An example: "All the evil men in New York cannot harm a hair of my head, were it not the will of God. If it be His will, what right have I or any one to say aught? I am only a speck, a mite, before God, yet not a hair of my head can be harmed unless it be His will. Oh, to live, to feel, to be—Thy will be done!" (pp. 84–5). Again: "I prayed that, if my bill might not pass, I might go back to New York submissive to God's will, feeling that it was for the best. I asked for forgiveness and asked that my bill might pass, if possible; but over and above all, that the will of God be done" (p. 6). Nevertheless, Comstock neglected no chance to apply his backstairs pressure to the members of both Houses.

[13] Now, with amendments, sections 211, 212 and 245 of the United States Criminal Code.

[14] *Vide* Anthony Comstock, Fighter, pp. 81, 85, 94.

[15] Now sections 1141, 1142 and 1143 of the Penal Laws of New York.

[16] U.S. *vs.* Casper, reported in the *Twentieth Century,* Feb. 11, 1892.

[17] The trial court dodged the issue by directing the jury to find the prisoner not guilty on the ground of insanity. The necessary implication, of course, was that the publication complained of was actually obscene. In 1895, one Wise, of Clay Center, Kansas, sent a quotation from the Bible through the mails, and was found guilty of mailing obscene matter. See The Free Press Anthology, compiled by Theodore Schroeder; New York, Truth Seeker Pub. Co., 1909, p. 258.

[18] U.S. *vs.* Bennett, 16 Blatchford, 368–9 (1877).

[19] *Idem,* 362; People *vs.* Muller, 96 N. Y., 411; U.S. *vs.* Clark, 38 Fed. Rep. 734.

[20] U.S. *vs.* Moore, 129 Fed., 160–1 (1904).

[21] U.S. *vs.* Heywood, judge's charge, Boston, 1877. Quoted in U.S. *vs.* Bennett, 16 Blatchford.

[22] U.S. *vs.* Slenker, 32 Fed. Rep., 693; People *vs.* Muller, 96 N. Y. 408–414; Anti-Vice Motion Picture Co. *vs.* Bell, reported in the *New York Law Journal,* Sept. 22, 1916; Sociological Research Film Corporation *vs.* the City of New York, 83 Misc. 815; Steele *vs.* Bannon, 7 L. R. C. L. Series, 267; U.S. *vs.* Means, 42 Fed. Rep. 605, etc.

[23] U.S. *vs.* Cheseman, 19 Fed. Rep., 597 (1884).

[24] People *vs.* Muller, 96 N. Y., 413.

[25] U.S. *vs.* Bennett, 16 Blatchford, 368–9.

[26] U.S. *vs.* Smith, 45 Fed. Rep. 478.

[27] U.S. *vs.* Bennett, 16 Blatchford, 360–1; People vs. Berry, 1 N. Y., Crim. R., 32.

[28] People *vs.* Muller, 32 Hun., 212–215.

[29] U.S. *vs.* Bennett, 16 Blatchford, 361.

[30] U.S. *vs.* Moore, 16 Fed. Rep., 39; U.S. *vs.* Wright, 38 Fed. Rep., 106; U.S. *vs.* Dorsey, 40 Fed. Rep., 752; U.S. *vs.* Baker, 155 Mass., 287; U.S. *vs.* Grimm, 15 Supreme Court Rep., 472.

[31] Various cases in point are cited in the Brief on Behalf of Plaintiff in Dreiser *vs.* John Lane Co., App. Div. 1st Dept. N. Y., 1917. I cite a few: People *vs.* Eastman, 188 N. Y., 478; U.S. *vs.* Swearingen, 161 U.S., 446; People *vs.* Tylkoff, 212 N. Y., 197; In the matter of Worthington Co., 62 St. Rep. 116–7; St. Hubert Guild *vs.* Quinn, 64 Misc., 336–341. But nearly all such decisions are in New York cases. In the Federal courts the Comstocks usually have their way.

[32] St. Hubert Guild *vs.* Quinn, 64 Misc., 339.

[33] For example, Judge Chas. L. Benedict, sitting in U.S. *vs.* Bennett, *op. cit.* This is a leading case, and the Comstocks make much of it. Nevertheless, a contemporary newspaper denounces Judge Benedict for his "intense bigotry" and alleges that "the only evidence which he permitted to be given was on the side of the prosecution." (Port Jervis, N. Y., *Evening Gazette,* March 22, 1879.) Moreover, a juror in the case, Alfred A. Valentine, thought it necessary to inform the newspapers that he voted guilty only in obedience to judicial instructions.

[34] *Vide* Newspaper Morals, by H. L. Mencken, the *Atlantic Monthly,* March, 1914.

[35] As a fair specimen of the sort of reasoning that prevails among the consecrated brethren I offer the following extract from an argument against birth control delivered by the present active head of the New York Society for the Suppression of Vice before the Women's City Club of New York, Nov. 17, 1916:

"Natural and inevitable conditions, over which we can have no control, will assert themselves wherever population becomes too dense. This has been exemplified time after time in the history of the world where over-population has been corrected by manifestations of nature or by war, flood or pestilence. . . . Belgium may have been regarded as an over-populated country. Is it a coincidence that, during the past two years, the territory of Belgium has been devastated and its population scattered throughout the other countries of the world?"

[36] For example, the printed contract of the John Lane Co., publisher of Dreiser's The "Genius," contains this provision: "The author hereby guarantees . . . that the work . . . contains nothing of a scandalous, an immoral or a libelous nature." The contract for the publication of The "Genius" was signed on July 30, 1914. The manuscript had been carefully read by representatives of the publisher, and presumably passed as not scandalous or immoral, inasmuch as the publication of a scandalous or immoral book would have exposed the publisher to prosecution. About 8,000 copies were sold under this contract. Two years later, in July, 1916, the Society for the Suppression of

Vice threatened to begin a prosecution unless the book was withdrawn. It was withdrawn forthwith, and Dreiser was compelled to enter suit for a performance of the contract. The withdrawal, it will be noticed, was not in obedience to a court order, but followed a mere comstockian threat. Yet Dreiser was at once deprived of his royalties, and forced into expensive litigation. Had it not been that eminent counsel volunteered for his defence, his personal means would have been insufficient to have got him even a day in court.

37 The chief sufferers from this conflict are the authors of moving pictures. What they face at the hands of imbecile State boards of censorship is described at length by Channing Pollock in an article entitled "Swinging the Censor" in the *Bulletin* of the Authors' League of America for March, 1917.

38 For example, the magazine which printed David Graham Phillips' Susan Lenox: Her Rise and Fall as a serial prefaced it with a moral encomium by the Rev. Charles H. Parkhurst. Later, when the novel appeared in book form, the Comstocks began an action to have it suppressed, and forced the publisher to bowdlerize it.

39 An account of a typical prosecution, arbitrary, unintelligent and disingenuous, is to be found in Sumner and Indecency, by Frank Harris, in *Pearson's Magazine* for June, 1917, p. 556.

40 For further discussions of this point consult Art in America, by Aleister Crowley, *The English Review,* Nov., 1913; Life, Art and America, by Theodore Dreiser, *The Seven Arts*, Feb., 1917; and The American; His Ideas of Beauty, by H. L. Mencken, *The Smart Set,* Sept., 1913.

41 *Vide* The Cambridge History of English Literature, vol. XI, p. 225.

42 The point is discussed by H. V. Routh in The Cambridge History of English Literature, vol. XI, p. 290.

43 In Boon; New York, George H. Doran Co., 1915.

44 In a letter to Felix Shay, Nov. 24, 1916.

INDEX

SUGGESTED READING

ADLER, BETTY J. *H. L. M.: The Mencken Bibliography.* Baltimore: Johns Hopkins University Press, 1961.

BULSTERBAUM, ALISON. *H. L. Mencken: A Research Guide.* New York and London: Garland, 1988.

COOKE, ALISTAIR, ED. *The Vintage Mencken.* New York: Vintage, 1955.

DORSEY, JOHN, ED. *On Mencken.* New York: Knopf, 1980.

DUBASKY, MAYO, ED. *The Gist of Mencken: Quotations from America's Critic Gleaned from Newspapers, Magazines, Books, Letters, and Manuscripts.* Metuchen, NJ: Scarecrow Press, 1990.

FITZPATRICK, VINCENT. *H. L. Mencken.* Macon, GA: Mercer University Press, 2004.

HOBSON, FRED C., JR. *Mencken: A Life.* New York: Random House, 1994.

———. *Serpent in Eden: H. L. Mencken and the South.* Chapel Hill: University of North Carolina Press, 1974.

JOSHI, S. T., ED. *H. L. Mencken on American Literature.* Athens: Ohio University Press, 2002.

———. *H. L. Mencken on Religion.* Amherst, NY: Prometheus Books, 2002.

———. *Mencken's America.* Athens: Ohio University Press, 2004.

MARTIN, EDWARD A. *H. L. Mencken and the Debunkers.* Athens: University of Georgia Press, 1984.

MAYFIELD, SARA. *The Constant Circle: H. L. Mencken and His Friends.* New York: Delacore, 1968.

4004

MCHUGH, ROBERT, ED. *The Bathtub Hoax and Other Blasts & Bravos from the Chicago Tribune.* New York: Knopf, 1958.

MENCKEN, H. L. *My Life as Author and Editor.* Ed. Jonathan Yardley. New York: Knopf, 1993.

MOOS, MALCOLM, ED. *H. L. Mencken, A Carnival of Buncombe.* Baltimore: Johns Hopkins University Press, 1956.

NOLTE, WILLIAM H. *H. L. Mencken: Literary Critic.* Middleton, CT: Wesleyan University Press, 1966.

NOLTE, WILLIAM H., ED. *H. L. Mencken's Smart Set Criticism.* Ithaca, NY: Cornell University Press, 1968.

RODGERS, MARION E., ED. *The Impossible H. L. Mencken: A Selection of His Best Newspaper Stories.* New York and London: Doublday, 1991.

SCRUGGS, CHARLES. *The Sage in Harlem: H. L. Mencken and the Black Writers of the 1920s.* Baltimore: Johns Hopkins University Press, 1984.

SCHRADER, RICHARD J. *H. L. Mencken: A Descriptive Bibliography.* Pittsburgh: University of Pittsburgh Press, 1998.

———. *H. L. Mencken: A Documentary Volume.* Dictionary of Literary Biography, vol. 222. Detroit: Gale Group, 2000.

SINGLETON, M. K. *H. L. Mencken and the American Mercury Adventure.* Durham, NC: Duke University Press, 1962.

STENERSON, DOUGLAS C. *H. L. Mencken: Iconoclast from Baltimore.* Chicago: University of Chicago Press, 1971.

STENERSON, DOUGLAS C., ED. *Critical Essays on H. L. Mencken.* Boston: G. K. Hall, 1987.

WILLIAMS, WILLIAM H. A. *H. L. Mencken Revisited.* Twayne's United States Authors Series 694. New York: Twayne, 1998.